Racism, Latinos, and the Public Policy Process

Latinos and American Politics

Series Editor: Henry Flores

Editorial Board: Tony Affigne, Edwina Barvosa, Benjamin Marquez, and Rodolfo Torres

Latinos and American Politics is concerned with the role Latinos, of all national origins and races, play in the American political process. Latinos are the largest minority group in the United States and have become the single most important group in presidential politics. This series, interdisciplinary in nature, seeks to advance the knowledge of Latino politics in the academy. The series includes works that focus on racial identities and their impact on intra-Latino relations and politics, Latina politics broadly defined to include the politics of gender, institutional and identity politics, electoral politics, community level politics and activism, the shifting types of politics Latinos have played in order to have their agendas entertained by political institutions, the behavior of Latina/o politicians, and the effects of the Civil Rights Acts on the political participation of Latinos. Contributors are encouraged to submit book length manuscripts that encompass besides the above named topics those focusing on gender, identity, racial politics, and all areas of public policy.

Titles in this Series

Latinas in American Politics: Changing and Embracing Political Tradition, edited by Sharon A. Navarro, Samantha L. Hernandez, and Leslie A. Navarro, 2016

Assault on the Mexican American's Collective Memory, 2010–2016: Swimming with the Sharks, by Rodolfo F. Acuña, 2017

Racism, Latinos, and the Public Policy Process, by Henry Flores, 2019

Racism, Latinos, and the Public Policy Process

Henry Flores

LEXINGTON BOOKS
Lanham • Boulder • New York • London

Published by Lexington Books
An imprint of The Rowman & Littlefield Publishing Group, Inc.
4501 Forbes Boulevard, Suite 200, Lanham, Maryland 20706
www.rowman.com

6 Tinworth Street, London SE11 5AL, United Kingdom

Copyright © 2019 by The Rowman & Littlefield Publishing Group, Inc.

All rights reserved. No part of this book may be reproduced in any form or by any electronic or mechanical means, including information storage and retrieval systems, without written permission from the publisher, except by a reviewer who may quote passages in a review.

British Library Cataloguing in Publication Information Available

The hardback edition of this book was previously catalogued by the Library of Congress as follows:

Library of Congress Cataloging-in-Publication Data Is Available

ISBN 978-1-4985-9973-3 (cloth)
ISBN 978-1-4985-9975-7 (pbk)
ISBN 978-1-4985-9974-0 (electronic)

Contents

Introduction—Racism: Some Introductory Thoughts		1
1	Racism Defined	9
2	Racism and the Public Policy Process	53
3	The Socioeconomic-Psychological-Ideological Elements of the State Matrix	99
4	How the Public Policy Process Creates a Racial Shield	133
5	Racial Intent Revisited and Some Concluding Thoughts	159
Bibliography		179
Index		187
About the Author		191

Introduction

Racism

Some Introductory Thoughts

The courtroom was well air-conditioned as Washington, DC, was in the throes of its usual balmy summer and the state senator from Texas sweated. The longer the trial went, the redder the senator's complexion got, the more his jaws locked, his facial grimace became tighter and, it appeared, the angrier he got. He had been upset since the beginning of the hearing and what made him so intensely angry was unclear except that the longer he sat in the gallery the angrier he appeared to get. At times he shook; his complexion turned a vivid red as testimony and evidence against his bill mounted. Perhaps his anger was because he was witnessing the expiration of his "child." He had worked so hard to see voter ID become law in Texas and now some federal court in distant Washington, DC, was on the verge of striking it down.

The three judges were asking hard questions of all witnesses and making it clear that they were not looking favorably on the senator's law. In the end, the panel unanimously ruled that the Texas voter ID law violated Section 5 of the Voting Rights Act (VRA) and would have to be rewritten if the state wanted to implement it. Their ruling, however, was negated later in the year when the Supreme Court issued its opinion in *Shelby County*.[1] Still, the question remained, What made the Texas state senator so angry throughout the hearing? Why did his anger reach such an intense level as the proceedings went forward?

The answer to these questions left me contemplating whether the senator was angry because his arrogance prevented him from accepting that his authority was being challenged by the US government and a couple of teenage Latinas. Another possible answer was that perhaps the senator was angry because he felt that without the law large numbers of Latinos would cast votes that would lead to his party's loss of control in the not too distant future. It was clear from evidence brought forth in the earlier congressional redistricting law suit, *Holder v. Texas*,² that Latinos were not favorably disposed to voting for Republican candidates and that voting generally was racially polarized in the state and had been since records began being kept on this issue. A confidential source indicated to the intervenor defendant expert that the senate sponsor's principle rationale for putting forth SB14 (voter ID law) was to lower the voting participation rate of Latinos.³ So, then was the senator's anger fueled because his anti-Latino legislation was failing? The senator was never interviewed about this issue and the confidential source had to be protected; the individual works in the state capitol and feared retaliation or the loss of her job so this nexus could never be explored empirically.

Nevertheless, SB 14 was passed during a legislative session that saw more than 100 pieces of anti-immigrant legislation submitted for consideration, at least five attempts at curbing the use of Spanish in various state governmental venues as well as making English the official language of the state, and the passage of congressional and state house redistricting plans that were clearly designed to dilute the Latino vote. The 2011 state legislative session was replete with anti-Latino demonstrations by the Tea Party on the capitol's grounds and racially hateful tirades by several elected state officials during various committee hearings throughout the session. The atmosphere in Austin that year was a cauldron of racial hatred fueled by the legislature itself and simply added amplification to the questions that arose as I observed the senator throughout the Section 5 hearing. These incidents, coupled with the spate of officer involved shootings of young persons of color, the continuing riling of anti-immigrant feelings, and the never-ending voting rights litigation over both congressional redistricting and voter identification laws, simply lend depth to the intensity and persistence of racism in America.

These incidents, however, are only the obvious. Currently, across the nation you have debates over whether to allow the Confederate battle flag to wave over public offices or whether statues of famous Confederate generals should be allowed in public places, struggles over gun control laws and same-sex marriages.⁴ Although only the battle flag issue is directly connected to racism, the other issues are reflective of the still deeper intolerance that underlies all prejudices and is an integral element in the understanding of the permanence of racism. This volume attempts to speak to the depth, intensity, and persistence of racism and how this infects the public policy process. The focus will primarily be in defining racism and developing an understanding as to why it is so deeply engrained in US political culture generally and in Texas' specifically. Adding is also an attempt at understanding why racism persists and why it is so intense of a feeling. Racism's place in the policy process will culminate this discussion. *In toto* this book is designed as a starting point for further research and not designed as the final or ultimate statement on racism. Racism's life and persistence in US political culture deserves more attention and depth of analysis than what I am offering here. Still, I strongly feel that little time has been spent in developing a thorough understanding of what racism is and how deeply engrained in our political process it has become.

I do not intend composing a traditional scholarly tome on racism rather I feel that the best way to begin a conversation is to present thoughts on what racism is and how and where within the US political cultural structure it resides. As a result, consider this a scholarly research and exploratory essay encompassing my thoughts on what comprises racism, what role it plays in US cultural structure, how it finds its way into the public policy process, and why this is the case. A review of the histories of racism that have been composed, including Gossett, Fredrickson, and Sussman[5] among others, have served to outline the pervasiveness of racism with most authors suggesting that it began as a justification for the institutionalization of slavery. Some scholars have pointed out that although slavery has existed for millennia, not until the middle of the seventeenth century was the race of enslaved people used as a rationale for their unique indenture. Generally, because the vast number of enslaved individuals imported into the United States came from Africa their color was used as an excuse for their subordination. These individuals were seen as less than their enslavers in every way. Even some of the revered "Fathers" of the United States, men such as Thomas Jefferson, saw African slaves as mentally defective or, at least, far below the intellectual levels of white persons.[6] This intellectual inferiority was deemed as the reason Africans were judged to be unfit for any other type of labor other than menial. This same rationale was used in Texas for not allowing Latinos to get more than a third grade or sixth grade level of education.

The first research in scientific racism was justified, against his wishes, by the explication of Darwin's theory of evolution as set forth in his *Origin of Species*.[7] Of the scientists of that era, many had no formal scientific training. Only their genteel status gave them license to spout their ideas and develop racial theories that construct social hierarchies with Whites at the top of the scale and blacks at the bottom. Francis Galton, a cousin of Darwin, created his now famous and much used correlation coefficient as a way of lending "scientific rigor" to his racial theories. Without apologizing for their efforts these early anthropologists developed their methodologies in order to understand the differences between what they saw as separate races of human beings. This eventually evolved into the field of eugenics or "scientific racism." Of course, much of the early research in eugenics has since been discredited or disproven. Still, it formed the basis for modern day racism.

In discussions with colleagues over the years I have concluded that racism includes the belief that race imbues individuals who are defined differently with dissimilar characteristics. As the Oxford English Dictionary (OED) definition reveals though, racism also includes the feelings and beliefs of fear, xenophobia, and ethnocentrism. The OED definition will be the starting point of this volume. As discussions with my colleagues unfolded, however, it became clear that no one could or can explain to me what the term "race" means. Some will argue there is only one race, the human, and that the pigmentation of one's skin is some variation of brown. Yet no one can explain, nor has any research uncovered, why some groups of people or individuals have differing hues of pigmentation. Everyone appears to carefully "tip-toe" around any discussion of the relationship between skin pigmentation and human behavior or intellectual differences except for those who insist there are differences, such as Charles Murray.[8]

There is sufficient evidence throughout US history that public policy decisions have been made based on perceived racial differences; for instance, the laws governing education of African American, Latino, and Asian children throughout the country, racial covenants dictating residential patterns in cities, and differing types of public accommodations in transportation, housing, and various social venues.[9] Still, questions remain as to why racial social policies were created in the first place. When these laws were first instituted the explanations were generally based in beliefs that those not identified as "white" were inferior and that to mix racial groups would only lead to the deterioration of civilized society. This was the principle argument against interracial marriages.

Although contemporary sciences have long since discredited eugenics theories, a large enough number of individuals, many well educated, still believe in the supremacy of "white" people over people of color. Many believers in the supremacy of white people are elected officials or play some other role in the public policy process and push forward agendas based on race without any other rationale other than the individuals affected, usually African Americans, Latinos, Asians, and Native Americans, do not support their agendas. Beyond the political rationale no other reasons for the differential legislation are given. One can understand discriminating against a group of persons who will not support your agenda, this is simply a game often played in many political arenas and has even been recognized as legitimate by the Supreme Court of the United States in *Davis v. Bandemer*, for example.[10] However, the Court has said that if it becomes evident that partisan discrimination crosses over into racial discrimination then it becomes unconstitutional as they decided in *LULAC v. Perry*.[11] Still the question remains, Why do some individuals discriminate against selected persons because of their race? What is it about race that instigates such strong feelings that the very thought of integrating with persons of other racial groups is abhorrent or unthoughtful?

My methodology begins with a technique I learned many years ago during my first year in graduate school at the University of California, Santa Barbara.

We were all required to attempt a seminar with the imposing title "Inquiry" taught by an Oxford don, Ragahavan Iyer. One of the most important lessons I learned in that class was how to ask a question. Before one can construct the question, however, one must understand every element of the question. The question itself must be properly constructed, based in theory, logical, and every concept within the question fundamentally defined before posing the question. Of course, the general rules of conceptual analysis must be imposed so that there can be no doubt as to what information is being sought. The first step in inquiry is to strip the concept under scrutiny down to its core element. This means, in a disciplined manner, peeling away each layer of the concept until you reach its essence. When asking the question "What is racism?," the most robust, disciplined way to reach the answer is to perform a conceptual analysis of this unique concept; this forms the starting point of this volume.

Several terms have already found their way into this conversation such as "political cultural structure" and "conceptual analysis" to name two that will be defined in the first chapter. The initial chapter includes the conceptual analysis of racism as well as what other elements comprise the concept at the heart of this discussion. The chapter begins with a discussion of the analytical process and concludes with an analysis of racism. Included in this discussion is the role played by xenophobia, fear, hatred, and evil. It is my perception, after a great deal of investigation and thought into some of the darkest pages of Western civilization's histories, that although thinking racially in its essentiality is not necessarily bad or evil, when racism is exercised to disadvantage a group of people because of their race then the motivation for a racial decision is founded in the four concepts I just identified. Each of these four concepts and their relationship to racism will form important subsections of this initial chapter.

The next chapter is dedicated to understanding how racism developed and became an integral element of public policy decisions. A brief overview of how racism evolved from one where race was the explicit raison d'etre for public policies to what it has become today, an unspoken assumption protected from public view by "racial shields." Racial shields, as defined in my earlier volume where I discuss the Texas voter ID law,[12] are rationales for a public policy that appear on the surface as race neutral but substantively have deleterious effects on people of color. These shields protect the racist substance of the policy from outside criticism, camouflaging the racial intent of public policy decision makers. Where "code words" are substituted for racial slurs or crude racial references, racial shields are conceptual constructs appearing racially neutral superficially but, when implemented as public policy, have disparate effects on minority populations. These shields, like the "equal protection clause" or the Second Amendment to the Constitution for instance act as mystification mechanisms or devises allowing racism to become imbedded in the policy itself and the process generally. For example, the "equal protection clause" is used to protect the rights of victims during redress of grievances while at the same time act as protection for the perpetrators receiving a fair hearing. If the perpetrators have more resources available with which to fight the complaint, however, their rights are qualitatively on a higher plain than those of the victims. So, the perpetrators can utilize every possible strategic permutation to fight a complaint than a victim can to pursue the complaint. In this instance the equal protection clause acts as a shield protecting the perpetrator from punishment and allowing them to continue injuring future victims. The First Amendment can be used as a shield protecting the rights of those spewing venomous and hurtful speech against racial minority groups, women, and other vulnerable groups, to cite just another example of how a legal device can be used as a shield to protect wrongful and racist behavior. Thus, these, among other laws and processes, can play a "shielding" role hiding racial purpose or intent from the public and provide cover for those attempting to use government to discriminate against others.

The subsequent chapter speaks to what constitutes the public policy process in the United States and Texas. Although a great deal has been written about the policy process, what I am proposing here is a reevaluation of the structure and processes of how policy is formed. Here emphasis is placed on where and how racism fits within the structures and processes that make up the public policy matrix of both the country and Texas. My assumptions here are that both the actions of the political leadership of the nation and state and the manner in which public policy is formed act as catalytic agents for the exercise of racism. For instance, I make the argument that activities of white supremacists are on the rise only because our nation's leadership does not speak up and discourage it. Rather, mostly politicians on the Right, conservatives specifically, tend to make statements in their efforts at seeking a political advantage creating the illusion that it is appropriate for individuals to perpetuate racist language and actions arguing that such reprehensible language is protected by the First Amendment. In this instance the First Amendment acts as a "racial shield" protecting racist language which, I argue, is inherently harmful and should not be afforded constitutional protection. Simultaneously, the precedents of law and previous racist policies tend to act as perpetuating influences in the policy processes of both the nation and Texas. This has become known as the institutionalization of racism.

The empirical data used to present the theoretical arguments set forth in the last two chapters will be based upon a discussion of national immigration policy, the general laws surrounding gun control in the nation, and the efforts to eliminate constitutional protections from voting rights. How laws in each of these policy areas are designed, written, passed, and implemented will provide evidence as to the institutionalization of racism in the United States.

Finally, in the last chapter it will be noted that the infusion of racism in the public policy process does not just affect domestic or internal politics, it possesses bigger implications that have affected foreign policy for decades, particularly since World War II. Racism itself is evil, vile, and harmful, intended to oppress people from accessing their constitutionally protected rights. The harmful intent that is essential for racism to exist can also be considered a defilement of international laws against human rights and a fundamental violation of Christian principles.

NOTES

1. *Shelby County v. Holder*, 570 US __ (2013).
2. 1:2012cv00128 (2012).
3. This informant must remain anonymous for fear of retribution as this individual works within the state government. Nevertheless, this person contacted me because he/she indicated shame at the attitude of this senator and his allies toward Latinos.
4. It appears that the State of Alabama is falling back on an old Jim Crow law that was used to prevent interracial marriages as a statutory basis for the refusal to issue marriage licenses to same-sex couples. *San Antonio Express-News*, October 4, 2005, p. A9.
5. T. F. Gossett, *Race: The History of an Idea in America* (New York: Schocken Books, 1965). George M. Fredrickson, *Racism: A Short History* (Princeton, NJ: Princeton University Press, 2002). Robert Wald Sussman, *The Myth of Race: The Troubling Perspective of an Unscientific Idea* (Cambridge, MA: Harvard University Press, 2014).
6. Thomas Jefferson, *Notes on the State of Virginia*, 1781.
7. Charles Darwin, *On the Origin of Species by Means of Natural Selection* (London: John Murray, 1859).
8. See the debates that raged around the publication of Charles Murray and Richard J. Herrnstein's *The Bell Curve: Intelligence and Class Structure in American Life* (New York: Free Press, 1994).
9. Thomas Adams Upchurch, *Legislating Racism: The Billion Dollar Congress and the Birth of Jim Crow* (Lexington: The University Press of Kentucky, 2004).
10. 478 US 109 (1986).
11. 548 US 399 (2006).
12. Henry Flores, *Latinos and the Voting Rights Act: The Search for Racial Purpose* (New York: Lexington Books, 2015).

Chapter 1

Racism Defined

INTRODUCTION

Perhaps the best way or at least a productive one, to begin this conversation is by going straight to the best-known arbiter of the English language for a definition of the concept we are most concerned. According to the Oxford English Dictionary (OED) racism is

> A belief that one's own racial or ethnic group is superior, or that other such groups represent a threat to one's cultural identity, racial integrity, or economic well-being; (also) a belief that the members of different racial or ethnic groups possess specific characteristics, abilities, or qualities, which can be compared and evaluated. Hence: prejudice, discrimination, or antagonism directed against people of other racial or ethnic groups (or, more widely, of other nationalities), esp. based on such beliefs.

The first step is to unpack the OED definition of racism that states that racism is fundamentally a belief driving the perception of one's race or ethnic group as superior to other groups or races. The OED definition of racism also includes the notion that those who believe they are superior to other groups also believe that the inferior groups present a threat to the "cultural identity," "racial integrity," or "economic well-being" of the superior group. The perceptions of superiority and threat are underlain by another belief, that the threatening and subordinate group is possessed of "characteristics, abilities, or qualities" unique to the inferior group. The final element of the definition is that the specific characteristics, abilities, or qualities of the inferior group(s) may be compared or evaluated using the characteristics, abilities, or qualities of the superior group as the standard or norm of comparison. This automatically places the subordinated group in a permanently inferior position. This permanent inferiority provides justification for the ensuing prejudices, discrimination, or antagonisms, even contempt for, against the inferior group(s). The OED definition, then, possesses five principle elements: racism is a belief; the belief includes the notion that there are unique differences between groups; one group believes it is superior to the other group(s); the group that believes it is superior assumes their general culture is the societal norm and all other group cultures are deviant; and, the superior group believes the inferior group(s) present cultural and political threats to the hegemony of the superior group. The definition of racism, then, includes a belief that one group is superior to others culturally and politically and the inferior groups threaten the qualitative integrity of the superior group's dominance.

Although the OED does not speak to the psychological dimensions of a belief in one's racial superiority, it does appear that one conclusion that may be drawn from the definition describes an individual or group who may suffer from some combination of narcissism, arrogance, a need to dominate, fear, and paranoia. This chapter is not intended as a behavioral or psychoanalysis of a prejudiced personality or individual, however, a fundamental understanding of the psychology underlying racism is important for a thorough comprehension of racism in order to understand the behavioral characteristics that drive discriminatory actions or behavior. An individual's perception of his or her culture and its place relative to others potentially may be traced back to a society's general definition of relations within that culture. An individual or group who believes in their racial superiority then sees their culture as possessing values that will lead a society to higher levels of civilization and political superiority because this is a perception propagated within that society. Various authors have argued that one core cultural American value, for instance, is based upon a perception that the United States has often described itself in biblical terms as "a city upon a hill."[1] The insinuation is that the United States is a country, nation, and people that are the cultural and political exemplars for the world to emulate. This solipsistic allusion is both arrogant and narcissistic because it assumes that this country and its way of life is the envy of the world's people and because Americans view themselves as the best culture as well as having the best governmental system in the world. This perception presumes that all other cultures and political systems are inferior and because the cultures and systems are inferior their people are as well.

The OED definition also speaks to the notion that those who believe in their racial superiority believe, by definition, in a racial hierarchy—that some races are better than others culturally and politically. Embedded in this belief, and clearly set forth in the OED definition, are feelings of fear and, subsequently, a type of cultural paranoia. Essentially, those who believe in their own cultural superiority are afraid that their culture will be contaminated or superseded by inferior races. This perceived threat eventually leads the superior race to institute discriminative policies in efforts at preventing the cultural and political contamination by the inferiors and their social and political ascension. Extreme examples of these reactions are found in the histories of the passing of the Nuremburg Laws in 1935 by Nazi Germany eliminating citizenship for Jews and the Jim Crow Laws passed throughout various former Confederate states following Reconstruction that lasted into the 1930s in the United States. In both instances, the Nazi regime and the southeastern United States saw Jews and African Americans as culturally, socially, and politically inferior, respectively. These groups in their respective times and places were held in low esteem, were viewed with a great deal of contempt, and feared culturally. As a result, laws were passed to insure these racial and social groups were separated from the greater society. Perceptually, separation protected against social and cultural contamination. Thus, the superior culture felt that the passage of racial laws protected their hegemonic position in society as well as in the world. As a result, Nazi Germany passed laws stripping Jews of the right to vote. While the southeastern states passed voting laws making it extremely difficult if not impossible for African Americans to participate in elections. Before proceeding to a discussion of how cultural and political discrimination is enacted in the policy process by those who perceive themselves racially superior, a more detailed discussion of the elements in the OED definition of racism is important here. The public policy process and how it is manipulated to pass racially based laws are the subjects of the next two chapters.

RACISM AS A BELIEF

Fundamental to the OED definition is that racism is a belief. The definition does not speak to whether the belief is based on empirical information, is an artificial construct, or derived from some form of reasoning. Racism is simply a belief. As most beliefs, racism can be considered a matter of faith passed on from generation to generation through various ideological mechanisms such as the family, religion, the educational system, one's peers, or the media.

A belief is a mental act of placing one's trust in someone, some idea, or something even if erroneous. The legitimation of the belief is founded in the understanding that, whether correct or incorrect, the belief is substantiated by someone or something that an individual trusts implicitly. Beliefs can be in abstractions, individuals, empirically based notions, concepts or ideas, or a concept that began as an abstraction and later empirically verified. In the first category one finds concepts such as deities or other similar abstractions such as "heaven, hell, angels, the devil, good, bad, evil," and so forth. Many concepts in this category are learned initially from the family and then reinforced through religious education. These types of abstractions can never be empirically verified. One cannot touch a deity or experience heaven or hell. One can only believe that they exist because one has been taught that they do and, consequentially, one comes to believe in their existence. Concepts such as good and evil may appear as manifested in human acts such as the beneficent or deleterious behavior of one human to another living being. In themselves evil or good cannot be seen concretely only as behavioral manifestations as defined by society.

Beliefs in other human beings are fostered through either what one thinks or comes to learn of the other individual. This person may have performed some heroic act or served as a role model of sorts, such as a teacher or religious leader or may be the expresser of ideological beliefs that a person finds particularly impressive. One can be led to believe in almost anything another person says simply because one becomes susceptible to that other person's charisma or personal charm, what is perceived that the other person represents or promises. This may be the case when speaking of national or international personalities such as religious leaders or well-respected individuals in particular fields of endeavor. Unless an individual or idea is well-known, through thorough research or personal interaction, the belief may be based in only a superficial and not substantive understanding of that person or idea and does not necessarily represent the truth. As a result, believers, those being manipulated, may be subject to demagoguery as well. Unfortunately, many of the beliefs used to manipulate the votes of the lesser educated and informed are based on stereotypically untruthful opinions or perceptions. Individuals or institutions that believers respect or appear important to the believer's ideological and philosophical orientations legitimize the importance of these less than truthful beliefs. Therefore, any attempts to discredit the untruthful belief may not be constructive or effective. Believers will build protective perceptual screens preventing them to allow for any open and free exchange of ideas.

Beliefs in emotions such as love, empathy, hate, fear, intolerance, and so forth are learned through the normal socialization processes. For instance, one's parents and family unit is the socialization environment for individuals to learn about familial or filial love and the parents may serve as role models for a child's understanding of platonic or marital love. This, subsequently, is reinforced through variable exposure to the popular media or one's peers and through interpersonal relations developed during one's lifetime. The same can be said about other emotions such as hate and intolerance. One learns to hate something, someone, or specific groups of humans at an early age through what parents or other adults say or how they behave around children. These feelings generally have no substance except that awarded by the authority figures teaching the young person or child at that moment. The substance of the belief evolves becoming stronger and, in some cases, more sophisticated as one receives more intense negative and ideologically deeper propaganda as one matures emotionally and politically. Negative, stereotypical, and untruthful propaganda are created and inseminated by and through authority figures, peers, and professional groups, through all socialization mechanisms that comprise one's daily social or psychological environment. Feelings of hate or love are irrational and not necessarily based in any type of empirical evidence but become ingrained in an individual so deeply that they will affect and dictate the way a person constructs the interpersonal relations with those they hate or love, like or dislike for the remainder of their lives. One cannot understand the depth of these feelings unless one performs some level of psychoanalysis on that individual.[2]

Finally, one can believe in an abstraction that eventually becomes an empirical reality. Here the most cogent example can be found in the world of military experience. Soldiers, when they are initially trained, are made to believe in an "enemy." This enemy is an abstraction concocted by the military trainers to give their young acolytes a rationale for the hardships they endure in training and later in combat. The trainers cajole and encourage their neophyte soldiers to kill these imaginary enemies in the most forceful and final way possible. An essential element in this training is using racial slurs and negative images of the enemy and illusions of inhumanity and cruelty perpetrated by that enemy that partially alleviates any ethical or moral quandary a young soldier may have when confronted with the necessity of killing another human being. This technique accomplishes several goals simultaneously. First, it instills a sense of teamwork and creates a team ethos among the young soldiers. Then it creates a sense of survival that leads the group to want to kill those deemed the "enemy." The enemy, at this stage, remains an abstraction made real in the imaginations of young soldiers by their military instructors and only becomes real when confronted on the battlefield. Many soldiers, however, never really engage an enemy combatant, only soldiers in actual combat encounter individuals who have been defined as the enemy, and then the enemy becomes a real person. Still the enemy does not become an actual human being, is not humanized until an up-close encounter occurs and the enemy is captured, wounded, or killed. Then, the enemy's humanness unfolds particularly as his personal possessions are rifled through in the process of intelligence gathering or looting.

Beliefs, then, can be held about abstract ideas or concepts or the word of another. Nevertheless, beliefs are created, transmitted, and perpetuated by individuals acting as their own agents or representatives of institutions. For instance, when one is young one believes various ideas, concepts, or values transmitted by one's parents or immediate authority figures. One believes what these individuals say because they are held up as the protectors and teachers of first resort for children. As an individual passes from childhood to adulthood they form their own belief systems based on their life experiences yet the acceptance and substance of any beliefs are founded in the beliefs that have been passed on to them by their parents or others who the children define as appropriate authority figures or legitimating agents. For some persons a legitimate authority figure could be a religious, civic, political, or professional figure that is in a position of influence. As an example, a parent or religious authority, such as a preacher, priest, or other similarly situated individual, may teach the young person that a certain deity exists that guides that young person's life. These individuals also assist in the creation of a value system, together with a structure of rewards and punishments, for that young person to follow throughout their lifetime. These religious or moral beliefs evolve and change as the individual matures in life but fundamentally remain imbedded in the subconsciousness on the individual.

In another phase of an individual's life one develops a system of political and social beliefs through their parents, reinforced by other individuals such as teachers, political, or other legitimated individuals that assist in the formation of one's ideological orientation. Essentially, a socialization structure that governs one's ideological orientation is slowly constructed throughout one's lifetime as they interact with others, observe, and experience political and social phenomenon. For instance, a child listening to how adults, particularly those in positions of authority, refer to individuals of other races will begin to develop biases for or against persons of those groups. As one grows older and lacking substantive knowledge of individuals of other races or nationalities those perceptions become hardened and more deeply imbedded in one's psyche. Or, a person, particularly a child, observing a calamity such as the terrorist attack on New York City's Twin Towers on September 11, 2001, may begin developing beliefs about Muslims and immigrants and whether wars, deportations, or racial restrictions are justified. Beliefs make up an essential element of one's overall ideological perceptual screen. The perceptual screen allows an individual to sift through and filter out any beliefs or ideas that oppose or that contradict those that make up an essential core of her ideological and belief structure. This structure allows an individual to define the world around them, their own essentiality, and their place within the world.[3] The ideological structure that one constructs around oneself and the individuals and institutions one interacts with throughout one's lifetime assists in the determination of one's relationship with and to others, other nation-states, other belief systems and so forth. Most germane to this discussion is that imbedded within one's ideological belief structures is one's understanding of who one is socially, including racially. One's ideological orientation also allows an individual to understand their gender and age essentiality and their particular place in a given historical moment.

One's ideological structure determines whether one is politically conservative, liberal, socialist, libertarian, or other. These types of orientations then help in determining the way in which an individual defines social problems, relations, and whether and how some political entity may address any issues associated with the problems or relations. For instance, individuals of differing ideological orientations define the concept of poverty and its causes differently. Conservatives may place more blame on the individual while a socialist may see the economic structure as the principle cause of poverty. Some conservatives may even not see poverty as a problem but only as a normal aberration of the economic system from which any individuals can extricate themselves eventually. For example, the Supreme Court in a now infamous decision *Rodriguez v. San Antonio Independent School District*, 411 U.S. 1 (1973) found that the only legal definition for poverty up to that time was a class of individuals who were completely without any economic resources and unable to pay for any legal representation. In fact, the court pointed out that no "discernable" or "identifiable" class of poor people existed because there lacked a mechanism to define such a class in the evidence the plaintiffs submitted to the court. Poor parents who claimed that the Texas state school financing system discriminated against property poor school districts brought the case itself. The majority opinion was composed by Associate Justice Lewis Powell who spent his legal career, before ascension to the Supreme Court, as a corporate attorney defending tobacco interests. At one time, he wrote the very conservative Powell Memorandum attacking organizations that opposed the tobacco interests over whether tobacco consumption led to cancer.[4]

RACE AS A BELIEF

Conceptually, racism falls within the analytical category of a belief that is an essential element of an overarching ideological system. The OED points out that racism as a belief is based in the conception that one accepts as a truth "that one's own racial or ethnic group is superior." It follows, then, that one must believe that they belong to some social category called a "race" and the race they belong to is superior to all others. As a logical consequence one also must believe that there is some hierarchy of races. In earlier historical eras and as late as the twentieth century, the belief in racial superiority was considered as a normal way in which to view society generally.

Race, again as an analytical category, is an ancient notion and its origins are unknown to those who study this concept. Some, such as Fredrickson,[5] believe that the origins of race go back to ancient times but finds that there is no early evidence that any systematic belief existed based on a hierarchy of races. Race was seen as one way for a group of people to differentiate themselves from others. The notion that one race was superior to another grew as different groups of people began conquering and enslaving others believing that the race of the victors was superior to that of the losers, thus their ability to win and enslave the losers. This belief of racial superiority found its way into Western sociological and anthropological thought as black Africa found itself the source of slaves for the Americas. The Western powers, mostly European, began developing justifications for racial superiority in order to rationalize the development and expansion of the slave trade and the conquering of the Americas and their indigenous people.[6]

By the eighteenth century, the idea of racial superiority of whites over blacks and others evolved from a combination of popular cultural beliefs biblically based and substantiated through scientific racism. The biblical foundations of racism are founded in the Hamitic legend declaring that the descendants of Ham or Canaan would be marked for eternity because Ham had seen his father Noah in an inebriated and naked state and made fun of him. Others who argue that a biblical root for race exists point out that God created this group of people from "mud" and so they remained dark skinned. Goldenberg argues, on the other hand, that there is no linkage between the color of people and slavery in Jewish antiquity.[7] One still finds references to "the mud people" in the literature and propaganda of contemporary white supremacist organizations, particularly those that identify themselves with Christian beliefs. Regardless, this branch of racial superiority thinking is found less in academic circles and is attributed more to those of popular culture. The most exaggerated examples of beliefs of this can be found in the rhetoric of what is known as the Christian Identity movement that began in 1915 as a branch of the Ku Klux Klan and persists to this day.[8]

Not until the seventeenth century was an effort made to lend scientific rigor to a hierarchical structure of races. Of course, the scientific rigor of the seventeenth through early twentieth century varied in sophistication. Contemporarily these methodologies would not withstand academic scrutiny. The Age of Enlightenment's scientific methods were based on what little knowledge was available at the time and the discourse on race was rather amusing by today's standards. Some thinkers declared that all humans descended from one race and environmental factors, such as varying exposures to sunlight, caused the differences in skin pigmentations. Others believed that there were multiple origins for all humans. Sometimes the difference between races, particularly those between "blacks" and "whites," were attributed to diet, disease, or the environment. Several thinkers even indicated that "black" persons were really "white" and that under certain circumstances individuals would revert to their white nature such as staying out of sunlight for an extended period.

Not until the late nineteenth and early twentieth centuries were efforts made to conduct anthropological research on the differences between races, which led to the creation of a science that came to be known as eugenics, was created to lend intellectual legitimacy to the concept of race and the biological differences between races. Joseph Arthur, Comte de Gobineau, a French aristocrat writing in the latter half of the nineteenth century, is considered to be the "father" of contemporary scientific racism. He set forth his master race theory in his seminal work *Essai sur l'inégalité des races humaines (Essay on the Inequality of the Human Races, 1853–1855).*[9] In his work de Gobineau identifies Aryans as the master race and asserts that Whites were the direct descendants of Adam and that the other two major racial groups, Black and Yellow, were not. De Gobineau never does speak to the origins of Blacks and Yellows and it is clear from his essay that he had no formal training in anthropology or biology. This French thinker's work, though, is important because his was the first attempt at a cohesive and coherent theory of racial hierarchy. He also spoke to the implications of race mixing or miscegenation. De Gobineau felt that any racial mixing between whites and others would work to the detriment of white civilization and culture. De Gobineau was a French royalist and defender of the *ancien régime* and believed his racist theory explained the movement of France from a monarchy to a republic and the rise and evolution of both materialism and democracy generally. Essentially, his racial theory provided the "scientific" rationale for inequality required for a democratic society to exist. In other words, racial inequality was natural and not one imposed by a monarchy or the state. As a result, the state could not be held responsible for the inequality. The inequality was a condition brought on by the race of the specific individual. Initially, then, racism was defined hierarchically with the fear, lurking in the background, that miscegenation would lead to the demise of civilization and the destruction of culture.

The field of eugenics was treated as a science shortly after de Gobineau's theories were publicized and became a controversial topic at the founding of the discipline of anthropology. Nevertheless, by the time "modern" scientists and anthropologists engaged in debates about eugenics several concepts had already been accepted as doctrine. The first and most important concept was the creation of a social category called "race" and it became an assumption in professional sociological and anthropological discourse. There was never, it appears, an attempt to question whether such a category possessed merit. Discussions proceeded into the twentieth century that races existed and that individuals who were possessed of certain physical characteristics belonged in a specific racial category. Even today, race categorization can be found in all areas of society from census questionnaires to references in the local news.

Secondly, it was assumed that a hierarchy of races existed and that "whites" or "Aryans" were at the top of the racial scale. "White" civilization was the most refined in every way. It was assumed that "white" civilization and culture had been responsible for all advances in the sciences, arts, and politics. The other cultures, primarily "black," "yellow," "red," and "mongrelized" were not capable of achieving the high social, intellectual, or cultural standards or the achievements established by "whites." "Mongrelized" races were the mixed races and the result of miscegenation and those that didn't fit the other categories and were even less accomplished than the lesser races. The third assumption, a logical extension of the second, was that miscegenation or the mixing of races should not be encouraged or allowed. To do so would be the beginning of the end for "white" culture and civilization. Thus, some of the important elements in the study of eugenics were to justify the existence of racial groups, the justification of racial superiority of whites and inferiority of all others, and the rationalization of anti-miscegenation policies. Most importantly, however, was the allusion to the fear that allowing integration of the races would diminish the quality of white culture and eventually lead to the demise of Western civilization.

One of the earliest supporters of scientific racism and eugenics was an American named Madison Grant. Grant not only agreed with the basic assumptions of eugenics but he spent his entire life propagating them, culminating in the publication of his most important work *The Passing of the Great Race*.[10] In his book, Grant developed his Nordic theory that states that the Nordic or white race was responsible for all advances in Europe and that in order to insure the continuation of advances in the sciences, arts, and politics the races had to be kept separate. His writings were so influential that even Adolf Hitler declared *The Passing of the Great Race* as his bible.[11] Grant's work in eugenics is very important because he spent his entire professional life propagating white superiority and lobbying congress for restrictive immigration policies that only allowed white, northern Europeans to immigrate freely while placing harsh restrictions on all others. His influence was so great that he provided data to Congress as they considered the Immigration Act of 1924 and he advised the State of Virginia when it considered miscegenation as part of their Racial Integrity Act of 1924. The landmark *Loving v. Virginia* Supreme Court decision in 1967 overturned this latter act.[12] Eventually, Grant's ideas were essential to the passage of anti-miscegenation and sterilization laws throughout the United States.

Madison Grant also infused his theories into national and international academic debates that were so controversial that eventually Grant and his followers were forced to leave the American Anthropological Association, where he had been president. Following his departure from the National Anthropological Association, he founded the Galton Institute to carry on his eugenics research. Two of Grant's adherents, Charles B. Davenport and Harry H. Laughlin, founded the Eugenics Records Office in Cold Spring Harbor, New York, where they continued eugenics research and advocated for the forced sterilization of the "feebleminded." This research was used as a rationale for the forced sterilization of women and men of color throughout the South and Mexican women in California.[13] Many of these laws, some of which were not repealed until the late 1970s extended to thirty-two states in the union, and the victims were still being compensated as late as 2010.[14]

Eugenics research, then, became the foundation for early immigration, anti-miscegenation, and sterilization policies in the United States. Scientific racism and eugenics, which formed the core philosophy of these policies, fell out of favor at the conclusion of World War II after many of the atrocities perpetrated by the Nazis in Europe came to light. In one particularly disturbing occasion *The Passing of the Great Race* was introduced as a defense document during the Nuremburg war crime trials on behalf of Alfred Rosenberg who was the chief race ideologist of the Nazi Party to no avail. As a brief historical aside, Rosenberg in his most influential work *Der Mythus des zwanzigsten Jahrhunderts* or *The Myth of the Twentieth Century*,[15] develops the racial theory of the Nazis that features a racial hierarchy based upon the works of DeGobineau, Houston S. Chamberlain, and Madison Grant. The hierarchy adopts Grant's Nordic theory as its model and places Aryans at the top with Blacks and Jews at the bottom. Chamberlain was a British racial theorist whose work was an essential element of the anti-Semitism propagated during the pan-German pre-World War II era and also influenced the thinking of Joseph Goebbels, Hitler's minister of propaganda. Nevertheless, Rosenberg's racial ideology was an essential part of the laws that stripped German Jews of their citizenship and laid the foundation for the final solution. On September 15, 1935, the laws were passed in Nazi Germany forbidding the intermarriage of Jews and Germans. These laws that were collectively known as the Nuremberg Laws, the official name of the laws was the Law for the Protection of German Blood and German Honor, were preceded by a series of other laws such as the Reich Citizenship Law that striped German Jews of their citizenship and later was expanded to include Romani (gypsies) and Black persons. According to the speeches that accompanied these laws, they were to ensure that German culture was not tainted by inferior cultures. The Nazis had already begun a euthanasia program to "cleanse" their culture through the elimination of "defectives," that is, mentally retarded, emotionally diseased, and individuals with deforming diseases such as multiple sclerosis or hip dysplasia.

The belief that gave birth to the Nazi racial laws were founded in the writings of Adolf Hitler where he spoke to the notion that interbreeding between races, particularly superior to subordinate, would lead to the downfall of a culture and eventually all of mankind. He pointed out that interspecies and interracial breeding went against the Laws of Nature and would lead eventually to total chaos. As an example, he then pointed out that the "Teutonic" race of North America had maintained its racial purity by not allowing interracial breeding thus making the United States powerful as contrasted to the countries of South and Central America.[16] Preceding the Nazi's actions in the twentieth century, similar laws were passed in the United States. During the late eighteenth and nineteenth century anti-miscegenation laws were passed and enforced in forty-two states until the early part of the twentieth century and were ruled unconstitutional or overturned by various state legislatures. As noted earlier, the most important Supreme Court decision in this vein was *Loving v. Virginia*. Both the US and German racial laws were designed to protect what the lawmakers perceived as the core culture of their respective societies. Most importantly, however, assumptions of the racial superiority of whites underlay a great deal of this research, which has found its way into university textbooks and still rears itself occasionally such as in the work of Herrnstein and Murray[17] and propagated contemporaneously by apostles of white supremacy.

THE BELIEF IN RACIAL THREATS

The last element in the OED definition of racism is that those who believe in their racial superiority feel that those in the lower races pose a threat to the cultural hegemony of the superior race. This fear is most evident in the eugenics literature of the early part of the twentieth century. Obviously, the most prominent work was that of Madison Grant where he spoke against miscegenation and in favor of restrictive immigration laws. Grant was specific: any interaction between the higher and lower races would be to the detriment of the higher races and the diminution of a nation's culture. Madison Grant's *The Passing of the Great Race* influenced other social and political scientists and politicians as well as racial policies at all governmental levels. Grant's work influenced not just the restrictive immigration laws of the United States it also gave birth to an entire national movement and a body of literature that, in turn, inspired anti-miscegenation, sterilization, restrictive covenant laws, and educational policies in many states that were ruled unconstitutional in the twentieth century. Regardless, Grant's publication and the body of literature it spawned became the guiding light of white supremacist and racial thinking throughout the country.

The threat that civilization would fall and democracy would collapse if the lower races took over or, at least, if the lower races were allowed to amalgamate can be found throughout the white supremacist literature that has dominated public policy discourse during the twentieth and twenty-first centuries. Some examples of the prominent racialist literature inspired by Madison Grant's work included *White America: The American Racial Problem as Seen in a Worldwide Perspective*[18] by Earnest Sevier Cox. Cox was a white supremacist who advocated for anti-miscegenation laws and in his *White America* declared that a racial hierarchy existed in the United States with whites as the superior race. Additionally, he championed the cause of racial separation that included developing policies to deport all blacks to Africa. Cox felt that "amalgamation" or miscegenation would lead to the devolution of American culture and the eventual demise of the white race. He assumed that races existed because they had been declared as such in the literature of his era; he did not conduct any research attempting to substantiate his position. His link to Madison Grant's work is found in the introduction where he thanks Grant for reviewing his manuscript. Besides declaring Madison Grant as an inspiration, Cox also cited the work of T. Lothrop Stoddard who spoke to "the impending peril of the Asiatic to Europe as well as to America and the rest of the White world."[19]

Stoddard was a leading thinker in the eugenics movement that swept through Europe and North America from the late nineteenth century through the 1930s. His research and writing were particularly important to both the eugenics movement and white supremacist thinking because it carried scholarly weight. Stoddard held a PhD from Harvard, studied law, and was a member of several learned organizations including the American Political Science Association and the American Historical Society. His most influential work was *The Revolt against Civilization or The Menace of the Underman*.[20] Stoddard acknowledges Madison Grant as inspiration for his work and implies that it is an extension of the evolutionary research first proposed by Charles Darwin, although he credits Darwin's nephew Francis Galton as the "founder of the science of 'Eugenics' or 'Race Betterment.'"[21] Stoddard notes that Galton's contribution had motivated his research and declared "inborn differences between men" exists "but the fact existed that these differences could be controlled."[22] Eventually, Stoddard concluded that regulating these differences could be accomplished only through strict immigration controls, anti-miscegenation laws, and forced sterilization programs.

The manner in which Stoddard describes the inborn differences between men was based on a merging of data allowing him to conclude that the highest culture was a "white" European culture with a national hierarchy headed by England followed in order by Scotland, Holland, Canada, Germany, Denmark, Sweden, Norway, and Ireland. The countries with "inferior cultures" included, in order of the lowest, Poland, Italy, Russia, Greece, Turkey, Ireland, and so forth.[23] It appears that Ireland was the lowest of the superior cultures and best of the inferior ones. He then argues that the most important variable in culture is the level of intelligence in each culture followed by the differences between races. Stoddard provides evidence, in the form of grades attained in a military intelligence exam, that indicates that "whites" attained higher numbers of "As" and "Bs" while "blacks" attained higher percentages of grades "C-" and lower. Of course, the "As" and "Bs" were grades attained mostly by the officer ranks, which tended to be college educated and the other grades by enlisted personnel who were not particularly educated to any degree.[24] Stoddard's biased testing structure, that could not pass academic scrutiny today, further substantiated his own racial biases.

Stoddard claimed that if the lower classes and races were allowed to procreate with those of high culture, blacks with whites, then the result would be the eventual demise of Western civilization and culture. He concludes that the fall of many great empires such as Rome and Greece for instance, was the result of the "pure" Romans intermarrying with barbarian peoples. As a result, Stoddard felt that "white culture's" demise would result if the Northern European people intermarried with the Eastern European people and blacks. Stoddard's work was particularly attractive to the Nazis and he was invited to discuss his research in Germany before the implementation of the Nuremberg Laws and subsequent Holocaust. Although Stoddard found Germany's approach to the race question abhorrent, it is clear that his ideas helped rationalize the Nazi's racial philosophies.

The final example of the racialist thinking that dominated social policies in the United States at the beginning of the twentieth century can be found in Theodore G. Bilbo's *Take Your Choice: Separation or Mongrelization*.[25] Bilbo was a governor and United States senator from Mississippi and had been a member of the KKK. His signature book was designed to support his efforts at having Congress pass legislation to "separate the races" by encouraging the migration of African Americans to Africa. He also indicated that his work and thinking were inspired by Madison Grant's research; Earnest Sevier Cox penned the introduction of *Take Your Choice*. Bilbo echoed the same themes in his book that Grant, Cox, and Stoddard had in their works pointing out the qualitative differences between races, explicated with little or no data, insisting that culture and civilization that had been built by Caucasians was destroyed by the incorporation of lesser cultures.

Bilbo's discussion begins with a review of what he considers the great cultures of the world beginning with Egypt, Rome, Greece, and India declaring that all had been developed by Caucasians. Their decline occurred when each began intermarrying with blacks and other people of color from lower cultures. To Bilbo, "Civilizations, the product of race, have been maintained as long as the race which created them has maintained racial integrity. The Caucasian has founded all great civilizations, and this race, remaining white, has not lost civilization. But when the blood of the white man has become mongrelized, civilization has not been maintained."[26] He points out that "without the directing hand and creative genius of the white race, and any effort to destroy the blood of this race by contamination with the blood of Africa is an effort to destroy the Nation and its future."[27] For Bilbo and other white supremacist thinkers, the United States was and is a white nation and could only be preserved through the separation of the races. Although a segregationist, Bilbo believed this was only a temporary and unsatisfactory solution; absolute separation was the preferred solution to the race problem. To that end only through the implementation of anti-miscegenation laws, separation of the races and, in some cases, forced sterilization could the culture of the United States be preserved.

Eventually, the beliefs of racial superiority and separation found their way into the development of public policy in the United States culminating with the passage of the Immigration Restriction Act of 1924 that was designed to restrict the immigration of Eastern Europeans, Italians, and Jews and increase immigration of Nordic or Northern Europeans in order that "America . . . remain American."[28] The Act of 1924 was influenced by representatives of the Eugenics Record Office who based their arguments on the work of Madison Grant insisting that American civilization and culture could only be preserved by not allowing immigration from Eastern and Southern Europe and all parts of Asia. No provision was made to restrict immigration from Latin America. There appears no evidence of why Bilbo excluded Latin America from his analysis other than it was simply overlooked or inclusion would have argued against larger geopolitical issues of that era.[29] Nevertheless, in Grant's *Passing of the Great Race* he points out that the disorganized societies and nations of Latin America were the result of race mixing between the descendants of the European conquerors and the indigenous population. The catastrophes of Latin America served as examples of what could happen in the United States if lesser cultures were allowed to mix with that of native-born Americans. In his *Passing of the Great Race* Grant states his observation neglecting to point out that Mexico was still involved in,

> What the Melting Pot actually does in practice can be seen in Mexico, where the absorption of the blood of the original Spanish conquerors by the native Indian population has produced the racial mixture which we call Mexican and which is now engaged in demonstrating its incapacity for self-government.[30]

The decades' long civil wars would not effectively conclude until 1940. The government of Mexico indeed was not stable between 1910 and 1940 but this instability was not due to cultural deficiencies but rather to political and economic differences between warring factions. The white supremacist thinkers at the beginning of the eugenics movement through World War I saw race mixing as deleterious to the American way of life and the nation eventually leading to white culture's degeneration. Essentially, the propounders of eugenics saw anti-miscegenation laws, state sponsored sterilization, and separation of races as a matter of cultural survival and the improvement of the nation. Frankly, the eugenicists saw their position as making their race stronger by cleansing the gene pool of weak or lesser genetic material. What they did not foresee was how their theories carried to extremes by the Nazis in Germany could lead to terrible consequences; consequences that both horrified the public and led to the general shunning of eugenics by academic and political circles.

Prior to World War II white supremacy thinking based on the science of eugenics dominated sociological, anthropological, and political discourse but it did not go unchallenged. There were those who opposed the racialist way of thinking such as Franz Boas who was considered the "Father of Modern Anthropology." Boas taught at Columbia University and was vilified by Cox and Stoddard for his criticism of eugenics and their movement. Gossett notes that Boas was the most important fighter against racism at the beginning of the twentieth century.[31] The acrimony was so intense between Boas and his followers that they eventually drove the eugenicists out of the American Anthropological Association. As pointed out earlier, this resulted in Madison Grant and his followers leaving the association and creating a branch of the Galton Institute in the United States. Still, scientific eugenics eventually fell from grace due to the passing of Grant and other leaders of the movement, the retirement of Charles Davenport, new findings in biological anthropology, and the revelations of the Holocaust.[32]

Nevertheless, eugenics reappeared on the American scene in the 1960s becoming a powerful assumption in many public policy realms. The principle academic worlds, where research was conducted and findings published that were based on the assumptions created by eugenics, appeared in the fields of sociology, political science, and psychology in the United States. The early work on poverty pioneered by Oscar Lewis in his *Five Families: Mexican Case Studies in the Culture of Poverty*[33] where it was posited that the culture of poverty within which these families lived was the determining rationale for the inability of these subjects to lift themselves out of their dire social straits. The culture of poverty was fundamentally based in the conception that,

> People with a culture of poverty have very little sense of history. They are a marginal people who know only their own troubles, their own local conditions, their own neighborhood, their own way of life.[34]

This perception found its way into the sociological and political science literature of the late 1950s, into, and through the 1980s beginning with the research of Daniel Patrick Moynihan, Nathan Glazer, and Edward Banfield.[35] Each of these scholars concentrated their efforts on the "urban problems" of the day and found that blacks and Latinos, because they lived within a culture of poverty, would be trapped forever within their lower social class circumstances.

Adding to the racism in American scholarship was the work of Arthur R. Jensen and William Shockley. Jensen was an educational psychologist who conducted research on the relationship between race and intelligence by comparing the scores on the Stanford Binet IQ test of different races. He concluded that blacks were less intelligent than whites given their lower scores on the examination.[36] He deduced that intelligence variances were the result of genetic differences between races. Although he failed to empirically connect actual genetic testing with anything, Jensen's research spawned a great deal of research both supporting and opposing his perspective that lasts to this day and still underlays the objective examinations used for university admissions, graduate school, and medical and law school qualifying examinations. Jensen's racial difference assumptions found their way into Herrnstein and Murray's work that became *The Bell Curve* in 1994.[37] In Rushton's and Jensen's 2005 article they expand racial difference research to include more than those between blacks and whites adding Latinos and Asians. Rushton and Jensen remain devoted to the "classical" classification of races that had been created as early as those of de Gobineau and presented their hierarchy of racial groups based on IQ test scores, sizes of brain, sexual behavior, criminal tendencies, personality, and social organization.[38] These debates in academia went well into the twenty-first century in scholarly journals in psychology, sociology, and political science.

Racial threats, then, are perceived as an artifact created through the establishment of racialist thinking. Without racism there cannot be a perceived threat against one's culture. Nevertheless, the creation of racism resulted in a concomitant creation in fear that the lower races, if allowed to incorporate or amalgamate with the higher cultures, would lead to the contamination of the superior culture eventually leading to its demise. There appeared not to be any thinking associated with the possibility that the incorporation might lead to the improvement of the lower or both cultures only the diminution of the higher one. This fear then led to the creation of social and cultural barriers reinforced by political and economic barriers against individuals of the lower races from fully participating in the societies created by the higher cultures. So, fear became an essential element of racism.

FEAR AND RACISM

As the review of the racial thinkers' literature reveals it is clear that each indicate the consequences of racial mixing pointing out the dilution of and possibly the extinction of Western civilization. Racist thinkers fear a threat to their culture as a result wish to act proactively against the threat. Still, the question remains, Why fear and does this fear lead to pathological actions against individuals of races and cultures that have been defined as lower on the cultural scale than the dominant race? Although it may clearly appear that threat leads to action and, in the public policy arena, may lead to the passage of policies and laws that intended to discriminate against certain racial groups, a definite conclusion can be reached only through understanding the emotions and feelings of those threatened. Here I must tread lightly because I am not a psychologist or psychiatrist. Yet it does not require deep analysis to understand that what one feels when threatened is fear.

The psychology of fear is based in the notion that fear itself can either be an emotion or a feeling with some overlap.[39] Fear is "entirely subjective" and may be the result of seeing something or someone that triggers this feeling, the feeling of some "impending doom." The racist literature reveals that the "doom" is the demise of Western civilization. The problematic is that the "doom" or the unfounded fear of the "demise of Western civilization" goes unarticulated or described to a degree allowing those easily vulnerable to racist rantings falling prey to their own imaginations. Thus, xenophobic imaginings drive fear resulting in "fear as a feeling" changing to "feeling as an emotion" the difference being that emotions result in actions while fears do not.[40]

The fear generated by racist propaganda and thinking, then, is based upon the creation of feelings of uncertainty and a fear that one will lose what social status one has, even if this social status is perceived rather than real. Therefore, an uneducated white person of menial employment will react to racist thinking because they fear that their place on the social rung of society, a feeling based solely on the belief that being a white person is higher on the social scale than a black person, is endangered by social integration. This fear of losing what little perceived social status a person has, so moved by racist thinking and rhetoric, drives this person to action. The more politically helpless the individual the more susceptible that individual is to the fears generated by racist rhetoric. As such, these individuals will take political action in a manner that they feel appropriate. In some extreme cases the action took the form of lynching and killing people of color while in more subtle cases the action became the passage of various types of laws designed to diminish social, political, or economic opportunities for colored people. In this latter category, one finds the Jim Crow laws of the first and second reconstruction eras.[41] Some argue that the demographic changes of the late twentieth and early twenty-first centuries have given rise to a Third Reconstruction explaining the proliferation of new voter restrictions and the intensification of racial rhetoric by elected politicians generally. Even the Republican Party presidential nominees and, most importantly the party's 2016 presidential candidate freely used racist rhetoric to rally their followers. Donald Trump was even accused of encouraging individuals who attended his campaign rallies to perpetrate violent acts against people of color and those who did not agree with his ideological positions on race.

Several beliefs appear to drive racial fear. It is feared that allowing complete integration meaning insuring equal access to Latinos and African Americans to all accommodations, public and private, could lead to the downward mobility of whites. The social and economic elevation of blacks and Latinos creates the fear that these groups will replace white workers in the labor force leading to the loss of wages and opportunities as well. As alluded to earlier, full integration means that full equality in the election process could lead to Latinos and African Americans taking the reins of political power in many states. Already the United States has elected an African American president; the fear is that this phenomenon could spread to the national Congress and many state executive and legislative branches. With these institutions controlled by members of racial minority groups it would be just a matter of time before the judicial branches across the nation would fall as well.

There is also the continuing fear of white women intermarrying or entering into sexual relations with men of color. As an aside, there never appears to be a fear of white men entering into sexual relations with black women or Latinas. Still, interracial sexual relations and marriages are still taboo in many regions of the United States. Finally, there is the fear that if Latinos and African Americans take control of the government they may retaliate against whites for past injustices.[42] Consequently, the fear generated by racism drives the politics that gives rise to a discriminatory public policy process resulting in the birth of racially discriminatory programs, laws, statutes, and policies.

The conceptual element that links fear as a feeling to fear as an emotion may be that those who will act to discriminate against people of color react to the stereotypes, even architypes, of the lesser defined races that anchor their perception and understanding of the other races.[43] Essentially, an individual who lacks knowledge or information of another person or phenomenon will "anchor" their perception in a past notion or idea, regardless of whether it is true or not, in order to make a value judgment of the unknown phenomenon or individual they are encountering. For example, in a 2015 incident in Austin, Texas, which was captured by a police video camera and uploaded to YouTube, an African American woman, a second-grade teacher, was forcefully pulled from her parked car by a police officer, thrown to the ground, handcuffed, and transported by another officer to jail. It is not clear what the offense was, but it appears as if the first police officer wished to issue a traffic ticket. The removal of the black woman was violent, and the police officer alleged that he had to treat her violently because she tried to hit him.

The video did not show her trying to hit him. Nevertheless, once in the other police vehicle she engaged the second officer in a conversation indicating that she was just trying to understand her situation. She felt that she was treated violently because of her race and the second officer avoided agreeing or disagreeing with her. After she indicated that she did not understand why white police officers treated black people so violently the officer said that 99 percent of all violence was perpetrated by black persons because they had violent tendencies.[44] The officer made it clear that white people feared black people because black persons had violent tendencies. In the conversation with the young woman, whose name is Breaion King, the officer admitted that being a police officer may make nonracist individuals believe in a racist manner.

In this example, the police officer indicated that white persons feared black persons because of their violent tendencies. The encounter reveals fear as a feeling, fear that black people are inherently violent; the police officer believes that violence is a natural characteristic of black people. As a result, white persons need to be vigilant around black people because whites fear the violence blacks may perpetrate against them since violence is within the nature of black persons. The black person may not perform any violent act, it is the mere physical presence of a black person with the inherent possibility of being violent that creates the fear in the white person. Here the threat is not against the destruction of culture but of the possible physical destruction of the white person. In the end, Ms. King, the second-grade teacher, had to be placed brutally under control by the white police officer because her very presence presented him with a perceived threat to himself or that of other white persons. In the final analysis, racism is based in perceived threats to the cultural integrity of the race deemed superior that, in turn, leads to fear of behavior labelled socially taboo and the loss of political, economic, and social control. Thus, the ideological construct of racism must include the attendant fear, threat, and political and social reactions that arise out of racism. Fear is the direct linkage between racism as a social and abstract concept and the physical action of composing racist laws or actions.

The element that creates or brings fear forward is the anchoring effect[45] that perceived characteristics of colored people have on white persons. These characteristics or qualities are anchored usually in stereotypical beliefs of the colored group, perpetrated and solidified through generations of socialization. Many of these stereotypical beliefs are not based in fact yet are brought to bear during the public policy process by individuals who lack real knowledge or understanding of people of color. In order to understand Latinos, Blacks, Asians, or Native Americans, an individual lacking knowledge of these people of color will interpret the needs and social conditions of them through biased perceptual lenses based on generations of socialization. This holds not only for social categories such as race but also in situations between genders and social classes.

Nevertheless, a white person encountering a person of color, lacking knowledge and understanding of the person of color's culture, social, or political situation, will rely on some stereotype they are anchored in to judge that person's character, values, or personality. They will use this anchor to try and understand why that person speaks the way they do, how they will or do behave, how educated that person is, or even what their occupation is. For instance, some individual meeting a young female intern, dressed in a doctor's coat and wearing a stethoscope around her neck may not believe that the young person is a doctor. In one incident at the University of California, San Francisco Medical School, one of the most prestigious in the nation if not the world, a young, female psychiatrist was told by a male patient or visitor that psychiatrists were not medical doctors. The young woman, a medical student at the time now a practicing neuro-psychiatrist, could not convince the male encountered in an elevator at the teaching hospital, that psychiatrists were medical doctors. The male "mansplained" to her that she was wrong. Here the male was claiming ownership of knowledge and expertise of the situation over the woman simply because he was a male and knew, in his own mind, that his maleness gave him superiority of knowledge and expertise over the woman even though, in reality, the woman was the expert in this area.[46]

Misunderstandings that are the result of the ownership of knowledge or expertise also was the cause of Professor Louis Gates being arrested trying to enter his own home by university police because they thought he was "breaking and entering" a white person's home. It appeared that black persons "were not supposed to be living" in that particular neighborhood. Or, Cornel West not being able to hail a cab on the way to a meeting with his publisher in New York City. Or, this author being mistaken for a gardener by a utility meter reader asking my daughter, who was very young and sitting on the porch watching me plant gardenias, where her father was as she pointed to me. The meter reader did not even look in my direction but kept asking her two more times where her dad, the homeowner, was and she kept pointing to me. After I let him keep talking enough to verify that he had objectified me, I revealed my identity to him, a white man, who appeared very surprised when I unlocked the gate to our backyard and allowed him to read our meter. Apparently, he found it difficult to believe that a Mexican could own a home in this particular neighborhood.

Cornel West in his seminal work *Race Matters*[47] notes that people of color are objectified and made to feel as the outsiders in American society because they do not fit the cultural image of what is an American. The same can be said about the "raced" situation Latinos find themselves in and the "gendered" situation women are relegated to. None of these groups of individuals fit the social norms created by the stereotypical beliefs established through history and perpetuated through socialization. These stereotypes, sometimes architypes, drive the policy processes of a society resulting in the creation of laws that are imbedded with barriers resulting in uneven policy effects. The infusion of race into public policy is the subject of the second to the last chapter of this book. At this point of the discussion, however, it is important to understand how race and racism have become an important thread in the tapestry of the American ideological imagination.

RACISM AND IDEOLOGY

Racism became an essential element in the national ideology from the founding of the nation and became a central variable in the manner American decision makers saw the world, identified public issues that required addressing, defined and designed public policy, and implemented those same policies. The formation of a national ideology is difficult to demonstrate, still it has been the topic of a great deal of research and it is formed through the intersection of a great number of variables. As Therborn, he is not the only one who has written in this area the body of literature in this area is broad,[48] clearly articulated an ideological framework as complex and includes not just an understanding of how ideology is formed and oriented but how it functions.

Göran Therborn notes that ideology possesses a dialectical character in that it is more than simply conceptual it is also a dynamic social process that possesses a psychodynamic dimension. He points out that ideologies do not only organize societies and individuals to fit into the order of those societies, ideologies prepare for and propel people into participation within a given society. Simultaneously, ideologies allow humans to interpelate what they observe and then determine the sort of action or inaction required by the interpellation. Essentially, interpellation is the act of an individual to stop and question language, verbiage, images that control her behavior in order to proceed to a deeper analysis of that language. Interpellation allows a person to move beyond the superficiality of any image, language, or belief, challenge the image, and deconstruct it for its true meaning. This permits the individual to draw a conclusion about that language, image, or belief and lets the individual make a determination as to the appropriate action to take.

Ideology, then, functions as a dominating force because it is structured in order to determine the dominant beliefs of a society. It determines how individuals orient and incorporate themselves into a social and political order; how they see themselves; how they see others; and how they interpret the world. In other words, the ideological structure of any given society determines what one believes socially, economically, and politically. This unique structure also assists in creating the self-definition of an individual emotionally, politically, and socially and determines how one orients oneself to other individuals in their society. Fundamentally, ideology assists one in defining themselves socially to include how they interpret themselves racially, sexually, as members of a profession, and how they see themselves within that profession, how they see themselves as members of a social class and their place within that class. Ideology also has the obverse function of assisting the individual in interpreting how others are members of a racial group, members of a specific gender, social class, nation, professional status, and so forth. The interpretation of others allows one to interpret one's own social, political, and, in some cases, emotional essence.

Ideology also functions to structure the belief system of a society a certain way including scientifically, religiously, and legally. In this regard there exists in any given society, here we are limiting the discussion to the United States, but the same analysis can be applied to any country or society, ideological mechanisms that define, diffuse, and make semi-permanent the beliefs and belief structures that control and maintain ideology. These mechanisms, labelled as socialization mechanisms by some, begin establishing ideological belief systems from the moment one arrives within society until their departure. So that the moment one enters the world within which one will live, work, raise a family, and contribute to the advancement of that society they are subjected to the ideological beliefs of that society. The qualitative effects of the socialization vary depending on the age and social status of the individual. For instance, one is taught about the racial categories of a society as soon as one encounters persons of other races. The teaching, in the beginning performed by one's parents, determines a great deal of how one sees oneself as a member of a particular race and how one defines others as members of their respective races. For instance, when a black child first encounters white children the initial interaction, lacking definition, may not necessarily be determinative but once that child asks their parents about the child of the other race then race, and specifically that race, is given definition. The definition may also include behavioral characteristics, some based on assumptions that may not be founded in fact but rather stereotypical images or stories that have been passed to the parent from their own parents or other members of their race or even of individuals of other races. Sometimes a child is "raced" and returns home to inquire as to what they had experienced seeking a rational explanation for the "racing." Here, again the parent will discuss the incident with the child resulting in the child forming a perception of themselves and that of others.[49] Although the discussion on how ideological mechanisms are structured has been covered earlier and elsewhere,[50] a brief presentation is important for clarity's sake here and is the subject of the next chapter.

RACIAL THREAT

A very important component of racism that requires elucidation is the notion of "threat," which is part of the OED definition. The definition stipulates that those who have racial feelings toward others understand them, consciously or unconsciously, as a threat to the dominant culture, "racial integrity, or economic well-being." Underlying this issue is the simple but most difficult question to answer, "Why is threat part of the OED definition of racism?" If threat is an essential element of the definition, then "fear" must also be included in the discussion or, at least, "apprehension" because to feel threatened one fears that some harm is expected against one's personal, social, political, or emotional condition.

The literature review, as brief as it was, of the scientific racism literature reveals that thinkers such as de Gobineau, Grant, Stoppard, Cox, and Bilbo all spoke of fear that white civilization would be lessened or destroyed if miscegenation were allowed. This same fear is still evident today in the white supremacist literature one finds on websites throughout the internet such as Stormfront.com, swa43.com (Supreme White Alliance), American Renaissance, and nsm88.org (National Socialist Movement) to name a few.[51] The American Renaissance website presents a list of hot links to other racist, racialist websites and blogs including the Human Biological Diversity web page that has a long series of citations on current research and thought pieces on scientific racism by academics and pundits. All are argumentative and subjective displays of research designed to attack what are called "political liberal" positions on race and reiterate much of the arguments of the older scientific racists except using new and current data and methodologies. Several articles also "imply" that racial segregation and closing borders to immigration are important to protecting the intellectual levels of Americans.[52]

Threat and the accompanying fear are essential political tools, as Fromm points out,[53] in order to move a society or population to espouse a certain set of beliefs and even to participate or support violence.[54] An essential goal of scientific racism is simply not to propagate their theories but also to influence public policy at various governmental levels. By using fear to develop support for certain public policy positions scientific racists, or simply racist politicians and government leaders, can gain at least tacit support from a percentage of the population sufficiently large enough to ensure racial policies can become law. Two examples will demonstrate this proposition.

THE 1924 IMMIGRATION ACT OR JOHNS-REED ACT

According to all available information, this was the first immigration law that was directly influenced by scientific racists, specifically Harry Laughlin who served as an "Expert Eugenicist Agent" to the House Committee on Immigration and Naturalization during the hearings.[55] The proponents of the law argued that immigrants from Asia and Southern and Eastern Europe, if allowed to enter the United States, would threaten the cultural foundations of this country. Prior to 1924 there had already been policy directly excluding Asians from all countries except the Philippines, which were an American protectorate (commonwealth status) until 1945. Prior to 1945 and after the Spanish-American War all Filipinos were granted American citizenship and free to come and go to the United States.

The supporters of the 1924 Immigration Act claimed that Asian, and Eastern and Southern European immigrants, would bring filth, disease, crime, radical politics, and lower native intelligence levels into the United States if their numbers were not severely restricted.[56]

Seller argues that the only reason Latin American immigrants were not included in the 1924 law was because growers had lobbied Congress to exclude this group from coverage in order to protect the cheap labor supply that had been crossing the southern border of the United States since the middle of the nineteenth century. Nevertheless, the arguments of the supporters for stricter quotas were clear. Immigrants who were not white and northern European were not welcome in the United States. The perceived threat was that non-white immigrants would dilute American culture as well as the hegemony of white Americans in all facets of society. There were even arguments against Catholic and Jewish immigrants coming into the United States for fear that American Protestantism's dominance would be challenged. The fear was based not only on the numbers of immigrants coming into the country but the claim that the immigrant populations had high birth rates. The only perceived solution at this juncture was the imposition of strict immigration quotas. The fear of a perceived threat resulted in the creation of an immigration policy that was specifically racial in nature.

During the consideration of the bill, it was decided that immigration from Asia and non-independent countries would not be allowed, and after the quotas for various European countries were established the discussion turned to immigration from countries of the Western Hemisphere. There was almost immediate consensus that there would be no quotas on immigration from Canada. However, when the topic of immigration from Mexico and the countries of Central and South America arose, racial attitudes rose to the surface. For instance, Fitzgerald and Cook-Martin note that U.S. representative John Box (D-TX) introduced a bill to include Mexico and other Latin American countries into the quota system that would place their numbers very low. He claimed that the influx of Mexicans created "the most insidious and general mixture of white, Indian, and Negro blood strains ever produced in America."[57] Harry Laughlin, who insisted that immigration from the Western Hemisphere be restricted to Whites, supported Box's position.[58] In the end, however, no restrictions were placed on immigration from countries in the Western Hemisphere. This decision was based, most likely, on several considerations including economic and political.

The economic rationale behind not placing immigration restrictions on individuals from Western Hemisphere countries was that there were simply too many trade agreements in place, and if the United States wished to continue adhering to the dominance claimed under the Monroe Doctrine then any restrictions could possibly be harmful to that hegemonic relationship. On the other hand, the equation that governed the imposition of quotas created a situation where white Europeans were advantaged over all other countries including those of the Western Hemisphere. The final version of the 1924 act established quotas for all countries based upon 3 percent of the total number of national origin individuals so identified in the 1890 census. This is an interesting point given that they first considered using the 1910 census numbers but changed their mind given the changing ratios of immigrants from Northern Europe and Southern and Eastern Europe. The 1890 census indicated a higher ratio of white to non-white population in the United States while the ratio was diminished in the 1910 census. By using the 1890 ratio this gave white Northern Europeans an arithmetical advantage over the Southern Europeans.

The composers of the 1924 legislation were driven by several assumptions that were racially motivated. The first assumption was that the impending immigration law needed to be designed to favor White Europeans defined as those arriving from Great Britain, the Netherlands, Sweden (including Norway and Denmark at that time), Germans, and "*even* [my emphasis] the Scotch-Irish."[59] This was to insure the cultural and social hegemony of "same stock" "Anglo-Saxon-Germanic in blood and Protestant in religion—of the same stock as that which originally settled the United States, wrote our constitution and established our democratic institutions."[60] Therefore, the first assumption is that however the immigration quotas were to be established they would be biased toward Northern Europeans as opposed to Southern and Eastern Europeans. These latter groups of immigrants were described by Garis as the "new" immigrants because they had arrived after 1890. Before proceeding further, it should be noted that Professor Garis, who was an associate professor of economics at Vanderbilt University when he composed his work, was one of the principle consultants and architects of the Immigration Act of 1924. He was the principle developer of the equation that gave birth to the quota system that lay at the heart of the new law. Prior to 1890 the "old" Anglo-Saxon-Germanic immigrants had far outnumbered the "new" immigrants who originated in "Russia, Poland, Austria, Hungary, Greece, Turkey, Italy, and the Balkan countries."[61] According to Garis, these "new" immigrants constituted "*the* [italics in original] immigration problem of *today* [italics in original]."[62]

Another assumption under which the congressional composers were laboring was that any immigrants who would be allowed to enter must be easily assimilateable. This meant that whatever groups were admitted had to possess the social capacity to absorb the cultural, social, and political values of the United States. In the perceptions of the writers of the 1924 immigration law only those immigrants arriving from Northern Europe, the Anglo-Saxon-Germanic stock of peoples, fit this category. As the author Garis notes, allowing individuals of the "new" immigrant countries resulted in the "emigration to America of many whose low standards of living, whose ignorance and racial hatreds have made it impossible for us under present conditions to assimilate and have marked them, in the minds of those who favor immigration restriction, along with the Italians and Russians, as undesirable immigrants."[63] Professor Garis drew his conclusion after a review of comments made by other leading academics commenting on the congressional hearings surrounding the passage of the 1924 immigration law.

The preponderance of the reports submitted during the house committee's work on the development of the 1924 law spoke to the racial superiority of "old" immigrant stock over the "new." The reports argued for strong restrictions on the "new" immigrants to ensure that a higher percentage of "old" immigrant stock would be admitted after passage of the law. The argument in favor of instituting restrictions against the "new" immigrants was based upon the "scientific racist" reports submitted by Harry Laughlin and others together with the results of the US Army tests referred to earlier in the discussion of Stoppard's scientific racism contributions. There were reports submitted by various psychologists and anthropologists who argued against using data from Laughlin and his cohorts as the basis for immigration quotas. The arguments against scientific racism were based on the methodological inadequacies of the various reports.[64] For instance, Young, Hexter, and Myerson point out that the tests were administered under adverse test-taking conditions for the colored test takers. They also argued that language played a role in the test results between native English speakers and immigrants who barely had a passing knowledge of English.[65] This latter group argues that regardless of the outcomes of any tests, race should not be used as the major determining factor for the construction of the quotas. Some even argue that "instead of specifying the qualities considered desirable the law favors those nations whose representatives we like, and debars others by general provisions."[66] In the final analysis, those who objected to the racial scientific analysis and use of intelligence testing to justify immigration restrictions concluded, "On this basis it would seem that the 'old' immigration is more desirable than the 'new,' being more easily assimilated because of a cultural background more nearly akin to our own."[67] Needless to say, this last group of social scientists was not listened to by the members of Congress or the Senate who passed the final bill overwhelmingly.

The final result was an immigration law that established quotas allowing immigrants from Northern Europe a situational head start, a place at the front of the immigration que that would give them a numerical advantage well into the twentieth century. This equation was not modified until 1965. As Garis points out, "Under the 3 percent law of 1921 the old immigration was entitled to 56.33 percent, while the new immigration had 44.64 percent. Under the new law of 1924 the respective percentages are 84.11 and 14.88."[68] Professor Garis's percentages refers to the percentage that each group of immigrants would have of the total quota of immigrants for any given year. Each country would be assigned a set quota based upon 2 percent of their national origin as it stood in the 1890 census. This new quota system would "help us to become more homogenous by sending to us every year a miniature or replica of that which we are already according to original national stock. The 1890 measure is the soundest, the healthiest, the fairest, and the best."[69] Essentially, those supporting stricter immigration quotas were afraid of the changing global demographics and turned the clock back enough to ensure that only white Europeans would be admitted in greater numbers than those of other countries.

RACISM AND VOTING RIGHTS

The second example of how racism finds its way into the public policy process may be found in the struggle of African Americans and Latinos for voting rights during the second half of the twentieth and the early part of the twenty-first centuries.[70] Much has already been written and reported on the struggles of the African American community in this policy area but little has been written of the suffering and struggles Latinos have endured to win the right to vote. As a result, the discussion here will be dedicated strictly to the history of what Latinos have had to overcome insuring access to the ballot in the United States.

Racially embedded policy designed to prevent Latinos from voting or, at least, to diminish the strength of the Latino vote is a legacy of the manner in which the franchise has been extended reluctantly to new groups throughout the history of the United States. In the beginning the framers did not wish to allow just anyone to vote. Rather the initial arguments indicated that the writers of the Constitution wanted only the elite or, at a minimum, only those property owners worth a certain amount to have the right to vote. As history unfolded, the same reluctance was seen to extending the vote to women, African Americans, and now Latinos.

Each group newly added to the voter rolls has a separate history. The unique relationship between Latinos and the United States involves a rather long and involved discussion that is not appropriate here but has been covered extensively elsewhere.[71] Unlike women's suffrage that of African Americans and Latinos has been underlain by racism. The reluctance to extend the franchise to both groups was and is still based on the perception that African Americans and Latinos are the products of alien cultures. These groups belong to the category of "unassimilateable cultures." African Americans and Latinos are both perceived as culturally inferior to whites. African Americans and Latinos adhere to alien cultures, not Western, speak different languages, and may have stronger allegiances to other countries or religions other than the United States and its core religion, Protestantism.

The historical trajectory of both African Americans and Latinos is markedly different. Where the ancestors of the former were brought to the United States as slaves or indentured servants the latter arrived or were incorporated in a variety of ways. History has recorded that individuals of Spanish speaking descent fought in the American Revolutionary War as either American citizens or as members of the Spanish military. Spanish officials in Cuba provided financial and logistical support to Washington's forces at Yorktown and Texas vaqueros herding Longhorns from Texas even supplied beef to George Washington's troops.[72] Mexicans became citizens of the United States after the signing of the Treaty of Guadalupe Hidalgo in 1848 that ended the war between Mexico and the United States. An essential element of this treaty was that Mexico ceded approximately half of its entire land mass, including all or part of the states of New Mexico, California, Nevada, Colorado, Wyoming, Utah, and Oregon. Texas became part of the United States in a separate annexation. Mexicans who chose to remain behind rather than repatriate to Mexico after the war were granted US citizenship together with all rights including voting.[73] Other national origin Latino groups such as Puerto Ricans, Cubans, and others were admitted into the United States at various other times, under different historical and treaty situations but eventually all were given access to US citizenship.[74]

Although Latinos have played significant roles in the history of the United States since the beginning, the first recorded instance involving a Latino petitioning for voting access after it had been denied because of his race appears in *In Re Ricardo Rodriguez*.[75] This was a petition by a Latino from San Antonio, Texas, requesting US citizenship and his right to vote. Mr. Rodriguez was forced to submit his petition to the federal court because Texas' state and local officials were in the process of denying Latinos the right to vote. Shortly after Texas had become an independent republic in 1836 there had been expulsions of Latinos from many towns and cities in the northern, central, and eastern parts of the state, including San Antonio, regardless of their citizenship status. Texas had granted Mexicans citizenship after liberation but there were efforts at "ethnic cleansing" and disenfranchisement throughout the state in order to minimize Latino political participation.

A striking example of the history of how race forms the most important social assumption underlying the manipulation of the Latino vote can be found in South Texas. Racial tensions have always been high between Anglos (Whites) and Latinos (Mexican Americans or Mexicans) since their first encounters in the early part of the nineteenth century. The killing of Mexicans, land-grabbing, and racial cleansing of certain parts of Texas have marked the low points of the intense racial animosity between both groups.[76] At the same time, Mexicans were awarded citizenship in both the Republic of Texas and the United States as the result of various treaties after the War of Secession (Texas Revolution) in 1836 and the Mexican American War of 1848 and the Gadsden Purchase of 1854.

Accompanying citizenship was the right to vote; however, voting for Mexican Americans was not a simple matter. Most Mexicans of the nineteenth century, probably like many of their uneducated white fellow citizens, knew little about the US Constitution or the structure and functioning of the US government so the manipulation of their vote was easy. In some cases, particularly in rural areas, Mexicans were rounded up, corralled, marched to the polls, and told who to vote for by local ranchers and power brokers. In South Texas the Mexican vote formed an important voting bloc for some of the state's most famous or infamous political bosses.[77] As the turn of the twentieth century approached, political reformers attempted to break the bosses' hold over local politics by pursuing tactics to disenfranchise Latino voters. This effort is exemplified by evidence and testimony presented in a federal court hearing of Ricardo Rodriguez, a resident of San Antonio, Texas, when he petitioned the court for citizenship allowing him to vote. Local politicos who represented two political parties and whose platforms reflected a reform agenda objected to the petition.[78]

Mr. Ricardo Rodriguez who was functionally illiterate, he could neither read or write English or Spanish, but was considered, by way of several character witnesses including Anglos, to be a "very good man, peaceable and industrious, of good moral character, and law abiding to a remarkable degree" was allowed to apply for his citizenship. It was also noted that Mr. Rodriguez had resided in Texas for ten years and he considered the United States home with no intention of ever returning to Mexico. Opposing the application were Messrs. T. J. McMinn and Jack Evans, attorneys with ties to the Republican and Populist parties, who were at the forefront of the reform movement's efforts at breaking the hold of the South Texas bosses. An essential element of this effort was the disenfranchisement of Mexican voters.[79] The Rodriguez petition hearing was the exemplification of this effort, but the most important aspect of this case lies in the role race and racism played in both the effort at disenfranchisement and the court's ultimate decision.

McMinn and Evans, in an effort at bolstering their case against Rodriguez, cited the work of a French ethnologist Dr. Paul Broca, whose research was principally in physical anthropology and focused on the relationship between the size of the brain and the intelligence of an individual. Dr. Broca's research was presented as proof that Mr. Rodriguez was not "white," not Asian, and not Black therefore ineligible for citizenship.[80] Many years later Stephen Jay Gould in his 1981 work *The Measurement of Man*[81] accused Broca of being heavily influenced by the scientific racist thinking dominating the field of anthropology in that era. Broca's evidence was simply a table that represented a hierarchy of skin hues with white at the top representing Northern European descended peoples including Americans. At the bottom of the racial hierarchy were the "Hottentots" an aboriginal people from West Africa. Immediately above the Hottentots were Mexicans and it was noted that this was the category to which Mr. Rodriguez belonged. In short "Rodriguez clearly belonged with the six million pure-blooded Mexican Indians and plausibly with the several Indian tribes," therefore not white.[82] Essentially, Mr. Rodriguez did not belong to any of the recognized races, he was a Mexican, yet no one could be sure as to what race Mexicans belonged, therefore Mr. Rodriguez belonged to some mixed group of individuals called Mexicans. This group, whose membership was not covered by any laws, fell into a racial or ethnic "netherworld" and, therefore, not eligible for citizenship.

The federal judge, Thomas S. Maxey, ruled that even though Mr. Rodriguez was clearly not white he was Mexican and Mexicans had been offered citizenship by the United States through a series of treaties beginning as far back as 1803, beginning with the agreement with France over the cessation of Louisiana, the Adams-Onis Treaty of 1819, the treaty with Texas over its annexation in 1845, the Treaty of Guadalupe Hidalgo in 1848, and finally in the treaty over the Gadsen Purchase in 1854. Judge Maxey noted that in each of the cited treaties Spaniards or Mexicans remaining behind in what became the territory of the United States were granted citizenship in the stipulations of each treaty. Judge Maxey also ruled that the Fourteenth Amendment "conferred citizenship upon persons of all races and colors born or naturalized in the United States and subject to its jurisdiction."[83] As a result, he ruled in Mr. Rodriguez's favor and allowed him to proceed with his citizenship application.

The *Rodriguez* case marked the first recorded legal effort to use race in defining the right to vote for Latinos. Although the actions of the progressives were blocked by the federal judge, the only result is that it left control of the Latino vote in the hands of South Texas political bosses. As a result, Latinos retained the right to vote but their vote would still be manipulated well into the 1960s in South Texas by various county judges, ranchers, and farmers. An unusual artifact of Judge Maxey's decision was that it established Latinos in a unique racial category; they were not considered to belong to any specific race but were categorized as a nationality by the court. Interestingly enough this unique status was brought up before the court in a later case where the unique racial categorization of Latinos allowed for the fullest extension of Fourteenth Amendment protections.[84] Throughout the twentieth century, the State of Texas attempted to dilute or disenfranchise African American and Latinos through various means from declaring political parties as private organizations disallowing open participation in primaries to the establishment of draconian voter identification laws.[85] Here only the most recent example of how race is infused in the state's voter identification law will be discussed.

There are several reasons for this choice. The first is that there are so many instances of attempts on the part of the State of Texas to disenfranchise Latino voters that they, together with an appropriate analysis, would fill a large volume and detract from the gist of this discussion. The second reason is that it is the most recent example of Texas's efforts at disenfranchisement. In addition, the voter identification process that Texas has put in place is the most interesting racists have employed to hide their use of race during the public policy decisional process. This last reason lies at the heart of the most recent tactic used by Texas in its long-standing conflict with Latino voters. Essentially, the legislative decision makers avoided all mention of race during their deliberations even to the extent of avoiding direct questioning as to whether their actions violated any federal law or the Voting Rights Act of 1965. When confronted by various legislators on this very issue the sponsors of the legislation refused to answer, a colleague would move to table the discussion, or the sponsor would simply declare that they had not been advised on the topic.[86] At one point one of the sponsors stated that it was not their responsibility to determine whether the voter ID law violated federal law. Instead, she declared, it was the responsibility of the Supreme Court to make the decision as to the legality of Senate Bill 14. The avoidance of any reference to race during the legislative deliberations over Senate Bill 14 represented a new chapter in the evolutionary development of racial rhetoric and served as an attempt at hiding the racial intentions of the voter identification bill's sponsors. The Texas state legislature passed a bill that was clearly intended to dilute the voting strength of Latino voters without even mentioning the words "race," "Latino," or "Hispanic."[87] Before the state could implement the voter identification law, however, it was forced to seek a review under Section 5 of the VRA that was still valid. The lieutenant governor, Greg Abbott, refused to send the law directly to President Obama's Department of Justice, indicating that he felt Texas could not receive a fair review and instead opted to send the bill to a three-judge panel of the US District Court for the District of Columbia for review. This hearing occurred in July 2012.

The state argued that it had guaranteed, using appropriate databases, that no specific voter group would suffer disenfranchisement under Senate Bill 14. However, the defendants, the US government, showed how flawed the databases used by Texas were. Additionally, evidence was brought forth indicating that the decisional process, although not explicitly racist, resulted in the creation of a law that was racist and would deleteriously affect minority voters, in this case Latinos.[88] This latter argument was put forth by defendant intervenors with the intention of proving that Texas had acted with the explicit intention of discriminating against Latinos. In the final analysis, the judges ruled unanimously against Texas saying that the databases they used were flawed and would result in discriminatory effects against minority voters. The court ignored any discussion as to whether Texas acted with racial purpose or intent.

The evidence of racial purpose or intent was based upon a qualitative evaluation of the decisional process through which the law passed from its initial creation to the final form it took. The first attempt at a voter identification law was in 2005 and specifically designed to "prevent illegal aliens" from crossing the southern border and casting ballots that would disrupt Texas's election process. The same intent behind the passage of identical laws appeared in the legislature in 2007 and 2009. The objective of the act was changed in 2011 from one that was intended to prevent illegal aliens from voting to a law said to protect the security and integrity of the ballot. It was also pointed out to the court that this same strategic initiative had been part of the Republican Party's Southern Strategy since 1964[89] and specifically designed to suppress the votes of racial minority voters. The first evidence of the Republican Party's involvement in voter suppression activities, as an essential element of their Southern Strategy, occurred in 1964 in Arizona. Republican operatives were sent to precincts having large numbers of minority voters to intimidate primarily Latino voters by asking questions about their citizenry and residency. At one location a young attorney singled out Latino voters and would read a passage of the Constitution and ask the potential voter to interpret the passage, essentially conducting a "constitutional literacy test" before allowing the voter to cast a ballot. The name of this attorney was William Rehnquist who later sat as chief justice of the Supreme Court and ruled in the infamous *Gore v. Bush* decision that determined the outcome of the 2000 presidential election.[90] The Southern Strategy was designed to maximize white voter turnout, particularly in the southeastern United States while ignoring or suppressing minority turnout. The strategy was initially inspired by Barry Goldwater but not implemented until Richard Nixon ran for the presidency. The fundamental idea was that the Republican Party would rely on white voters to form the core of their support while ignoring minority voters. The GOP felt that the party lost minority voters after the passage of the Civil Rights Act of 1965.[91]

These types of activities and their variations proliferated throughout various states through 2003. After 2003, the battle to diminish the Latino vote shifted to various legislative bodies. In Texas, after the Republican Party took over both chambers of the state legislature in 2003, they began pursuing the creation and implementation of a voter identification process. To say that race was at the heart of this effort is an understatement. The initial attempts during the 2005, 2007, and 2009 sessions advertised the voter identification bills as legislation that would prevent "illegal aliens" from crossing over from Mexico to cast fraudulent votes.[92] Eventually, a voter identification bill was passed during the 2011 session over the objections of Democratic Party members. These members attempted to bring to the attention of their Republican colleagues the possibility that the substance of Senate Bill 14 violated federal statutes or the VRA to no avail and a bill was passed and signed by Governor Rick Perry in June 2011.

In July, Senate Bill 14 was reviewed by the three-judge panel of the US District Court for the District of Columbia and was found to violate Section 5 of the VRA because the databases the state used to verify voter identification cards were flawed. The court concluded that the flawed databases would have the effect of placing an undue burden on poor, young, old, and minority voters. Although defendant intervenors on the side of the federal government petitioned the court to rule that the state had acted with racial purpose or intent, the panel sidestepped this issue and did not even comment on it. Nevertheless, the court forbade Texas from implementing the law until it could correct the flawed data files. Later, during the summer of 2012, the US Supreme Court ruled that the enforcement provisions of Section 4 that triggered coverage under Section 5 were outdated and therefore unenforceable in the *Shelby County* decision. This resulted in vacating the district court's ruling in the Senate Bill 14 petition and Texas immediately implemented the original version of the law, flaws and all.

Meanwhile, African American congressional representative Mark Veasey, representing a district in Fort Worth, Texas, sued the State of Texas charging that Senate Bill 14 violated Section 2 of the VRA.[93] The case was heard in the US District Court for the Southern District of Texas, Corpus Christi Division, in front of a Latina judge Nelva Gonzalez Ramos. The plaintiffs argued that "Senate Bill 14 contravened the Fourteenth and Fifteenth Amendments because of its discriminatory purpose . . . was unconstitutional under the First and Fourteenth Amendments for placing a substantial burden on the right to vote . . . and constituted a poll tax in violation of the Fourteenth and Twenty-Fourth Amendments."[94] Judge Ramos agreed with the plaintiffs on all three points ruling that SB 14 was enacted with discriminatory purpose and resulted in discriminatory effects. Texas immediately sought relief before the most conservative appeals court in the country, the Fifth Circuit sitting in New Orleans. The Fifth Circuit ruled 9 to 6 against the State of Texas and ordered SB 14 be fixed to remedy the discriminatory effect of the law. The court ruled that discriminatory purpose did not exist under the *Arlington Heights Factors*,[95] however, the Fifth Circuit did rule that SB 14 as configured could have a disparate impact on more than 600,000 minority group members and thus be in violation of Section 2 of the VRA and had to be amended. *Veasey* was remanded to Judge Ramos's court to oversee the restructuring of SB 14. The state appealed to the Supreme Court who denied *certiorari* in January 2017. Writing for the Court was Chief Justice Roberts who noted that the Fifth Circuit had found the voter ID law violated Sec. 2 and had remanded *Veasey* back to the District Court for a remedy. As a result, the case had not run its course judicially, besides the question of racial intent had not been addressed completely so was still in need of a decision on the part of the District Court. The Supreme Court noted, however, "petitioners (the state) may raise either or both issues after entry of final judgement. The issues will be better suited for *certiorari* at that time." Judge Ramos accepted a negotiated SB 14 restructuring that would allow voters who did not possess the state-approved voter identification card to sign an affidavit as to their identity supported by any number of documents including "voter identification card, utility bill, bank statement, government check or 'some other form of government document' that shows the name of the voter."[96] It was unclear as to whether the State of Texas would appeal to the US Supreme Court because the best-case scenario would be a 4–4 split as Justice Scalia's seat was empty at this time, which would have the effect of allowing the Fifth Circuit's decision to stand.

Although the various levels of the federal courts in the voter ID case indicated that racial purpose was not at the heart of their decisions, only the disparate effect standard, they did indicate that if the District Court had applied the appropriate methodology as outlined in *Arlington Heights* then maybe evidence of racial purpose may have been uncovered. The *en banc* 5th Circuit did indicate that although the District Court did base her opinion on the *Arlington Heights Factors* her decision was still based on old data that was the same evidentiary argument used by the Supreme Court in *Shelby County* and therefore inappropriate. The Fifth Circuit pointed out that although the data were appropriate, they weren't of enough recent vintage. The timely data were anecdotal at best but not of sufficient quality as to be relevant to the proof of discriminatory purpose.[97] Consequently, the Fifth Circuit remanded the discriminatory purpose part of the case to the District Court for reconsideration but declared for the plaintiffs under the discriminatory effect standard. Although no direct evidence of sufficient quality substantiating the claims of racial purpose was found during the discovery stage one avenue of investigation was never pursued. Not one expert or attorney sought to discover whether or not there had been private confidential meetings among the sponsors of the bill where discriminatory purpose was discussed. Still, the court admitted that Texas did have a history of racism and racial tensions throughout its history that determined a great deal of public policy in many issue areas besides voting. None of the courts stated that racism was over and times had changed for the better only that the appropriate data had not been brought forth in the trial.

CONCLUSIONS ABOUT RACISM IN BOTH EXAMPLES

Both examples reflect elements of the OED definition of racism. They show that the policy makers objectified people of color and feared the repercussions of what would happen to the United States, in the case of immigration reform, and Texas, in the voter ID case, if access in both policy areas were broadened. In the case study of immigration policy, it is clear that the policy makers were influenced by the spokespersons for scientific racism whose racial beliefs included a social hierarchy with whites at the top and people of color at the bottom. The case studies also reveal that the policy makers felt that increasing the numbers of immigrants deemed less desirable would threaten the cultural integrity of the United States that was defined as white and Protestant and allowing increases in minority voters could lead to a loss of political power.

In the final analysis racism is a belief that has become an integral thread in the tapestry of the American political cultural ideology. In other words, racism has embedded itself in the way decision makers view a policy issue, how they interpret the issue, and how they develop policies or choose not to address the issue. At the same time, racism assists decision makers in determining how the policies are designed to address an issue and how these policies may or may not be implemented. Racism is an essential element in how Americans generally and Texans specifically view the political and cultural worlds around them.

It goes without saying that racism is based on a belief that social constructions labelled "race" exist. Yet, a thorough reading of the available scholarly literature indicates that there is little, if any, biological or scientific evidence that some artifact, thing, or *quelque chose* that one might call race exists. Race is a social construct developed in the seventeenth century as a way of distinguishing one social grouping from another. As this categorization continued various thinkers such as de Gobineau and Grant developed hierarchies of these groupings and credited each with various categories of skin pigmentation, behavior, and intellect. This culminated with the belief that a social grouping called Nordic, Caucasian, or white was the highest ranking of all social groupings. Below this august grouping laid several others with their home on the social ladder defined by darker degrees of pigmentation, more unpredictable types of behavior, and lower levels of intelligence.

The concept of racism, then, began with a belief that the world or one's society was composed of racial groups with whites at the top of the social ladder and all the rest arrayed beneath arranged in descending order depending on the darkness of their skins and perceived behaviors and lack of intellectual achievement. Racial beliefs have passed down through history during the normal socialization process that expand and spread beliefs of all sorts throughout society. Racial beliefs evolved into racial thinking and that, in turn, evolved into racism the act of making decisions concerning the well-being of groups and/or individuals based upon their racial categorization.

The interesting aspect of this social construction is that it was created and propagated by individuals from the highest social grouping; individuals who defined the social hierarchy and also determined that if racial groups were not segregated then cultural anarchy would ensue. In other words, those who described the racial social structure came from the Nordic, Caucasian, or white social grouping according to their racial classifications. As some of the literature has indicated this grouping gave itself credit for all the discoveries that advanced civilization in the arts, sciences, and industry. As a result, it fell to whites to be the defenders of the social order and given that whites were in control of the political, economic, and social systems of American society it was easy to propagate these racial beliefs. Racial beliefs found their way into classrooms, the popular media, everyday social interactions, and so forth. One of the consequences of the propagation of racial beliefs was that those in the lower social groupings found themselves channeled or tracked into various work occupations and were educated only to the extent necessary to fulfill their use to society as a whole. Worse, many in the lower social groupings believed this social mythology and led, in some communities, to an almost fatalistic perception of the future for themselves and their children.

In the case of African Americans, this meant that until the middle of the twentieth century they were not given many opportunities to educate themselves to any level of sophistication or to compete for occupations that were paid very well. Latinos were also perceived as only being useful for menial, manual occupations and were educated appropriately. Continuing decades of this treatment resulted in both of these groups falling further and further behind whites in the economy of the United States. Essentially, the characteristics attributed to the lower social groupings were interpreted in such a way as to allow for whites to officially discriminate against them in almost every area of public and private accommodations. Therefore, African Americans until the 1960s in various parts of the United States were educated in Black schools and Latinos were educated in either separate classrooms from white students or, as in South Texas, in schools especially designed for them, Mexican schools. In Texas, specifically Latinos in rural areas were only schooled through the third or sixth grade because it was deemed all the education required to work on ranches or farms. Conscious educational segregation led to the establishment of a permanent economic underclass.

Besides being relegated to certain low-paying and low-status occupational strata the social groups on the lower rungs of the racial hierarchy were forced to live in certain enclaves and generally were, until later in the twentieth century, also not allowed to patronize all restaurants, places of social gatherings, even churches. This segregation enforced through legal means as well as social convention was designed to insure that the lower and higher social groupings did not intermingle. Intermingling meant contamination, contamination resulted in the dilution of the higher social grouping's culture and, some felt, would lead to the demise of Western civilization.

The social separation of races became an absolute requirement to prevent the lower social groups from contaminating the higher group. Contamination, according to racial theories, would result in the denaturing of higher culture and the subsequent end of that culture. Consequently, social and political barriers were constructed to prevent the lower social groupings from intermingling with the higher grouping. The combined structuring of social and political barriers created and maintained a racially segregated society. Segregated education resulted in socially stratified and segmented communities that, in turn, created racially segregated neighborhoods. Racism, embedded in one policy area cascaded over into another resulting in an orchestrated, systemic, and highly structured segregation process. All parts of the system worked in a synchronized fashion and has become systematically institutionalized to the extent that the very nature of the structure mystifies the realities of racial segregation. Although one may argue that all of the endemic inequality is not racial but social and economic, it goes without saying that the effects of inequality fall more heavily upon the shoulders of the African American and Latino communities than whites. Poor whites are socially segregated from rich or well-to-do Anglos as well but they are still separated from people of color into their own occupational strata, schools, and residential enclaves.

In the next chapter we explore how racism found its way into the public policy decisional structures of the United States and why it is so difficult to uncover. Addressed is also the question as to why it is so difficult, if not impossible, to untangle this Gordian knot.

NOTES

1. Mathew 5:14. From Jesus' Sermon on the Mount. "You are the light of the world. A city that is set on a hill cannot be hidden." This is a theme that appears throughout American intellectual history beginning with Jonathan Winthrop (1630) in his *A Model of Christian Charity*. Several US presidents including Ronald Reagan, George Bush, George W. Bush, and Bill Clinton have all used the metaphor in speeches extolling the greatness of the United States. A critique of this notion is presented by Richard M. Gamble in *In Search of the City on a Hill: The Making and Unmaking of an American Myth* (London: Continuum International Publishing Group, 2012).

2. See the seminal research of psychoanalysts such as Erich Fromm in his *The Heart of Man: Its Genius for Good and Evil* (New York: Harper and Row Publishers, 1965).

3. See Göran Therborn's discussion in chapter I of his *Ideology of Power and the Power of Ideology* (London: Verso Editions and NLB, 1980). See also the early work on internalization by John Scott, *Internalization of Norms: A Sociological Theory of Moral Commitment* (London: Prentice-Hall, 1972). George Mead, *Mind, Self, and Society: The Definitive Edition* (Chicago: The University of Chicago Press, 1934, 2015).

4. Jane Mayer, *Dark Money: The Hidden History of the Billionaires behind the Rise of the Radical Right* (New York: The Knopf Publishing Group, 2016).

5. George Fredrickson, *Racism: A Short History* (Princeton, NJ: Princeton University Press, 2002).

6. For a comprehensive overview of this history, see Thomas F. Gossett, *Race: The History of an Idea in America. New Edition* (Oxford: Oxford University Press, 1997).

7. David M. Goldenberg, *The Curse of Ham: Race and Slavery in Early Judaism, Christianity, and Islam* (Princeton, NJ: Princeton University Press, 2009).

8. One need only Google any KKK or white supremacist website to see how the organization refers to itself as Christian with the objective of fighting for and maintaining a country based in Christian values. For instance, www.theuka.us, www.originalknightriders.net, www.texaskkk.net, www.traditionalistamericanknights.com, and www.kkk.bz all reference the notion that they are Christian, refer to Jesus Christ as their exemplar, and seek to return the United States to a "Christian culture."

9. Gobineau's work was published in English as *The Moral and Intellectual Diversity of Races*, J. B. Lippincott, 1856 (rep. by Garland Pub., 1984).

10. Madison Grant, *The Passing of the Great Race* (New York: Charles Scribner's Sons, 1916).

11. Jonathan P. Spiro, *Defending the Master Race: Conservation, Eugenics, and the Legacy of Madison Grant* (Burlington, VT: University of Vermont Press published by University Press of New England, Lebanon, NH, 2009).

12. 388 U.S. 1.

13. Carolina Garcia, "*Los mexicanos, principales víctimas de la esterilización forzosa en California* (Mexicans, the principal victims of forced sterilization in California)," *El País*, July 12, 2013.

14. Ibid., "*39.000 euros para cada víctima de la esterilización forzada* (39,000 Euros for each victim of forced sterilization)," *El País*, May 25, 2012.

15. Publisher unknown, 1930.

16. Adolf Hitler, *Mein Kampf.* English translation, March 21, 1939, Deitrick Eckart (London: Hurst & Blackett LTD.), 222–25.

17. Richard J. Herrnstein and Charles Murray, *The Bell Curve: Intelligence and Class Structure in American Life* (New York: Basic Books, 1994).

18. First published in 1923, revised in 1937. Mr. Cox self-published the first edition. Wickliffe Draper, a white supremacist, philanthropist, and textile machinery manufacturer published the subsequent edition.

19. Ibid., v.

20. T. Lothrop Stoddard, *The Revolt against Civilization or the Menace of the Underman* (Burlington, VT: Ostara Publications, 2012).

21. Ibid., p. 27.

22. Ibid.

23. Ibid., p. 44. Stoddard lays these out in two tables.

24. Ibid., pp. 41–43.

25. Theodore G. Bilbo, *Take Your Choice: Separation or Mongrelization* (Poplarville, MS: Theodore G. Bilbo, 1947). (Burlington, VT: Ostara Publications, 2012).

26. Ibid., p. 19.

27. Ibid., p. 8.

28. Statement by President Coolidge at signing ceremony. (Pub.L. 68–139, 43 Stat. 153, enacted May 26, 1924).

29. President Franklin D. Roosevelt announced the "Good Neighbor Policy" on March 4, 1933. First inaugural address. In this address, the president stated that US foreign policy philosophy toward Latin America would change from one of intervention and imperialistic exploitation to one of assistance and support and the encouragement of trade relations. Bilbo's inclusion of Latin America might have had deleterious implications for President Roosevelt's pronouncement.

30. Grant, *The Passing*, p. 17 cited in Pat Shipman's *The Evolution of Racism: Human Differences and the Use and Abuse of Science* (New York: Simon & Schuster, 1994), 123–24.

31. Thomas Gossett, *Race*, p. 418.

32. A particularly rich work on the relationship between the American eugenics movement and Hitler's eugenic scientists. Stefan Kühl, *The Nazi Connection: Eugenics, American Racism, and German National Socialism* (Oxford: Oxford University Press, 1994).

33. Oscar Lewis, Ruth M. Lewis, and Margaret Mead, *Five Families: Mexican Case Studies in the Culture of Poverty* (New York: Basic Books, 1959).

34. Oscar Lewis, 1963, "The Culture of Poverty," *Society*. Reprinted January/February 1998. p. 7.

35. Nathan Glazer, *Beyond the Melting Pot: The Negroes, Puerto Ricans, Jews, Italians and Irish of New York City* (with Daniel P. Moynihan) (Cambridge, MA: Massachusetts Institute of Technology Press, 1963, second expanded edition 1970).

Edward Banfield, *The Unheavenly City Revisited* (Prospect Heights, IL: Waveland Press, Inc., 1970. Reissued, 1990).

36. Arthur Jensen, "How Much Can We Boost IQ and Achievement," *Harvard Educational Review* 39 (1969): 1–123.

37. See the extensive discussion of the relationship between race, heredity, physical characteristics and IQ in J. Phillipe Rushton and Arthur R. Jensen, "Thirty Years of Research on Race Differences in Cognitive Ability," *Psychology, Public Policy, and Law* 11, no. 2 (2005): 235–94.

38. Ibid., Table 3, p. 265.

39. Daniel Gardner, *The Science of Fear: How the Culture of Fear Manipulates Your Brain* (New York: PLUME, 2009).

40. Sabari Roy, "The Psychology of Fear." Futurehealth.org, Oct. 5, 2010.

41. Some argue that we are now in a third reconstruction era. See William J. Barber and Jonathan Wilson Hartgrove, *The Third Reconstruction: Moral Mondays, Fusion Politics, and the Rise of a New Justice Movement* (Boston: The Beacon Press, 2016).

42. Patrick Phillips, *Blood at the Root: A Racial Cleansing in America* (New York: W. W. Norton & Company, 2016).

43. Kahneman, *Thinking, Fast and Slow* (New York: Farrar, Straus and Giroux, 2011).

44. See the entire YouTube video at www.youtube.com/watch?v=FBVt6blqhac.

45. Kahneman, *Thinking Fast and Slow*.

46. This incident was related to me by my daughter Dr. Julia R. Díaz. The male was a black man she incidentally encountered as she was making her rounds one day in the teaching hospital at UCSF in 2015.

47. Cornel West, *Race Matters* (Boston: Beacon Press, 1993).

48. The literature in this area usually falls into the categories of political psychology or socialization and began with extensive studies pioneered at the University of Michigan by M. Kent Jennings and others. A great deal of this research forms the basis of marketing strategies, political polling, and so forth.

49. Lani Guinier describes this happening to her son early on in his life and the subsequent discussion they had about his "racing" in Lani Guinier and Gerald Torres, *The Miner's Canary: Enlisting Race, Resisting Power, Transforming Democracy* (Cambridge, MA: Harvard University Press, 2002).

50. Henry Flores, *The Evolution of the Liberal Democratic State with a Case Study of Latinos in San Antonio, Texas* (Lewiston, NY: The Edwin Mellon Press, 2003). See the discussion in chapter 2.

51. Both the Federal Bureau of Investigation and the Southern Poverty Law Center have an extensive list of hate organizations of various types sorted by hatred toward gay persons, non-whites, Jews, women, and so forth. How many total number of hate organizations exist in the United States today is difficult to estimate because some on the various lists are defunct, some have changed their names, and some have yet to be identified.

52. Joh Fuerst, "The Nature of Race: The Genealogy of the Concept and the Biological Construct's Contemporaneous Utility," *Open Behavioral Genetics*, June 2015

and Jerry A. Coyne, "Are There Human Races?" *Why Evolution Is True*, Feb. 28, 2012.

53. Fromm, *The Heart of Man*.

54. Ibid., pp. 25–26.

55. Elizar Barkan, *The Retreat of Scientific Racism: Changing Concepts of Race in Britain and the United States Between the First World Wars* (Cambridge: Cambridge University Press, 1993), 118. Cited in David Scott Fitzgerald and David Cook-Martin, *Culling the Masses: The Democratic Origins of Racist Immigration Policy in America* (Cambridge, MA: Harvard University Press, 2014), p. 100.

56. Stuart Creighton Miller, *The Unwelcome Immigrant: The American Image of the Chinese* (Berkeley: University of California Press, 1969). Clifford Kirkpatrick, "Intelligence and Immigration," *Psychoanalytic Review* 14 (1927): 363–64. Maxine S. Seller, "Historical Perspectives on American Immigration Policy: Case Studies and Current Implications," in *U.S. Immigration Policy*, edited by Richard R. Hofstetter (Durham, NC: Duke University Press, 1984), pp. 148–55.

57. 70 Congressional Record, S2817-S2818 (daily ed. Feb. 9, 1928). Cited in Fitzgerald and Cook-Martin, p. 105.

58. Ibid.

59. Roy L. Garis, *Immigration Restriction: A Study of the Opposition to and Regulation of Immigration Into the United States* (New York: The Macmillan Company, 1927), 203.

60. Ibid.

61. Ibid., p. 204.

62. Ibid.

63. Ibid., p. 213.

64. Garis's book contains a great number of tables and graphs, particularly chapter VII, justifying the restriction of immigrants from various Eastern and Southern European countries as well as Asia and some countries in the Americas. These tables and graphs were submitted as evidence during the congressional hearings and assisted congress in reaching decisions that eventually led to the development of the restrictive equation.

65. K. Young, *Science*, Vol. LVII, No. 1484 (June 8, 1923): 660–70. Maurice B. Hexter and Abraham Myerson, "A Study in Probable Error: A Critical Review of Brigham's *American Intelligence*," *Mental Hygiene*, Vol. VIII (January 1924).

66. Howard Woolston, "Wanted—An Immigration Policy," *Journal of Social Forces* Vol. 2 (1923–1924): 666–70.

67. Henry P. Fairchild, *Immigration*, reprinted from original 1925 (Charleston, SC: Nabu Press, 2009), pp. 451–53.

68. Ibid., p. 207.

69. Speech given by the Honorable Henry H. Curran, a former commissioner of immigration at Ellis Island, at the Hotel Astor, March 25, 1924. Cited in Garis, 1927, p. 284.

70. See for instance J. Morgan Kousser's *Colorblind Injustice: Minority Voting Rights and the Undoing of the Second Reconstruction* (Chapel Hill: The University of

North Carolina Press, 1999) or Ari Berman's *Give Us the Ballot: The Modern Struggle for Voting Rights in America* (New York: Farrar, Straus and Giroux, 2015).

71. As an example, see Rodolfo Acuña's *Occupied America: A History of Chicanos* (8th edition) (New York: Longman Publishing Group, 2015).

72. Archives, Sons of DeWitt Colony Texas @ 1997–2012, Wallace L. McKeahan, *Nuevo España, Nuevas Philipinas—Provinicia de Tejas, 1528–1821.*

73. *In Re Ricardo Rodriguez*, 81 F. 337 (W. D. Tex. 1897).

74. These histories are covered in Ronald Fernández, *The Desenchanted Island: Puerto Rico and the United States in the Twentieth Century* (2nd ed.) (New York: Praeger Paperback, 1996). Olga Jiménez de Wagenheim and Kal Wagenheim, *The Puerto Ricans: A Documentary History* (Markus Wiener Publishers, 2002). Arturo Morales Carrión, *Puerto Rico: A Political and Cultural History* (New York: W. W. Norton & Company, 1984). Aviva Chomsky, Barry Carr, and Pamela Maria Smorkaloff, eds., *The Cuba Reader: History, Culture, Politics* (Durham, NC: Duke University Press, 2004).

75. 81 F. 337 (W. D. Tex. 1897).

76. David Montejano, *Anglos and Mexicans in the Making of Texas, 1836–1986* (Austin: The University of Texas Press, 1987).

77. Ibid., pp. 110–12, 130, 136, 139–40, 147–49, *passim*.

78. Ibid., *In Re Ricardo Rodriguez.*

79. Arnoldo DeLéon, *In Re Ricardo Rodriguez: An Attempt at Chicano Disfranchisement, 1896–1897* (San Antonio, TX: Caravel Press, 1979), 1.

80. Ibid., p. 8.

81. Stephen Jay Gould, *The Measurement of Man* (New York: W. W. Norton, 1981).

82. De Léon, *In Re*, p. 8.

83. Ibid., p. 11.

84. *Hernandez v. Texas*, 347 U.S.475 (1954).

85. These are all discussed and identified in Henry Flores (2015).

86. Ibid.

87. See chapter 2 in Flores, *Latinos and the Voting Rights Act*, for a complete discussion of the legislative debate on Senate Bill 14, which was the legislative designation for the "Voter Identification and Verification Act of 2012."

88. Ibid., pp. 143–210, *passim*.

89. James Boyd, "Nixon's Southern Strategy 'It's All in the Charts,'" *New York Times*, May 17, 1970, p. 215.

90. Chandler Davidson, Tanya Dunlap, Gale Kenny, and Benjamin Wise, "Republican Ballot Security Programs: Vote Protection or Minority Vote Suppression—Or Both?" *A Report to the Center for Voting Rights & Protection* (Washington, DC, September 2014).

91. James Boyd, "Nixon's Southern Strategy 'It's all in the Charts'." *New York Times*, May 17, 1970, p. 215.

92. Flores, *Latinos and the Voting Rights Act*, see the discussions in Chapters 2 and 5.

93. *Veasey v. Abbott*, 796 F. 3d 487 (5th Cir. 2015).

94. *Veasey*, 796 F. 3rd at 698, 684, and 703.
95. *Village of Arlington Heights v. Metropolitan Housing Development Corporation*, 429 U.S. 252 (1977). The Arlington Heights factors are outlined in the case but can also be found in *Latinos and the Voting Rights Act*.
96. Statement of Chief Justice Roberts, *Greg Abbott, Governor of Texas, et al. v. Marc Veasey, et al.*, No. 16-393. Decided January 23, 2017.
97. *Veasey v. Abbott*, 503–504.

Chapter 2

Racism and the Public Policy Process

The myth of the Gordian knot reveals a great deal of how difficult it is to understand the complex nature of the interconnectedness and multilayeredness of the state that I call the "matrix." Matrix has been chosen to describe the state because it is an appropriate metaphor for elaborating the complexity of the state. Unlike "The Matrix" of popular culture the state as matrix is not a virtual reality world in which the struggle for humanity is fought. The "matrix" of the state possesses finite limits, is real, and is the creation of human beings over a certain time period. The state as matrix simply describes how intricately complicated the interconnectedness of the various institutions of the state are as well as the many layers of the state, that is, national, state, and local governments and their interconnections.

The myth of the Gordian knot is a metaphor for untangling a complex, complicated, and difficult problem. The knot itself, according to Greek mythology, was designed to protect the connection of an oxcart to the palace of ancient Phrygia. The oxcart had been offered as a gift to Zeus as thanks for the ascendancy of a peasant named Gordias to the throne of Phrygia. Later, an oracle declared that the individual who could "unravel" the knot would be king of Asia. Many tried and failed until 333 BCE when Alexander the Great arrived in Phrygia during the conquering of Persia. He tried many times but became exasperated, so he drew his sword and sliced through the knot. Some scholars have noted that this was an Aristotelian response to the problem; others claim it was the wrong response. Nevertheless, Alexander eventually became king of all Asia, however, upon his demise his empire fell apart. Perhaps if he had had the patience to untangle the knot using his intellectual capabilities his empire would have had a different future.[1]

Combining my definition of the state with the myth of the Gordian knot describes the problematic of understanding the intricacy of the state as well as difficulty and patience one requires to thoroughly understand the structures and functions of the state. So, the principle tasks of this chapter are to describe the complex state structure referred to here as the "matrix." Secondly, we will attempt to unravel the matrix to develop a thorough understanding of how racism can become infused within the structure. My assumption is that racism, although belonging to the human psyche, can also find itself as an essential element within the structure affecting public policy in ways not intended resulting in the uneven distribution of services provided by the state.

Much of what will be presented here I have already discussed in detail elsewhere[2] but what I said earlier requires some reiteration, elaboration, and modification if we are to unravel the matrix. Although I have not retreated from my earlier comments on the state, I have reached what, I feel, are richer conclusions thus the need for elaboration. Essentially, I pointed out that the structure of the liberal democratic state was a flexible and amorphous entity that is ideologically structured to insure the maintenance of the socioeconomic-politico strata and status quo of our society. Here I wish to add the role racial thinking and racism play within the ideological structuring of the state. In other words, I wish to expand the matrix to include the historical and psychological as well. Essentially, we only thoroughly comprehend the complexity of the socioeconomic-political matrix by understanding why individuals working within the matrix make decisions the way they do. What motivates individuals to decide, for instance, to fund certain social programs a certain way and to a certain extent, such as education, immigration, gun control, and so forth is important to understanding why policy outcomes are oriented in a certain manner. The easy answer is that all policy outcomes are negotiated among all institutions and institutional actors. The subsequent and more important question is, What motivates the institutional actors to take the negotiating positions they do in the first place? Only the inclusion of the psychological and ideological elements of the matrix will allow us to understand this question.

THE SOCIOECONOMIC-POLITICAL-PSYCHOLOGICAL STRUCTURE

The socioeconomic-political-psychological structure is a complex matrix describing the interaction between all institutions in society, both private and public, that, when functioning, construct, structure, and maintain the social structure of our society. This assumes that an individual's place within a social stratum is the direct result of these interactions and human beings have no choice into which social strata they are born. Many sociologists beginning with G. William Domhoff conclude that most individuals, some even cite percentages, will not move out of their strata throughout their lifetime.[3] Upward movement is possible and some individuals do manage to move up the social ladder but it is not the norm and highly improbable; moving downward is easier and happens often given the fragility of the financial and economic situation under which much of the lower-middle, working-, and poor classes live.

Essentially, most contemporary sociologists conclude that the United States is now a well-structured class society with some indicating that the middle class is disappearing altogether.[4] The largest assumption is that once one is born into their social strata, they are subject to the policy and programmatic functions of the matrix. For instance, if one is born to a rich or wealthy family one has both a financial and economic "head start" because one is then educated in schools and subject to socialization mechanisms available to them because of their birth. The same holds true for individuals born into all classes. The higher the social class the more advantages one has available to them, which opens more opportunities in their lifetimes, including social connections that will help them maintain their lifestyles and social standing keeping them within their own social strata throughout their lifetime. Of course, falling from the social strata is also subject to the machinations of the matrix. In the event of a catastrophic financial failure those in the upper classes of society will lose a great deal or some of their assets together with the social standing that goes with them and may find themselves among the ranks of the lower classes. However, in the event of such a crisis, such as a global depression, the rich possess more assets and may be able to weather the crisis to a certain extent better than the other classes. On the other hand, a major financial disaster would devastate what little social standing the lower classes have and would result in very large numbers relegated to the streets such as was the case in the Great Depression.

So, what does the socioeconomic-political-psychological matrix look like? How would one go about unraveling the Gordon's knot rather than slashing through it to understand its complex network? One issue that must be overcome in order to understand the matrix is that the various institutions and their layers tend to overlap and, in some cases, become integral parts of each other. For instance, the health care of the nation is a combination of institutions controlled by both the private and public sectors, professional associations, and manufacturing companies. The interdependencies of all these institutions weigh heavily in determining the price and costs of health care in the United States. Most insidiously, without one of these institutions others cannot perform their function; without one the entire social matrix is threatened. Health care is an essential part of the matrix because of the jobs that depend on this industry and the money this industry pores back into the general economy and revenues of the state coffers at all levels. Additionally, the health care industry insures that those who work within and without the industry are healthy, insuring they can play their parts in the construction and reconstruction of the general matrix. This same brief example can be replicated for all economic, financial, and political institutions as each institution plays a vital role within the matrix's functioning and long-term survival.

THE STATE

I pointed out in an earlier work, *The Evolution of the Liberal Democratic State*,[5] that the state is composed of three abstract structures: ideological, process, and decisional. Each structure oversees the structuring and functioning of all institutions within each of the structures simultaneously. In other words, the ideological or socialization processes and decisional structures of any matrix function together as they produce policies and reproduce conditions necessary for society's continuation and survival. This statement requires additional unpacking to better understand this theory of the state. All state institutions, regardless of whether they exist at the national, state, local, or special governmental levels are ideologically structured in such a manner as to oversee and maintain the existing social conditions of our society. The institutions, ideologically structured at the beginning of the republic or when they were initially created, have been added onto and restructured in such a way as to insure the diffusion of social, political, and economic tensions that arise from time to time. The continuous ideological and consequent institutional restructuring, together leading to the diffusion of tensions, result in the maintenance of the social structures of society. In short, as each tension is defused the institution evolves or morphs into another version of itself exemplified by the history of how each cabinet ministry was added, insuring that the national government could bring sufficient emphasis and resources to bear in order to deal with a given crisis at that moment in history. For instance, in the twentieth century the Departments of Commerce and Labor were created in 1917 to deal with the tensions between capital and labor that some felt threatened the existence of our nation. There were those during that historical period who felt that the tensions between industrial corporations and labor unions were so tense that a revolution similar to one in Russia could occur in the United States.[6] In 1948, the Department of War's name was changed to the Department of Defense because the United States wanted to move away from the emotionalities generated from the ravages of World War II and project a more peaceful face to the world and also to mark a new era of global peace. Finally, in 1965 the Department of Housing and Urban Development (HUD) was created to confront the economic and social crises facing our nation's large urban areas and the rapid urbanization of the entire country. The creation of HUD fashioned an image or perception that the national government was deeply concerned with urban issues. It was also the recognition that the population in the United States had primarily become concentrated in large urban areas and the United States was no longer a rurally based society. Finally, the creation of HUD was also a reaction to the riots that had become annual occurrences every summer in big cities across the United States. These are but a few examples of the state's expansion to meet social or economic challenges facing the nation in those moments; similar rationales can be found for the creation of each ministry that comprise the national government. Each cabinet office was designed to confront and defuse a crisis that threatened the stability of the United States at that moment in history. The other national ministries have histories reflecting the same relationship between the rise of a national crisis and the creation of a bureau designed to confront the crisis because the Executive Branch or Congress felt an agency dedicated to tackle the consequences of the crisis was required. Most importantly, the creation of an agency to focus on a specific crisis is an indicator to the people of the nation that the government or state is attempting to solve the problems created by the crisis if not the crisis itself. Just as importantly, as each ministry was added it marked the evolution of the matrix. An additional bureaucracy increased the budget, expanded the number of jobs and laws, regulations, and extended the reach of the national government. Essentially, adding to government markedly changes the face of government. In short, the government, the state apparatus, evolves to a new and different state matrix. The matrix adds additional layers, levels and interconnections to the state matrix increasing the complexity of the state.

An important consideration is that the ideological structuring of each institution within a liberal democracy is important because the political, economic, and social structures of any given society must be compatible and complimentary or the social system will collapse. This was made abundantly clear by both Adam Smith[7] and Karl Marx.[8] Generally, when nation's fail it is because of the institutional incompatibility caused by the mismatch between the social, economic, and political structures. The ideological difference, which generally occurs at the creation of the state, leads to a degree of instability during the initial stages of the state's existence. I would argue that the United States was relatively unstable from 1789 through World War II due largely to the differences between how the national state was structured and the rapid growth and expansion of industry and commerce as well as the need for spatial expansion. In short, it may be the case that the state evolves slower than the economy and society, as a result its evolution, is reactive rather than anticipatory. The establishment of the public/private sector nexus and finalization of the Bretton Woods Agreement following World War II solidified and united all three sectors—political, economic and social—of the United States. Additionally, US global dominance reinforced the sense of superiority of US political and cultural institutions. Several historical examples exist where political systems have failed including the French and Russian Revolutions of 1789 and 1917, respectively, where the political, economic, and social systems of both countries were not structurally compatible or integrated.

Even the United States has faced the possibility of collapse in both the nineteenth and twentieth centuries. During the nineteenth century, the US collapse resulted in a devastating civil war that saw at least two major factions fighting for control of the national government because one faction felt that the national economy should be agriculturally based while another saw the burgeoning industrial era as the future of the nation.[9] There have been other moments in the history of the United States where various social groups have caused enough disruption that the national government has had to make major policy decisions in order to subdue the dissent such as those concerned with ending the Vietnam War, and placing immigrant, gender, and civil rights on the national agenda, and so forth. In each instance, the national government was forced to change public policy direction or enhance the national discussion in order to appease the demands of a large segment of US society. These changes in policy direction served to absorb or diffuse the social tensions that arose due to a lack of policy in the contested area or a policy incompatible with the wishes and needs of society.

It is also important to note that the age of administrators and politicians may create other tensions. For example, the current disagreements of those who feel that issues such as climate change, health care, technological innovations, marriage choices, and the civil rights of Latinos, black Americans, and women are not being fully addressed. An essential element of this tension is that senior decision makers are trapped in their beliefs and perceptions formed in earlier ideological eras. These older administrators, lawyers, politicians, and leaders fail to recognize the realities of social and financial changes occurring while they are in positions of power. As a result, many important current policy areas are not addressed or completely ignored or interpreted through aged perceptual lenses. This will result in intergenerational tensions that may affect the way in which policy decisions are raised or altogether ignored. This may also explain why the state is reactive rather than anticipatory in that older decision makers may interpret problems such as climate change or technological innovations through older ideological lenses as opposed to the way younger generations perceive the problem. As a result, either a problem is overlooked or postponed until a crisis forces the decision makers to respond.

Although internal stressors such as the economy or some social issue can cause government to act and change its structure, external stressors can also cause or add to institutional stress. One of the most interesting examples of the effects of an external stressor on the US state was the influence of the denigration to our national image over congress's reluctance to pass the Civil

Rights Acts of the 1960s. The United States faced charges of hypocrisy, principally from the Soviet Union and other communist bloc countries, on how we treated African Americans as we propagated the virtues of democracy internationally. Although internal stressors as well as demonstrations by civil rights activists were important to the passage of these much needed laws, the criticism of our Cold War enemies bolstered the momentum of the activists. Although times were ripe for the passage of these important laws additional impetus came from the nation's ideological enemies that assisted in moving an intransigent congress.

When governments change policy their structure also changes because the new policies either cause government structures to expand or contract. For instance, removal of our military from Vietnam changed the size and eventually the internal structure of the military. Another example of institutional change due to a change in policy can be found in the history surrounding the implementation of the Civil Rights Acts of 1965. The Civil Rights Acts led to the creation of agencies and the restructuring of many others required for the implementation and enforcement of the programs and laws that evolved out of the 1965 acts. The passage of the Civil Rights Acts also created a cascading effect in the realm of political participation because it opened the floodgates to the participation and elections of more African Americans and then later Latinos that, along with dramatic national demographic shifts, began changing the face of US politics. This culminated with the election of an African American president in 2008 and a highly competitive female presidential candidate in 2016. These electoral shifts allowed for the rearranging of the national public policy agendas that, again, resulted in changing institutions and institutional arrangements. Without the passage of the Civil Rights Act it is very conceivable that a great deal of social unrest would have resulted and one can only guess as to the extent of violence and damage to the nation this would have caused. Instead, the rise of Barack Obama and Hillary Clinton was marked with a minimal amount of racism and misogyny as compared to what they would have encountered in an earlier historical period. Still, after President Obama was installed there appeared to be more intransigence on the part of Congress to cooperate with the new president and a suspicion was that the leadership of both institutions, dominated by white southerners, was due partially to racism.

THE ROLE OF IDEOLOGY IN THE FORMATION OF THE STATE

Without a doubt, ideology is the "glue" that holds any society together. If one does not have all citizens thinking and believing in the same general principles and political direction, then the seeds for the political disintegration of a nation have been planted. Not everyone must believe in exactly the same principles or in the same political direction; there must be a consensus in a set of general beliefs in order that a society remains cohesive. There can be disagreements about specific types of policies, taxes, the role of public education, the role of government in the provision of health care, and so forth. However, there cannot be large segments of society disagreeing on principles that are deemed important for the proper functioning of society. For instance, large segments of our nation cannot believe in the total and complete nationalization of the banking, health, energy, or food production sectors. The nationalization of sectors that continually have problems but are essential to our everyday comfort and existence runs counter to the way Americans think about the role of government. Government can regulate, to a certain extent, but cannot interfere or become an active controller of an economic sector. Ownership of businesses and corporations are the sole purview of the private sector and not the government. This is a basic principle in American liberal democratic ideology. To think otherwise is unfathomable and intellectually foreign, particularly on the part of politicians or public decision makers. Any politician who champions the nationalization of any economic sector in a capitalist economy would never win their election or, if already in office, might face deselection in the next round.

Regarding the nationalization of banks or the general belief in capitalism the essential questions, then, arise as to how did this type of belief, the nexus between private and public sectors, arise and become such an integral element of our national ideological culture? In addition, what is it about the structure that allows a belief of this nature to take such a strong hold at all levels of society? A detailed discussion of how our national financial and economic structures were founded and how they have evolved throughout history will uncover the answers to these questions. Most important to this discussion, however, is to understand how this key principle, among many others, has become imbedded in our national ideological culture. Before moving to the substantive discussion of the issue, I must define what is meant by the national ideological culture. A national ideological culture specifies the basic values through which an entire country views the world, its place in the world, and defines its national identity. For the United States this includes beliefs in concepts such as the free enterprise economic system where private ownership of the means of production, property, and finance are the cornerstones of the economy. The concept of private ownership is a part of the general national belief system because it is legitimized through its inclusion in the economics or business curriculum in all schools both private and public that Americans attend during their lifetimes and come to understand as the manner in which the economy is normally and traditionally structured. The concept is employed in the business world and in the way in which public/private relations are conceptualized, eventually finding their way into public policy. Most importantly, the notion that private ownership is a paramount liberal democratic principle even plays a significant part in the daily lives of Americans. Private ownership underlies the way in which Americans see their relationship to home ownership and other types of properties. Even in a perverted manner, some men see this as the basis of their relationships with their spouses and their children.

Still another belief that is central to the national ideological culture is the belief that the United States is "exceptional" as some have referred to it and have described it as "a city upon a hill."[10] Belief in this notion has led Americans to view their country, government, and social system as the model for the entire world. Not only do Americans see themselves as the model for a nation's success globally, they also pursue their foreign policy positions with these assumptions in mind. Whether we deny it or not much of what we do when negotiating trade or aid agreements assume that any outcomes will bring our partners closer to what we look like socially and politically. Domestically, this assumption finds its way into many policy areas. For instance, an essential myth of residency in the United States is that individual ownership of homes is desirable. One can even obtain credit on their annual income tax from deducting the interest they pay on a mortgage loan and the property taxes paid to local governments. So, even the laws are structured under the assumptions of private ownership[11] governing how one pays for and pays rent to the state.

Elaborating further on the private ownership of property one may argue that the opposite of private ownership is public ownership. This concept is anathema to the ideological cultural values held by almost all Americans. The perception that the nationalization of the free enterprise system or of any institution within any sector of the system is not even included in curriculum or public policy discourse. Nationalization of the private sector is excluded from the national consciousness of any liberal democratic society. It is not out rightly rejected, although it may be depending upon the discourse, it is simply not thought of as a viable public policy option. Public ownership of the means of production, financial institutions, and so forth is not a value openly spoken of in public fora and completely excluded from curricula at all educational levels. In short, the concept or notion that the public can own the central institutions of the economy, within a liberal democratic society, is simply not in the ideological consciousness of Americans. As a result, public ownership as a possible policy alternative in solving problems in the economy is not even included on an institution's public policy agenda. Americans generally have not even heard of this concept except in some far off and distant socialist or communist country.

The history of the evolution of the banking system is instructive because it clearly demonstrates that banking was and has always been the purview of the private sector in the United States. The government steps in when the banking system falls prey to the avarice of various financial actors and speculators who sometimes threaten to bring down the national economy manipulating stock, bond, and loan markets in their pursuit of profits. Government action leads to the passage of new regulatory laws or the enforcement of existing ones, the banking system adjusts to the new laws, and business continues as usual until the next crisis. The most recent example of this was the housing bubble of the early twenty-first century when a few individuals took advantage of investment banking laws to generate billions in profits for themselves. The result, however, was the failure of some investment banking houses and the passage of new regulatory laws. On the consumer side, thousands of lower middle- and middle-class persons lost their homes and found themselves in debt that was impossible to manage on their modest incomes. Throughout this last crisis there was no talk of the government taking over the banking industry only that the government pass new regulations or punish the culprits who caused the damage. In this case, the government did not pass any new regulations only punished a few perpetrators for their over-zealousness. Greed or the growth of the bank's bottom line, regardless of the effects on their clients, was never an issue.[12]

The nationalization of banking or any other sector that is the purview of private ownership is not an idea that is taught in schools, discussed in boardrooms, or in the halls of government because it falls into a category of ideas that are not part of our national ideological culture. As a result, the public ownership of property, as a concept, is excluded from any list of options available to decision makers when considering policy alternatives.[13] The government's role in banking is a complimentary one, not one that determines how capital is managed or invested. The government acts more like a referee managing conflict between competing banking entities and creating standards that allow the various banking sectors to work smoothly with each other. Thus, the role ideology plays in this example establishes the institutional and structural relationships between the public and private sectors in the banking industry. It represents the way of thinking, which eventually becomes institutionalized as the way in which problems between institutions of this sector are managed.

Then the national ideological culture is the philosophical, almost metaphysical and consequently conceptual screen through which a society views the world. It determines the national identity of a country, the manner in which its citizens view other countries and cultures, and how they define their political place within the global context. A nation's ideological culture is composed of the values and beliefs that make Americans American, Mexicans Mexican, and Russians Russian. This culture defines how citizens and longtime residents of countries approach every aspect of their daily lives and how politicians, business persons, and various types of leaders of every country identify and define an issue to be dealt with, how the issue is to be dealt with, and how any solution is to be implemented. The specific ideological culture will then determine whether issues such as poverty, housing, investment strategies, taxation policy, and so forth are issues that should be dealt with by their respective government, what the specific policy in any given country will look like, and how that policy is to be implemented. It may be determined, for instance, that poverty in one country is the fault of the individual while in a different country poverty may be seen as a systemic consequence. The definition of the poverty problem will determine what role the national government will play in alleviating poverty or not and just how the poverty policy will be structured and what its intended goals are.

In the bigger picture, the matrix or state is held together by the national ideological culture of a country and becomes the metaphysical glue holding a country together, determines that country's economic and political direction, and is an important determiner of that country's well-being. In the end, the ideological culture of a nation plays an important role in determining the social and physical well-being of the persons subject to its rule. As an aside to those who espouse the pseudo-theories of the deep, dark, unfathomable administrate state, the state is only as deep as society allows it to be, it is not dark, however, its many parts and segments make it appear so and finally it is not unfathomable. The matrix can be understood if one possessed the patience Alexander the Great did not.

HOW IS THE NATIONAL IDEOLOGICAL CULTURE STRUCTURED?

The configuration of the national ideological culture is built around the structure and functioning of a society's ideological mechanisms, the society's political and decisional structures, and the various processes within that society that orient that society's general direction.[14] The ideological mechanism of every society, this cultural mechanism is essential to any society's existence, has become what political scientists, psychologists, and sociologists have come to call "the socialization process." I call it an ideological mechanism instead to underline that, first and foremost, the institutions functioning within this mechanism play an important political role. Additionally, these institutions function almost automatically from generation to generation and from historical era to historical era, mechanistically, automatously. These mechanisms inculcate every individual within that society with the same general political and social values. So, individuals are indeed socialized but more importantly they are politicized as well in a very systematic fashion.

The institutions that make up the ideological mechanisms' structures include the family unit, the various peer groups one enters and exits throughout one's lifetime, the work setting, educational institutions, the media including political propaganda, and religion. As one progresses through life from before birth through death one is exposed to the forces of the ideological mechanisms allowing one to develop an understanding and orientation to a way of life that includes the political. The ideological formation process begins during one's childhood where the foundational belief structures and systems are embedded within the consciousness and subconsciousness of everyone. As an individual progresses through life, these belief structures and systems become reinforced or changed until one passes. The changes are more substantial earlier in life, but they still occur through one's mature years. The ideological formation of the individual is what determines one's orientation and identification as a progressive, conservative, reactionary, libertarian, socialist, communist, or moderate. Generally, one takes on some semblance of the ideological orientation of the parents but there can also be the opposite effect where, as one matures, one questions the beliefs that they have embraced their entire lives and may or may not change or modify them.

As one proceeds into the professional world, one brings her ideological belief system to bear as one interprets the political, economic, and social world and finds her place within that world. The belief system assists the individual in making her decisions about how to interpret the propaganda spewed by politicians and governments and how to cast a ballot in support or against politicians or policy initiatives. The belief systems also assist the individual in going about their daily lives professionally and socially. In some cases, one's ideological orientation may even assist an individual as they choose a life partner, a circle of friends, and organizations that one wishes to join.

As individuals move into and become part of important social and political institutions and ascend through the ranks of these institutions, they bring their ideological orientation to bear when making decisions or, at least, take part in the formation and implementation of those decisions. This phenomenon is most visible in the political world where politicians or bureaucrats tinge policy decisions with their own ideological orientation regardless of institution or situation. For example, ideology plays an important role in the way justices, at all levels of the US judicial system, make their decisions. It is most evident in the realm of civil rights cases that are adjudicated, for the most part, in the federal court system. Judges have even felt free to point out to plaintiffs and defendants their dislike for hearing civil rights cases. Justices or judges have been so blatant about their ideological orientation when making decisions that some judges have even been reported to various judicial ethics panels for their behavior or comments.[15] Elected officials also bring their ideological orientation to bear when considering policy positions on various issues whether in economic development, environmental, taxation, or defense policies. Politicians even present their ideological orientation as an essential element of their electoral bona fides to the electorate during their campaigns substantiating their "conservative," "liberal," or "progressive" values to their constituent bases.

The ideological orientations of political actors, whether elected or appointed, including career public servants, function as "selective mechanisms" or "sifting devices" that allow the individual to make choices among policy alternatives or implementation methods. These selective mechanisms act in three ways that determine the subjectivity of public policies and they function at all levels of government and the state. The first method of selection has already been discussed here. Simply, it is the exclusion of certain concepts, ideas, or policy alternatives during the ideological formation and socialization processes of society. Some ideas are simply eliminated in the normal course of learning through ignorance, neglect, or intention. Thus, any idea that does not conform to any of the accepted norms of a society will not even occur to those making decisions or considering policy alternatives. The second selective mechanism functions because of the fashion in which the political, social, and economic structures in a society are intertwined. The matrix created by the intersection of all the institutions representing the three principle social sectors of a society only allow policy alternatives, of those left over after the exclusion mechanism has functioned, to rise to the top of the decisional processes of society. For example, in the realm of economic development the nexus between the private and public sector dictates the policy alternatives that will be considered during the decisional process due to the size and expense of developments wished by local or regional governments. The sizes are of the magnitude normally that eliminates participation by small developers and financiers from the competition leaving only the large developers and bankers to gain from a local government's priorities. These policy finalists are then prioritized further with those more favorable to the ideological orientation of individuals in control of the decisional process to be given the most consideration. In the world of economic development this means that those alternatives that appear more attractive to the investment interests of those who control the capital necessary and the capability for successful development will choose the alternatives more favorable to their desired outcomes. Those in control of the public side of the decisional process will pass policies that make investment by the private sector more attractive. So, generally, for an economic development project to achieve success the investor, with a combination of the best cost structure and who is willing to agree to any government incentives and regulations (these are often negotiable), will win the government's request for a development proposal. Albeit there are times local or national political considerations that come into play, such as rules requiring that minority or small businesses perform a certain percentage of the development or work, allowing smaller organizations to participate in the process. Still the "lion's share" of opportunities always go in the direction of the larger investors. Smaller investors normally participate in activities peripheral to but associated with and complimentary to the larger investment activities such as parts suppliers to large automobile manufacturers, building material suppliers to subdivision developers, and so forth.

The third selective mechanism functions in tandem with the second in that the prioritization of policy alternatives, by definition, excludes consideration policies required to solve social problems endemic to society generally such as poverty, crime, educational attainment, environmental quality, and so forth. These latter issue areas are never addressed or addressed in a superficial manner only because until recently they have not been viewed as systemically produced social issues. Conditions such as poverty, illiteracy, crime, and so forth are seen as problems that are the result of individual failure and must be addressed by the individual not society. If society intervenes, it is only to seek a temporary solution buying time for the individual to address the problem. Generally, when these nonprioritized issue areas are addressed they are dealt with temporary policies that do not speak to the core causes of the problems but rather only provide temporary or superficial relief. For example, in the area of crime the causes of crime are not addressed, more police are hired, more sophisticated policing alternatives are created, and more secure jails and prisons are built. The root causes of the crime are never confronted only attempts at lowering the crime rates through increasing arrests, incarcerations, and intimidating communities become the foci of criminal justice policies. The same can be said when speaking of policies designed to lift the burdens of poverty. The root causes of poverty are never addressed only palliative poverty policies are considered. In every case, all policies that are supposed to address social problems not deemed of high priority by the government or society are generally only temporary in nature. Crime and poverty, among other social concerns, such as homelessness or public health, are deemed to be the fault of the individual and not that of the social or economic structure, as a result only programs or policies that speak to individual concerns are considered or passed by the decisional structures of the government or state. Neglected are the needs of various communities that are at the foundation of criminal behavior.

RACIAL THINKING AND RACISM IN THE IDEOLOGICAL MATRIX

It is understood that racial thinking is an important thread in the ideological matrix of US society. Racial thinking defines a principle way in which

Americans view the world both externally and internally. This is true both on the individual and national levels of perception. We begin thinking racially from a very early age, taught by our parents and reinforced by the other ideological mechanisms of society. The racial images that assist in defining our perceptions have varied from family to family, racial group to racial group, social class to social class, and geographical region to geographical region. These differing perceptions are dictated by the ideological culture dominating those regions, classes, and groups. The orientation and intensity of racial thinking and perception and its place in the ideological matrix has been determined by the various ideological mechanisms as they function(ed) throughout history.

As a result, the national ideological culture can best be described structurally as a matrix saturating the overall state matrix. One can imagine the national ideological culture as the blood coursing through the body of the state matrix allowing it to perform its normal daily functions. In other words, it is a network of interconnected perceptions, ideas, and notions that form one general orientation shared by a nation. As discussed earlier, this matrix gives a national identity definition and a nation's people direction. The matrix also assists the nation and its people to define its political place in the global community. In the United States, the matrix has given the American people a sense of international superiority in the global community. Americans feel that their type of democracy is the best in the world, pointing to the chaos and disorder in other countries. Sometimes the disorder and seeming chaos in other countries is attributed to the other country's culture as in the countries of Latin America, Africa, Asia, and the Middle East. The disorder in other countries is sometimes attributed to tendencies toward autocracies that other countries are purported to tend toward such as in Russia or Eastern Europe. Alternatively, sometimes the disorder is credited to the age of a democracy such as those in Europe. Overall, our democratic system, in the perception of Americans, stands as a "city on a hill" and an exemplar or model society of what other countries aspire to. Of course, many Americans have never been to other countries, studied the histories of other countries, or even met persons of these other countries. Americans, then, tend to project their perception of other people unto the other people and think that the other people feel just as the Americans think they do. Essentially, many Americans think that people of other countries see themselves as Americans see them and even wish to be just like Americans.

Internally, Americans view their nation in racial and social class terms and within each group lie gender identities as well as perceptions of social behavior. These perceptions, however, take on slightly differing definitions among the classes and racial groups. The racial hierarchical definition of US society created by the scientific racism movement of the early twentieth century persists still. Whites or Anglos still define themselves at the top of the racial hierarchy with the remainder of the races falling somewhere below them on other rungs of the racial ladder.

The racial thinking that is an integral fiber in the tapestry of the American national ideological culture is historically evident and can be attested to through an evaluation of public policy at all governmental levels. At the beginning of the republic one finds the slave population, which was almost totally of African descent, counted as three-fifths of a person,[16] American Indians were not even counted, and Mexicans or Latinos were not even in the country's consciousness. The master/slave relationship with African Americans remained until President Lincoln signed the Emancipation Proclamation[17] declaring the end to slavery. Actual freedom did not come until the passage of the Thirteenth, Fourteenth, and Fifteenth Amendments to the Constitution in 1865, 1868, and 1870, respectively. Finally, the nineteenth-century constitutional amendments were not fully implemented until the passage and signing of the Civil Rights Acts of 1965. Still, to this day, law suits are brought into federal court annually seeking redress under each of these amendments and laws for some racially discriminatory act someplace within the United States. In short, racial discrimination is an everyday part of life in the United States because the people of the United States and policy makers think racially and sometimes act in racist manners.

RACIAL THINKING AND THE SELECTION MECHANISMS

Without a doubt, racial thinking was included in the fashion in which the national ideological culture of the United States was structured from its founding and has played a prominent role in almost every nook and cranny of the nation's political world to date. Racial thinking has determined domestic social policy orientation in immigration, housing, education, criminal justice, voting, and poverty to name but a few. One can even argue that issue areas such as gun control or taxation policies, which appear race neutral, really have racial thinking structured into the substance of these policy areas. Three examples from the above list of policy areas will serve to substantiate my position: immigration, gun control, and voting.

The Exclusion Mechanism

The function of the exclusion mechanism is to exclude certain concepts or options as principle foci while this mechanism sifts through various policy alternatives and interpretations. The inclusion of racial thinking into the development and implementation of policies in immigration, gun control, and voting requires a comprehensive understanding of the historical development of each policy area. Perhaps the most important aspect of the exclusion process is that although the process excludes ideas it also excludes people. In the below examples it is abundantly clear that people of color are the main groups excluded from full participation in US society by the explicated policies. The first example used to describe how the exclusion mechanism operates is that of national immigration policy.

Immigration Policy

The nation's national immigration policy has always been composed with statements of exclusion in mind. Beginning with the 1790 Naturalization Act, which specifically excluded non-white people from naturalizing through the present day, exclusion has been specific as to particular types, races, and nationalities of individuals. Table 2.1 shows each act and the population the specific act excluded, restricted, or included. Some of the laws were amendments of previous laws and were intended as refinements such as the Immigration Act of 1891 that established broad provisions for screening while laying the foundation for the establishment of the now famous Ellis Island processing center. Others, such as the series of laws and acts from 1875 through the Geary Act of 1891 were designed specifically to exclude immigration from China and other Asian countries. These sets of exclusionary laws were intended to control the Chinese population in the United States and to discourage further emigration from China.

The data in Table 2.1 can be discussed from different perspectives but one of the easiest is to view it in terms of eras or phases. For instance, the initial phase of immigration laws focused on naturalization principally because the nation was young and still quite open to entry by any person from any country. Still, the nation needed to establish some fundamental statements on citizenship and it did this by closely following the constitutional provisions of only allowing "free white persons" to become citizens, a provision explicitly set forth in the naturalization laws from 1790–1870. Finally, in 1870, three years after the last of the famous "Civil Rights Amendments" to the Constitution that spread constitutional protections to the freed slaves between 1865 and 1868, Section 7 of the Naturalization Act of 1870 was added extending the right of citizenship to Africans and individuals of African descent. Essentially, all non-white persons, however defined in the historical era prior to 1870, were denied citizenship and excluded from full participation in American political society.

Immigration appears to have become an issue during the latter half of the nineteenth century, this is reflected in the next phase of immigration policies

Table 2.1 Immigration Policies 1790–Present

Year	Name of Legislation/Case	Major Highlights
1790	Naturalization Act of 1790	Established the rules for naturalized citizenship, as per Article 1, Section 8, of the Constitution, but placed no restrictions on immigration. Citizenship was limited to white persons, with no other restriction on non-whites.
1795	Naturalization Act of 1795	Lengthened required residency to become a citizen. This legislation spoke of immigration of white persons only.
1798	Naturalization Act (officially An Act to Establish a Uniform Rule of Naturalization; ch. 54, 1 Stat. 566) Alien Friends Act (officially An Act Concerning Aliens; ch. 58, 1 Stat. 570) Alien Enemies Act (officially An Act Respecting Alien Enemies; ch. 66, 1 Stat. 577)	Extended the duration of residence required for immigrants to become citizens to 14 years. Enacted June 18, 1798, with no expiration date, it was repealed in 1802. Authorized the president to deport any resident immigrant considered "dangerous to the peace and safety of the United States." It was activated June 25, 1798, with a two-year expiration date. Authorized the president to apprehend and deport resident aliens if their home countries were at war with the United States of America. Enacted July 6, 1798, and providing no sunset provision, the act remains intact today as 50 U.S.C. § 21. This legislation identified immigrants as white persons only.
1870	Naturalization Act of 1870	Extended the naturalization process to *"aliens of African nativity and to persons of African descent"* (Sec. 7). Other non-whites were not included in this act and remained excluded from naturalization, per the Naturalization Act of 1790.
1875	Page Act of 1875 (Sect. 141, 18 Stat. 477, 1873-March 1875)	The first federal immigration law prohibited the entry of immigrants considered as "undesirable." The law classified as "undesirable" any individual from Asia who was coming to the United States to be a contract laborer. Strengthened the ban against "coolie" laborers, by imposing a fine of up to $2,000 and maximum jail sentence of one year upon anyone who tried to bring a person from China, Japan, or any oriental country to the United States "without their free and voluntary consent, for the purpose of holding them to a term of service." Imposed a 50 cent head tax to fund immigration officials.

Table 2.1

Year	Name of Legislation/Case	Major Highlights
1882	Chinese Exclusion Act	Restricted immigration of Chinese laborers for 10 years. Prohibited Chinese naturalization. Provided deportation procedures for illegal Chinese. Marked the birth of illegal immigration (in the United States).
1885	Alien Contract Labor Law (Sess. II Chap. 164; 23 Stat. 332)	Prohibited the importation and migration of foreigners and aliens under contract or agreement to perform labor in the United States.
1891	Immigration Act of 1891	First comprehensive immigration laws for the United States. Bureau of Immigration set up in the Treasury Dept.[3] Immigration Bureau directed to deport unlawful aliens. Empowered "the superintendent of immigration to enforce immigration laws."
1892	Geary Act	Extended and strengthened the Chinese Exclusion Act.
1903	Immigration Act of 1903 (Anarchist Exclusion Act)	Added four inadmissible classes: anarchists, people with epilepsy, beggars, and importers of prostitutes.
1906	Naturalization Act of 1906	Made some knowledge of English a requirement for citizenship.
1907	Immigration Act of 1907	Restricted immigration for certain classes of disabled and diseased people.
1917	Immigration Act of 1917 (Barred Zone Act)	Restricted immigration from Asia by creating an "Asiatic Barred Zone" and introduced a reading test for all immigrants over fourteen years of age, with certain exceptions for children, wives, and elderly family members.
1918	Immigration Act of 1918	Expanded on the provisions of the Anarchist Exclusion Act.
1921	Emergency Quota Act	Limited the number of immigrants from any country to 3 percent of those already in the United States from that country as per the 1910 census. An unintended consequence of the 1920s legislation was an increase in illegal immigration. Many Europeans who did not fall under the quotas migrated to Canada or Mexico, which [as Western Hemisphere nations] were not subject to national-origin quotas; [and] subsequently they slipped into the United States illegally.

(Continued)

Table 2.1 (Continued)

Year	Name of Legislation/Case	Major Highlights
1922	The Cable Act of 1922 (ch. 411, 42 Stat. 1021, "Married Women's Independent Nationality Act")	Reversed former immigration laws regarding marriage, also known as the Married Women's Citizenship Act or the Women's Citizenship Act. Previously, a woman lost her US citizenship if she married a foreign man, since she assumed the citizenship of her husband, a law that did not apply to men who married foreign women. The law repealed sections 3 and 4 of the Expatriation Act of 1907.
1924	Immigration Act (Johnson-Reed Act)	Imposed first permanent numerical limit on immigration. Began a national-origin quota system.
1924	National Origins Formula	Established with the Immigration Act of 1924. Total annual immigration was capped at 150,000. Immigrants fit into two categories: those from quota-nations and those from non-quota nations. Immigrant visas from quota-nations were restricted to the same ratio of residents from the country of origin out of 150,000 as the ratio of foreign-born nationals in the United States. The percentage out of 150,000 was the relative number of visas a particular nation received. Non-quota nations, notably those contiguous to the United States, only had to prove an immigrant's residence in that country of origin for at least two years prior to emigration to the United States. Laborers from Asiatic nations were excluded but exceptions existed for professionals, clergy, and students to obtain visas.
1934	Equal Nationality Act of 1934	Allowed foreign-born children of American mothers and alien fathers who had entered the United States before age eighteen and lived there for five years to apply for American citizenship for the first time. Made the naturalization process quicker for American women's alien husbands.
1940	Nationality Act of 1940	Pertains chiefly to "Nationality at Birth," "Nationality through Naturalization," and "Loss of Nationality."
1943	Chinese Exclusion Repeal Act of 1943 (Magnuson Act)	Repealed the Chinese Exclusion Act and permitted Chinese nationals already in the country to become naturalized citizens.

Table 2.1

Year	Name of Legislation/Case	Major Highlights
1952	Immigration and Nationality Act (McCarran-Walter Act)	Set a quota for aliens with skills needed in the United States. Increased the power of the government to deport illegal immigrants suspected of Communist sympathies.
1965	INA Amendments (Hart-Celler Act)	Repealed the national-origin quotas. Initiated a visa system for family reunification and skills. Set a quota for Western Hemisphere immigration. Set a 20k country limit for Eastern Hemisphere aliens.
1966	Cuban Refugee Adjustment Act	Cuban nationals who enter, or were already present in the United States, legal status.
1986	Immigration Reform and Control Act	Required employers to attest to their employees' immigration status; Made it illegal to hire or recruit illegal immigrants knowingly; Legalized certain seasonal agricultural illegal immigrants, and; Legalized illegal immigrants who entered the United States before January 1, 1982, and had resided there continuously with the penalty of a fine, back taxes due, and admission of guilt; candidates were required to prove that they were not guilty of crimes, that they were in the country before January 1, 1982, and that they possessed minimal knowledge about U.S. history, government, and the English language.
1990s		Started sanctions for knowingly hiring illegal aliens. Provided amnesty to illegal aliens already in the United States.[14] Increased border enforcement. Made it a crime to hire an illegal immigrant.
1990	Immigration Act	More than 5.8 million illegal immigrants entered the United States in the 1990s. Mexico rose to the head of the list of sending countries, followed by the Philippines, Vietnam, the Dominican Republic, and China.
1990	*United States v. Verdugo-Urquidez*	Increased legal immigration ceilings. Created a diversity admissions category. Tripled the number of visas for priority workers and professionals with U.S. job offers.

(Continued)

Table 2.1 (Continued)

Year	Name of Legislation/Case	Major Highlights
1996	Illegal Immigration Reform and Immigrant Responsibility Act of 1996 (IIRaIRA)	The court reiterated the finding of *Kwong Hai Chew v. Colding*, 344 U.S. 590, 596 (1953), "The Bill of Rights is a futile authority for the alien seeking admission for the first time to these shores. But once an alien lawfully enters and resides in this country he becomes invested with the rights guaranteed by the Constitution to all people within our borders." Stated, "those cases in which aliens have been determined to enjoy certain constitutional rights establish only that aliens receive such protections when they have come within the territory of, and have developed substantial connections with, this country." See, for example, *Plyler v. Doe*, 457 U.S. 202, 212.
1999	*Rodriguez v. United States*, 169 F.3d 1342, (11th Cir. 1999)	Phone verification for worker authentication by employers. Access to welfare benefits more difficult for legal aliens. Increased border enforcement.
2002	Enhanced Border Security and Visa Entry Reform Act	An estimated 3.1 million immigrants entered the United States illegally between 2000 and 2005. From 1998 to 2001, Mexicans accounted for 68 percent of immigrants who entered the United States illegally. That percentage jumped to 78 percent for the years between 2001 and 2005, mostly due to stricter security measures that followed the September 11, 2001, attacks upon the United States (which more efficiently prevented illegal entry from nations that did not share a land or maritime boundary with the United States).
2005	REAL ID Act	Provided for more border patrol agents. Requires that schools report foreign students attending classes. Stipulates that foreign nationals in the United States will be required to carry IDs with biometric technology.

Table 2.1

Year	Name of Legislation/Case	Major Highlights
		Required use of IDs meeting certain security standards to enter government buildings, board planes, open bank accounts.
		Created more restrictions on political asylum.
		Severely curtailed habeas corpus relief for immigrants.
		Increased immigration enforcement mechanisms.
		Altered judicial review.
		Established national standards for state driver licenses.
		Cleared the way for the building of border barriers.

SOURCE: Author generated from the archives of the History Office and Library, United States Citizenship and Immigration Services.

set forth in Table 2.1. Beginning with the Page Act of 1875 and culminating with the first comprehensive immigration law in 1891, specific laws were passed to exclude people of color from entering the United States. In this series of laws Chinese immigration was prohibited. The Chinese initially immigrated into the United States during the gold rush era of the 1840s and then began working building the nation's rail industry. However, after a depression an outcry began among American nativists that eventually led to a set of laws that became known as the Chinese Exclusion Laws. These laws concluding with the Geary Act of 1892 were designed to not only prohibit Chinese immigration but also to diminish the existing population base by placing stringent prohibitions against the immigration of Chinese women. The Geary Act also prohibited the reentry into the United States of any Chinese who left to visit their families or conduct business outside the borders of this nation.[18] The last of the immigration laws specifically prohibiting immigration from all countries in Asia was passed in 1917 that excluded all persons from any country in Asia except the Philippines. The Philippines were a US colony so Filipinos were allowed free entry without restrictions.

The next phase of exclusionary immigration policy was what appeared to be more focused on the political, undesirable, and non-English speaking categories. For instance, in 1903, anarchists were specifically excluded with a refinement on the exclusion of this category in the 1918 law. These laws were passed to inhibit the importation or exclusion of potentially revolutionary thinking and actors who might threaten American capitalism and replay the Russian Revolution on US soil. The 1903 law also identified as "undesirables" individuals with deformities or illnesses reflecting a fear of foreign diseases from infesting the US population. Finally, an additional legal "hedge" against foreign influence, the Naturalization Act of 1906 made it a requirement that anyone becoming a citizen was required to know and speak English.

The rise of the scientific racism movement gave birth to the next phase of immigration laws that saw the first explicitly national origin laws passed in 1921 with a refinement in 1924 that lasted until repealed in 1965. The 1924 act was influenced by the research of Harry Laughlin of the Eugenics Records Office[19] that used race interchangeably with national origin. In the finalized law, quotas were established for total annual immigration and for nations although some nations were declared as non-quota distinguishing them from more stringently controlled nations. The way in which the formula that determined the quotas was structured resulted in preference given to the English-speaking nations of Europe and the racially white nations of Northern Europe. Immigrants from Eastern and Southern Europe were given smaller quotas thus restricting their numbers annually. Again, this gave "white" persons more priority and a place at the head of the immigration queue over all others. The rationale was based in the eugenics notion that white and English-speaking Europeans were more like Americans than others. As a result, intermingling between the "white" Europeans and Americans would not dilute American culture.[20]

The more restrictions that were placed on immigration the more the undocumented population grew, consequently the final phase of immigration policies and laws beginning in 1965 through the present concentrated on increasing enforcement of the existing laws, strengthening restrictions, verification of identities, and so forth. Increasing strictures in the latter half of the twentieth and first part of the twenty-first centuries were and are designed to restrict immigration, both documented and undocumented, from Latin America. The US government-built border barriers across its southern border as a symbol of the barriers against Latin American immigration principally from Mexico. Currently, the estimated undocumented immigrant population in the United States stands at approximately 11.1 million persons.[21] Although the majority of undocumented immigrants still come from Mexico, this represents only 52 percent of all undocumented persons as of 2014. By 2018, migration from Mexico had flattened but still the Department of Homeland Security estimates that there are between 11.1 and 12.1 million undocumented immigrants in the United States.[22] According to the same report, the remainder of undocumented persons are arriving from Central America, Asia, and Sub-Saharan Africa.[23] One of the most interesting items of information produced by the Pew Research Center is that they found that fully 67 percent of undocumented immigrants have resided in the United States for more than ten years with many in some geographical areas such as California residing for more than fifteen years.[24]

This brief history of immigration policy since the founding of the nation through the present clearly demonstrates that it began as a racially based policy and has remained so to date. Immigration policy, which grew out of the first naturalization laws, began as a law that favored white persons and did not consider any other groups for almost the first one hundred years when persons of African descent were specifically granted the right to citizenship. Since then the state created exclusionary laws against Asians, Eastern Europeans, and Latin Americans. The latter category of exclusionary laws was exclusionary because they were quota based and the formula used, which was based on a small percentage of individuals from those countries already residing in the United States, were designed to only allow a very small percentage of Latin American immigrants into the country. These exclusionary and quota-based laws gave rise to the large number of undocumented individuals currently residing in the United States because they forced more individuals to migrate illegally due to the long processing times for legal admission.

Keeping with our metaphor racial considerations became the central element in the lifeblood of the immigration policy process and became the principal raison d'être underlying bureaucratic decisions in this policy area. Race became the lifeblood that allowed the state matrix to function in this area. Currently, immigration decisions are made on the bases of national origin or criminality or specific types of professional occupations yet in each case the racial nature of the individual is the principle decision-making variable.

Gun Control

One of the most interesting areas of exclusion that is unique to the United States lies within the realm of our gun owning national ethos. The exclusionary mechanism of the state eliminated almost all controls over guns because of a cultural and racial bias that was built into the notion of gun ownership at the beginning of the nation. This same ethos became institutionalized and remains embedded within the framework of the public policy processes governing this policy area today. This culture is reinforced mostly through media manipulation by the firearms industry that continues through the present. The resistance to gun control laws began at the founding of the nation and metamorphosed to the extent that it has now become a crucial thread in the American national cultural ideology. This "gun ideology" has won legal legitimation as the Supreme Court has changed its interpretation of the Second Amendment throughout the more than two hundred years of its decisional history.

Gun ownership culture in the United States can be dated to the days of the Glorious Revolution in seventeenth-century England. King James II, a Roman Catholic, tried to disarm the Protestants only allowing Catholics to bear arms as a hedge against possible rebellion. The king's efforts went for naught, however, and in the English Bill of Rights of 1689 it openly states that Protestants may bear arms "for their Defence suitable to their Conditions and as allowed by Law."[25] This law allowed all, who could afford "suitable to their conditions," "arms" to do so. Essentially, if one possessed the financial wherewithal, which few could in that historical period, one could exercise the right of owning an arm. This codification of gun ownership became a "right" that found itself transplanted in the New World and found its way into the cultural and ideological ethos of English immigrants.

The early English settlers to the New World felt they had the right to bear arms for "common defense," which translated into being prepared to be an essential part of the colonial "militia" to repel "invasion." Some have argued that this right also included the "right" to protect oneself against attacks by "savages" on the frontier and, where appropriate, slave insurrections.[26] Concomitantly, specific laws were passed in colonies and the early states prohibiting African Americans from owning arms as a barrier against slave revolts.[27] Finally, on May 8, 1792, Congress passed a statute defining what a "well-regulated militia" was and required that "all free able-bodied white male citizen of the respective States, resident therein, who is or shall be of age of eighteen years, and under the age of forty-five years (except as is herein after excepted) shall severally and respectively be enrolled in the militia . . . [and] every citizen so enrolled and notified, shall, within six months thereafter, provide himself with a good musket or firelock, a sufficient bayonet and belt, two spare flints."[28]

As a result, what has been thought of as a civil right to bear arms for all white free males was initially a requirement by congressional mandate. Still this initial law, acting as an exclusionary mechanism, excluded all non-whites from the law. Only free white males, residents, and within a certain age range, were "required" to bear arms. The requirement to bear arms was then not only to insure for the defense of the nation from outside invasion but also defense against any type of potential insurrection from Native Americans who were being displaced from their lands and African Americans who were enslaved and continuously rebelling against their dehumanizing situation. The reluctance to allow African Americans the "right to bear arms" was stated by the Supreme Court in the now infamous *Dred Scott* decision.[29] Essentially, the Court concluded that if slaves were considered citizens then they would have all rights and privileges of citizenship including the right to bear arms. The Court cited the naturalization law of that time that specifically stated that citizenship was restricted to "free white males," which excluded not only African slaves but also all other groups that were not considered as "free white males." As a result, it is clear that at the inception of the nation and until African Americans were allowed naturalization by the Naturalization

Act of 1870 gun ownership was restricted to white males. Fundamentally, gun control laws of this nation were racially based at the beginning of the republic. Since then, however, the racial basis of gun ownership has been mystified, submerged if you will, particularly since the culmination of the civil war and the passage of the Civil Rights amendments of the nineteenth century. The mystification has come in the form of propaganda that has sold gun ownership as a constitutionally protected right under the Second Amendment of the Constitution. So, what of the Second Amendment? How has the Court interpreted the amendment? And, how has it become blended into the American ideological fabric?

The Second Amendment, as many commentators have pointed out, is vague and confusing to contemporary grammarians, linguists, legal scholars, academics, lawyers, jurists, and the general public. It may have made sense, grammatically, to those who penned it originally, but it certainly is confusing today. Nevertheless, there is a great deal of disagreement on exactly what it means among all of those who do try to comprehend its meaning. The confusion is understandable if one simply looks at it. The specific language of the Second Amendment reads as follows: "A well regulated militia being necessary to the security of a free state, the right of the people to keep and bear arms shall not be infringed."[30] The amendment's awkward sentence construction may not necessarily be a product of its times but rather the result of the intense politics being played behind the scenes of the amendment writing committee to insure an amendment protecting the state militia systems from infringement by the newly created central government.[31] Waldman points out that the first two public drafts had clear language stating that the "right to bear arms" was only meant for members of the state militias. As a matter of fact, the language of the first two drafts was very clear discounting the argument that the final version reflected the language and grammar of the times. Table 2.2 compares the language of each of the first two versions of what eventually became the Second Amendment with the final version appearing in the bottom cell of the table.

The final version cited above was the result of negotiations between the various writers, principally James Madison, Elbridge Gerry, Patrick Henry, George Mason among others. The final language was devised by the Senate as it was approving the entire Bill of Rights before submission to the states for ratification.[32] Waldman argues, after extensive original research into diaries and notes of individuals involved in arguing for certain versions of the amendment together with news articles of the day, the original drafters made the distinction clearly between a standing army and a militia. The original writers, not all participated in the Constitutional Convention only in drafting the Bill of Rights or serving on the various House or Senate committees, who rewrote the various drafts appeared to be concerned with making the distinction between "standing armies" and "militias." The "standing armies" were

Table 2.2 Evolution of Second Amendment

Madison's First Draft	*The right of the people to keep and bear arms shall not be infringed; a well armed and well regulated militia being the best security of a free country; but no person religiously scrupulous of bearing arms shall be compelled to render military service in person.*
House Committee Redraft	*A well regulated militia, composed of the body of the people, being the best security of a free State, the right of the People to keep and bear arms, shall not be infringed, but no one religiously scrupulous of bearing arms, shall be compelled to render military service in person.*
Final Version (reworded and reordered by the Senate).	*A well regulated militia, being necessary to the security of a free state, the right of the people to keep and bear arms, shall not be infringed.*

SOURCE: Michael Waldman, *The Second Amendment: A Biography.* New York: Simon & Schuster, 2014, pp. 52–56.

ugly reminders of the British Army that had been recently repelled while the "militias" formed the core of the revolutionary army. Of course, the "militias" without proper military training proved not very effective, undisciplined, refused to fight or report for duty, and many did not possess arms. In the end, the Continental Army together with assistance from foreign allies actually defeated the British Army. Throughout US history, the "militias" eventually fell into disuse and disappeared from the nation just after the turn of the twentieth century, replaced by the National Guard in 1903.[33]

In attempting to determine whether "the people" or the "militia" have the right to bear arms a comparison of Madison's version with that which came out of the House deliberations is helpful, to a certain extent. Madison's version separates "the people" into two separate clauses while the House version incorporates reference to the people into the "well-regulated militia." It is not clear in Madison's version whether all the people have the right to bear arms or only those people who are members of the "well-regulated militia." The House version makes it very clear that a "well-regulated militia" is composed of the people, not all people, so the select few have the right to bear arms as members of the militia. If you were a conscientious objector, Quaker or Mennonite, or not of the age of 18 and over 45 you were exempt from militia service. It was also quite popular that university students, the sons of rich persons, persons employed in "vital" work or services were exempt from service as well. The sons of the rich normally paid someone to register in their place.[34] In the end, the confusing version came out of the Senate and was ratified together with all the other amendments of the Bill of Rights.

The politics of including "gun protections," as confusing as they appear, were complicated by the fear of a large standing army, which the United

States did not maintain until after World War I and the need to have the Bill of Rights ratified by all the states. President Washington and the first Congress wanted absolute agreement to insure national unity behind the Bill of Rights. As a result, there was a great deal of politicking surrounding the writing of almost all of the amendments but those involving the Second Amendment revolved around the need to ensure that the western and southern states would be guaranteed that the central government would not have the strength or authority to interfere in state matters. This fear still lingers and is the rationale for those arguing in favor of small government, less regulation, and freer markets. Essentially, fear of large government is still very much part of the national ideological culture. The second reason was that the southern states particularly did not want African Americans to own guns. At the beginning of the nation slavery, although frowned upon by many, was still legal in the southeastern United States and slave holders specifically and whites generally were deathly afraid of slave revolts. Firearms in the hands of a large group of persons who had suffered inhuman, horrible, and violent treatment at the hands of slaveholders and others in the South did not appear to the Second Amendment writers and some members of congress as an appropriate combination. Frankly, the authors were afraid that if African Americans were allowed to own guns they would visit revenge upon whites. Therefore, many states passed laws specifically making it illegal for Blacks to own or bear arms.[35]

The same fears that gave birth to the notion that all white men between certain ages were required to own arms when the colonies were first established, fear of invasion, large standing armies, Indians, and slave revolts were the reasons for the creation and passage of the Second Amendment. The Second Amendment, then, was written and included in the Bill of Rights partially based on fear of Indian raids and attacks, the revolt of African American slaves, and foreign invasion. Racial thinking, xenophobia, and fear are imbedded within the logic and verbiage of the Second Amendment from the beginning. Additionally, these ideological, philosophical, and psychological assumptions remain imbedded in the Second Amendment to this day.

The national cultural gun ideology of the United States began as a requirement for all white male residents between the ages of 18 and 45 to own a flintlock or long rifle together with a good knife or hatchet, powder, and shot in the eighteenth century and evolved into one where it has become the constitutionally protected right to own a gun for protection. Some states have even allowed individuals to carry any sort of weapon one wishes openly. One can even purchase high-powered military caliber weapons in gun stores or at gun shows and still have Second Amendment protection in some states. Essentially, gun technology has evolved quite dramatically since the end of the eighteenth century, but the interpretation of the Second Amendment has not considered this. Finally, the conception of a well-regulated militia has been replaced by the creation of National Guard units in every state. Outside of each state's National Guard, there is no officially sanctioned militia in the United States.

An important aspect of the evolution of this strange paradox where the technology has evolved but the law has not is partially due to the way in which the Supreme Court has interpreted the Second Amendment through the years. Beginning with the first challenges through 2008 the Court has always seen gun ownership as it relates to militias or National Guard units. *Washington, DC v. Heller*, 554 U.S. 570 (2008) was the decision that ultimately defined gun ownership as a constitutionally protected right for every individual. The court ruled, Justice Antonin Scalia an ideological supporter of gun rights wrote the majority opinion, that one possessed the constitutionally protected right to own a gun for the protection of one's household. *Heller* was followed two years later by *McDonald v. Chicago*, 561 U.S. 3025 (2010) that extended the fundamental right to homeowners in every jurisdiction in the nation. This opened the floodgates to more than two hundred legal challenges to state and local gun control laws, many of which were financed by the National Rifle Association's (NRA) litigation arm, in every state.[36]

The facts surrounding *Heller* are important to discuss because they reveal the racial underpinnings of the case. The city of Washington, DC, had passed a stringent gun control law in an attempt at curbing the violence and shootings that appeared to occur daily in the city. The law specifically made it illegal to own a handgun and required that all rifles and shotguns used for hunting be kept disassembled or secured with trigger locks. Dick Anthony Heller was a security police officer in the federal government and lived in an area characterized as a high crime neighborhood. Heller challenged the DC law so that he could own a handgun to protect himself at home. There is evidence that the Cato Institute, a conservative think tank, used the Heller situation as a test-case against gun control laws. It appears that Heller could have registered his handguns with the city because he owned them prior to the implementation of the 1976 DC law, however, he refused to do so indicating he was suspicious of government interference in his private matters. Heller also indicated that he was afraid the government would confiscate his personal weapons, he owned four handguns, once they knew he owned them. After consultation with the Cato Institute attorneys, Heller purchased another handgun, a .22 caliber weapon, presented it for registration with the DC police and was refused registration after which he filed his suit.[37] The case wound its way up the judicial ladder and landed on the dais of the US Supreme Court. Justice Scalia, writing for the 5–4 majority, opined that the Second Amendment protected the right of an individual to carry a gun even without an affiliation to any militia or National Guard. Gun ownership, then, became a fundamentally protected right under the Second Amendment. Although Scalia pointed out that his opinion was based upon an originalist interpretation of the Second Amendment, he did not seek research into the original documents or arguments surrounding the writing and passage of the Second Amendment. Instead, he attempted a rather awkward linguistic analysis of the amendment, which appears twisted, stilted, and unconvincing. What Scalia was attempting to accomplish was to divine the meaning of the Framer's original intent. He did conclude that the Washington, DC, law violated the original intent of the Second Amendment of keeping guns in one's home to provide for personal defense. The majority opinion did, however, point out that there were limits to the right in that convicted felons and individuals who had a record of mental illness still could be denied a gun permit if the local jurisdiction deemed so.

Although *McDonald* extended constitutional protections nationally under the Fourteenth Amendment's "due process" and "equal protection" clauses it did leave intact the provisos of the Washington, DC, gun control laws. Essentially, a local jurisdiction for instance, could pass laws restricting gun ownership but it was left to the jurisdiction to determine what those laws were. This loophole created a great deal of uncertainty among local and state jurisdictions, so the State of California passed a law banning the carrying of guns in open while Texas went in the other extreme passing a law allowing "open carry." The California law allowed county sheriffs to issue a concealed weapons permit if the applicant could show "good cause." This law was challenged by an individual named Edward Peruta with his legal expenses being paid for by the NRA. The case came out of the Ninth Circuit Court of Appeals in San Francisco that ruled against Peruta pointing out that,

> The *en banc* court held that the history relevant to both the Second Amendment and its incorporation by the Fourteenth Amendment lead to the same conclusion: The right of a member of the general public to carry a concealed firearm in public is not, and never has been, protected by the Second Amendment. Therefore, because the Second Amendment does not protect in any degree the right to carry concealed firearms in public, any prohibition or restriction a state may choose to impose on concealed carry—including a requirement of "good cause," however defined—is necessarily allowed by the Amendment. The *en banc* court stated that there may or may not be a Second Amendment right for a member of the general public to carry a firearm openly in public, but the Supreme Court has not answered that question. Based on the overwhelming consensus of historical sources, we conclude that the protection of the Second Amendment—whatever the scope of that protection may be—simply does not extend to the carrying of concealed firearms in public by members of the general public.[38]

As the summary above points out, the Ninth Circuit ruling was made by the entire membership, it was a 7–4 ruling, and did not see Second Amendment protections being extended to the general public carrying a concealed weapon.

An important aspect of this decision, as it pertains to this discussion, is that in the final paragraph of one of the *McDonald* dissenting opinions a justice noted how gun control laws historically have been used to take arms away from minority groups. As a result, all persons should be allowed to own and carry arms.[39] Still in June 2017 the Supreme Court denied *certiorari* leaving the California law intact. In the same session, the Supreme Court refused to intervene in an appeal by the Department of Justice that would not allow individuals convicted of previous felonies to possess guns.[40] The Third Circuit had ruled that individuals who had been convicted of minor, nonviolent offenses could not be denied Second Amendment rights. As more and more cases appear before federal courts, there will be other Second Amendment challenges and it appears that the federal courts will continue to grant gun ownership more and more legal legitimacy.

Besides the legal system the other legitimizing force behind making gun ownership a constitutional right were the political machinations of individuals and organizations that have supported and lobbied for Second Amendment protections throughout the history of the United States. This history began shortly after the Civil War with the founding of the NRA. It was originally founded as an organization to teach and educate young men on how to shoot. The founders had been officers in the Union Army during the Civil War and were appalled at the lack of marksmanship ability among their recruits. As a result, two officers founded the NRA and began conducting shooting camps throughout the northeastern United States. The NRA remained an educational and training organization until 1975 when it created a lobbying organization and began traditional lobbying activities at all governmental levels.[41]

The NRA only began lobbying to change the interpretation of the Second Amendment in the late 1970s after libertarian forces took control of the organization. The tactics used by the reactionaries at the 1974 NRA National Convention so incensed President George H. W. Bush that he resigned his membership on its board of directors.[42] Nevertheless, once the gun extremists had taken control of the NRA, they changed the mission and tactics of the organization. They began intense lobbying activities at the national level, participating in political campaigns, politically organizing their constituency, and rewriting the Second Amendment. Interestingly enough, the NRA did not wish to join the Cato Institute in the *Heller* case for fear that the Supreme Court would rule against gun ownership.

The NRA's propaganda takes the form of gun educational programs for American youth groups such as the Boys Scouts of America, self-defense classes, police educational and safety programs, legislative lobbying at all levels of the government, and litigation support services wherever it appears that the Second Amendment may be under legal attacks. These activities are sponsored through the various foundations and litigation support units of the NRA, which receives funding from its membership and corporate sponsors.[43] The list of corporate donors to the NRA reflects a cross section of weapons, ammunition, outdoors equipment, hunting touring, and hunting technology industries. Nevertheless, the relationship between the concept of "right to bear arms," defined as it was at the beginning of the nation's founding, has morphed into a civil right defined as the collective right to bear arms. This conceptual evolution has been driven by various Supreme Court decisions throughout history culminating with Justice Scalia's now famous opinion in *District of Columbia v. Heller*.[44]

The nexus between gun ownership and race though still persists. The right to bear arms has led to the proliferation of gun ownership in the United States to the extent that fully 32 percent of all households have guns. This is a decline from 51.1 percent in the 1976–1982 period but attributed mostly to the decline in the interest in hunting.[45] Thirty-nine percent of all White households had firearms while only 18.1 percent of Black and 15.2 percent of Latino households had households with gun ownership. Therefore, Whites are twice as likely to own and possess firearms than African Americans or Latinos. The highest percentage of households where guns were present was in rural counties (55.9%) located in the west-north-central, east-south-central, and west-south-central regions of the United States.[46] Gun ownership was also more prevalent in households with incomes above $50,000 with the highest numbers of guns per households in those having the highest incomes above $90,000.[47] The NORC study, then, found that more affluent, white households in sparsely populated areas of the nation were more likely to be gun owners than in minority populations residing in urban areas.

Not only is the entire area of gun ownership, whether we're speaking of gun control legislation or the right to bear arms, one finds a major racial divide in public opinion. In a 2017 poll conducted by the Pew Research Center, 57 percent of all Americans were in support of some type of gun control measures. Mining this data, one discovers that there are sharp racial divisions concerning those groups in support of gun control and those who support "gun rights." Fully 55 percent of all Whites indicate that they support gun rights while only 28 percent of Hispanics and 31 percent of Blacks do. The percentages almost flip when it comes to support for gun control laws. Only 42 percent of Whites support some sort of gun control while 69 percent and 73 percent of Hispanics and Blacks, respectively, want gun control.

The differences of opinion for these two issues are also seen when looking at ideological orientation and party identification percentages in the same

Table 2.3 Support for Gun Control and Gun Rights by Race

	Support for Gun Rights	Support for Gun Control
Whites	55%	42%
Hispanics	28%	69%
Blacks	31%	73%

SOURCE: Pew Research Center, U.S. Politics and Policy. "Public Views about Guns." June 22, 2017.

poll. For instance, only 19 percent of liberals, 42 percent of moderates supported gun rights while 72 percent of conservatives did. The poll also found that only 25 percent of conservatives supported gun control while 56 percent of moderates and 79 percent of liberals did. The partisan divide was just as broad as 79 percent of Republicans supported gun rights while 47 percent of Independents and only 20 percent of Democrats supported the same issue. Finally, 78 percent of Democrats and 51 percent of Independents supported gun control while only 18 percent of Republicans did.

The racial divide on both of these issues may be partially attributed to the violence that has been visited on the two racial groups through the use of guns. According to the most recent Pew study of Centers for Disease Control data African Americans have a homicide from gun fatality rate ten times higher than Whites while Latinos have one that is three times higher than whites. Whites use guns more for suicide than either Hispanics or Blacks. Table 2.4 shows the rates per 100,000 of death by firearms by race for both homicides and suicides. Although the data is dated, it is the latest to date and reflects the effects on the use of firearms on all three major racial groups. As the data show firearms are used more in suicide deaths by Whites followed at a distance by both Hispanics and African Americans. When considering homicide rates, the data reveal a much different picture with African Americans having a much higher homicide by firearm death rate than the other two groups. One can easily surmise from a comparison of the data on death rates and public opinion polls why Latinos and African Americans are more in favor of gun control and less in favor of gun rights than Whites. In a rather jaundiced response to the suicide rate for Whites the NRA-ILA (National

Table 2.4 Deaths by Firearms by Race (2010)

Race	Suicides (per 100,000)	Homicides (per 100,000)
White	8.5	1.4
Hispanic	1.9	3.8
Black	2.7	15.3

SOURCE: Pew Research Center tabulation of CDC's National Center for Injury Prevention and Control Web-based Injury Statistics Query and Reporting System (WISQARS).

Rifle Association-Institute for Legislative Action)[48] points out that the availability of guns allows for the individual choice to commit suicide.[49]

Both Waldman and I see the conservative judicial review of gun control laws more and more constraining local and state governments from imposing restrictions on gun ownership and use coupled with the political activities of the gun lobby as the direct causes of a change in American political and social culture in this issue area. From a state theoretical perspective what this discussion was designed to do was illustrate the power of the exclusionary and inclusionary forces functioning within the state to form public policy. On one level, the dual forces of reactionary judges and extremist political activity principally by the NRA have changed the American national ideological culture within a very short time. Most importantly and more relevant to this discussion is how deeply embedded racial thinking is in gun policy. Both the notion that all individuals within society have a right to bear arms and the need for gun control have divided deeply along racial lines. The right to bear arms is driven by fear and anxiety among whites and white law makers, not all but those in important policy making positions. Because white conservatives have control over both the national, state, and local governmental apparatuses, they can exclude any notion of gun controls wanted and needed by the Latino and African American communities.

If one considers gun policies[50] in the United States from an historical perspective it is evident that important aspects of the development of these policies began substantively racially based. The arguments surrounding the composition and ratification of the Second Amendment include discussions of the rationale for the need for this amendment included as a hedge against Indian attacks and slave revolts. Waldman points out that Patrick Henry and other Southern framers felt that the Second Amendment was an appropriate safeguard against a strong central government wanting to "take our niggers away."[51] The Indians, of course, were fighting being dispossessed of their lands while African Americans were attempting to break the chains of slavery. According to an early history of African slave revolts in North America, principally the United States, during the seventeenth, eighteenth, and nineteenth centuries Herbert Aptheker discovered that there had been a total of 250 revolts. The most well-known of these was that of Nat Turner in Virginia but the largest occurred in Louisiana Territory in 1811 when as many as 500 slaves burned down three plantations. More than 200 slaves were executed after this revolt was put down by the militia and US military. Another 500 slave revolts occurred aboard ships headed to the Americas, most destined for the United States.[52] It goes without saying that Whites in the slaveholding areas of the United States felt the threat of slave revolts daily thus the need for armed militias and the requirement that all white men carry firearms.

Since the inception of the colonial era and the founding of the United States the framers and leaders of the nation purposely intended to use gun ownership and policies as a protective measure against Indians and African Americans. This "purposeful intent" became structured into law and all overt references to race were removed instead race became "structured intent" and the entire Second Amendment and gun rights arguments became racial shields hiding the racial intent of the Second Amendment. In the final analysis the "resultant intent," "effect" if you will, of gun laws resulted in ownership patterns and public opinions reflecting the sharp racial divides in American society. This "structured intent" then received the blessings of the federal court system and became an essential element of not just gun laws but of the strong ideological orientation of gun rights in this nation. Essentially, what began as a racist requirement, to own a firearm, at the beginning of the republic morphed into the belief on the part of almost the entire nation that each individual had a constitutionally protected right to own a gun and, in some jurisdictions, to carry one openly.

"Purposeful intent" and "structured intent" are terms I am introducing to argue that "intent" and "effect" in the legal sense are actually not separate elements or concepts but actually part of the same theoretical construct. So, in terms of gun policies the sharply divided racial differences in public opinion, gun ownership and death rates are actually the result of the framer's original intent when constructing the Second Amendment. The Supreme Court has deemed to separate the concepts of "intent" and "effect" making them two concepts in discrimination cases that at one time had to be proven when plaintiffs argued a case. As discussed earlier here and elsewhere[53] proving intent when there is no direct evidence of racist discussion during the writing of public policy is difficult in contemporary times because much racist sentiment is now hidden by "racial shields" or code words. Essentially, racial intent is structured into the law, thus it is "structured intent."

Purposeful intent is the conscious effort on the part of decision makers to intend that a specific outcome occur and design a policy, program, or law to produce the effects purposely intended. When composing immigration, gun control and voting laws decision makers purposely intended that specific racial or national origin groups be affected by the way the laws were written and interpreted. This purposeful intent then became structured into law resulting in the same unequal effects resulting every time the laws were implemented. The intent then becomes an essential element of the decisional process and structure leading to disparate or uneven effects.

My argument here is the result of an evolution in my thinking and many years of participation as an expert witness in civil rights litigation. Fundamentally, I see effect and intent as two sides of the same coin. Without intent, one cannot have effect. In any theoretical construct, one must always begin with presuppositions or assumptions directing the final outcome. The same holds true when discussing the "intent"/"effect" nexus. If, in conducting research that uncovers uneven, disparate, or unequal effects one cannot simply conclude that these are the result of an objective decisional process or the effects of unintended consequences emanating from the decision, then it is logical that something within the process or at the beginning of the process (intent) caused the effect to result in uneven outcomes. This argument and the theoretical discussion will be elaborated in the next chapter.

Voting

The last policy area to consider in this discussion is that of voting rights. Essentially, voting laws in the United States, since the nation's inception, were and still are racially oriented. Early in the nation's history, racially oriented voting laws were established that excluded the right to vote to all except white males. Obviously, African Americans were not citizens but slaves, those who were freedmen, were denied citizenship until 1877. Latinos did not exist as they do in the twenty-first century because the regions where the original Latinos lived, the Southwestern United States, were actually part of the Spanish Empire. Very few, if any Asians of any national origin resided in the original thirteen colonies. So, citizens of the United States were only white at the founding and the only individuals allowed to vote in the eighteenth and almost the entire nineteenth centuries until the ratification of the Fifteenth Amendment to the Constitution which formally granted voting rights to all persons regardless of "race, color or previous conditions of servitude."

Latinos, on the other hand, gained citizenship through the signing of various treaties. For instance, Mexican Americans who remained in the United States after the signing of the Treaty of Guadalupe Hidalgo in 1848 were awarded citizenship as part of the treaty provisions. Puerto Ricans were granted citizenship in 1917 through the passage of the Jones-Shaforth Act and are considered natural born citizens of the United States. Other Latinos gained their citizenship through the normal naturalization process. In each instance, regardless whether by treaty or naturalization, citizenship came with the right to vote. Exercising the franchise for both African Americans and Latinos has not been easy because of the passage of certain registration and voting laws in some states compounded by the way representational districts are gerrymandered and the movement to tighten voter identification laws. Each of these barriers has been racially motivated under the racial shield of partisanship behavior and legislative maneuverings. In other words, each group has been awarded voting rights to enhance the strength of the party in power who extended those rights. Simply put the party in power felt that the new racial group being given full voting rights would feel beholden to the party in power who politicked for those rights, a quid pro quo of sorts. In some instances, racial groups have also been subjected to racial gerrymandering to weaken the support levels for the party out of power.[54] Fundamentally, race has been used as a tool to achieve a partisan advantage. Minority voters' ability to participate equally has been abrogated giving white voters the advantage in election contests. The result is that the voting rights of minority voters have been trampled in order that one political party is given an electoral advantage over the other.

Other authors have produced a prolific body of literature identifying how after the passage of the Fifteenth Amendment various formally Confederate states passed a variety of Jim Crow laws that were used to inhibit African Americans from voting. Some of these devises included various "literacy tests," "interpretations of certain documents such as parts of the Constitution," "property qualifications," "character tests," and so forth.[55] As these overt dilutive activities were removed by various jurisdictions across the nation others, more subtle and sophisticated, replaced them. In voting rights law dilutive activities and devices are very specific and require the production of a great deal of empirical evidence before the Court accepts the allegation that a covered group's voting power has been "diluted."[56] The new dilutive devices included such practices as not locating polling places in voting precincts having large covered populations[57]; not producing enough voting machines to handle large numbers of voters; moving polling places at the last minute with little or no publicity; confusing instructions on proper identity cards; stationing police in the vicinity of polling places; not producing enough computers to insure that election judges can check voter registration status; assigning unknowledgeable election judges to various voting sites who misinform minority voters of their right to vote; shortening the number of early voting days; and more. All of these aforementioned activities have been uncovered through complaints to either the NAACP or MALDEF over the years and some have been subjected to litigation.[58]

In the final analysis, it is obvious that African Americans have been racially discriminated against since they first arrived in North America. At the beginning of their relationship with the Americas they were subjected to slavery and denied access to the franchise because of this condition, they were considered chattel and not eligible for citizenship thus denied the right to vote. It required the passage of a Constitutional Amendment to grant African Americans citizenship and the right to vote but implementing laws were absent until the passage of the Voting Rights Act of 1965. To this day African Americans are still bringing lawsuits in various jurisdictions to protect their right to vote because different states have passed laws in the twenty-first century that have dilutive effects on the power of their votes including racial gerrymandering and voter identification.

The effects of racism on the voting rights of Latinos have a much different historical trajectory than that of African Americans. As noted earlier Latinos are a heterogeneously defined social group who identify with their nation of origin. So, the overall designation of Latino includes Mexican Americans, Puerto Ricans, Columbians, Cubans, Dominicans among others. These racial and ethnic groups[59] include immigrants or descendants from every Spanish-speaking nation in the Western Hemisphere and Spain. Citizenship was awarded to Mexican Americans as a result of various treaties; Puerto Ricans gained citizenship through an act of Congress, the others through various types of naturalization processes. The common bond is language; all speak a dialect of Spanish that varies depending on country and region. Core vocabularies of Spanish are relatively the same but a great deal of variation exists among colloquialisms and the way various objects or actions are labelled. All groups of Latinos have suffered some degree and type of discrimination in the voting booth. In the historical eras prior to the 1960s racial exclusion from the voting booth was overt. As racial groups became more politically and socially active, racial candidness and overt racial behavior morphed into the use of code words or language and racial shields.[60] Attempts at diluting the Latino vote became secretive and objectively appearing particularly through the use of modern software technologies. Dilutive methods evolved from the explicit to the veiled and hidden. Legislators began operating behind closed doors in highly confidential meetings rather than act openly when creating the dilutive devices present today.

Racial intent in congressional redistricting can be difficult to prove because much of the overt language that was used in racial gerrymandering in the nineteenth and early twentieth centuries has evolved into the use of nonracial terms, such as the use of "scientific rigor," and "traditional redistricting standards." These racial shields are enhanced by the use of sophisticated and manipulated statistical techniques and software that bury the discriminatory nature of gerrymandering in the trappings of scientism and objectivity. The new technologies that are currently used in congressional and other types of redistricting efforts in all states can also be used because the software, generally software such as ESRI's GIS,[61] has geographical shading that can be used to identify precincts by level of racial density and performance in elections. These technologies were used in the 2011 round of redistricting in Texas to racially gerrymander US Congressional District 23 (USCD 23) to make it a Latino majority district that underperformed. In other words, although the district was a majority, 54.1 percent Latino, the effective Latino citizenship turnout rate stood at approximately 38 percent. This outcome was the result of redistricters going throughout the boundaries of USCD 23 and replacing majority Latino precincts that had high turnout rates with majority Latino precincts having low turnout rates historically. Although the State of Texas denied that they had drawn the district, there were others, USCDs 29 and 35 for instance,[62] an email between two redistricting attorneys uncovered during discovery revealed that they intended to pursue the above strategy during the redistricting process that they proceeded to do.

The racial intent underlying the creation and passage of the Texas voter ID law proved difficult to uncover because throughout the decisional process the legislators refused to mention race or use the terms such as Hispanic or Latino. They indicated that they were only passing the bill, SB14, to prevent anyone from casting "an illegal vote." The legislative record the day during which SB14 was debated on the State House floor reflects a refusal on the part of the bill's sponsor and her defenders to even engage in a discussion of whether the bill's provisions would violate the civil or voting rights of Latinos.[63] Nevertheless, when the voter ID bill was first introduced during the 2005 session its intent was to prevent "illegal immigrants" from crossing the border and casting illegal votes. This xenophobia is identically the same as that expressed during the attempts at passing the restrictive immigration laws preventing immigrants from Mexico, after the 1845 war with Mexico, to return to the United States vote and create a government in their own image and culture as some Texas legislators feared.

RACE AND PUBLIC POLICY

As the discussion throughout this chapter has demonstrated the only manner in which to understand the infusion of racism or racial thinking into an area of public policy is to understand the relationship between the two historically. One must begin by asking if there were racial considerations when the policy was being initially discussed and then determine whether these concerns were included as one of the reasons for the creation of the policy or law. The brief reviews of the three policy areas presented here—immigration, gun control, and voting rights—have demonstrated that racial thinking was an essential element in the arguments surrounding the need for policies in these areas. The policies eventually changed with the times. The language used at the beginning of the deliberations was overtly racial, the stated intent of the legislation or policy was overtly racial with the laws and policies designed to protect "white privilege."[64] As time marched on each of the laws in the respective policy areas changed and lost all semblance of racist thinking, which had become blended and infused into the laws. Instead, the laws in each area that are in place today have non-racial appearing rhetoric describing their goals and objectives. So, immigration policy is designed to control crime and keep illegal immigration at bay. Liberalized gun laws are designed to address the phobias against everyday crime that appear so all pervasive in this day. Finally, it appears that voting laws are becoming more restrictive in order to protect against the fear that large numbers of undocumented voters will sway elections in ways foreign to the American way of governing. The underlying theme it would appear is that fear seems to have driven laws in these three policy areas. If racial intent was behind the initiation of these laws, then the fear is racially based but not overtly stated, implied with a "wink and a nod." The role of fear as being fundamental to racial intent is discussed in the next chapter.

Still, the conundrum underlying the niche of race in public policy remains. The Supreme Court has created a problem because of the way it demands evidentiary proof of discrimination. The Supreme Court's logic reflects how racism becomes institutionalized within the public policy decisional processes of the government even if the Court does not realize it. The rationale the Court uses in forcing plaintiffs to prove racial discrimination has become another example of a "racial shield" hiding discriminatory practices by legislators because the standards are vague and open to interpretation granting the courts a great deal of latitude when deriving their decisions. This shield has become imbedded in the precedential history of the Court and has acted as a barrier against those seeking relief from discriminatory practices before the court while protecting the privileged position of white voters, gun owners and the general white population. Allowing the majority white population to maintain control of the levers of public and private power. With the addition of more conservative and reactionary judges to the federal court system, there is no change possible in the foreseeable future. Further untangling the Gordian knot of the state matrix is the subject of the next chapter with the roles played by both the economic and psychological institutions of the matrix. This is highlighted with a discussion of the roles xenophobia and fear play in the matrix and their effects on both victims and discriminators.

NOTES

1. Arrian, *The Campaigns of Alexander* (New York: Penguin Group, 1971), 105; and Plutarch, *Life of Alexander*, p. 19; E. A. Fredricksmeyer, "Alexander, Midas, and the Oracle at Gordium," *Classical Philology* Vol. 56, no. 3 (July 1961): 160–168.

2. Henry Flores, *The Evolution of the Democratic State with a Case Study of Latinos in San Antonio, Texas* (New York: Edwin Mellen Press, 2003).

3. Domhoff (1967) at one time noted that only about 12 percent of the working class would have, given opportunities and circumstances, the possibility of moving into the middle class.

4. Dennis Gilbert, *The American Class Structure: In An Age of Growing Inequality* (Belmont, CA: Wadsworth, 2002). William E. Thompson and Joseph V. Hicky, *Society in Focus* (Boston, MA: Pearson, Allyn & Bacon, 2005). Leonard Beeghley, *The Structure of Social Stratification in the United States* (Boston, MA: Pearson, Allyn & Bacon, 2004). John Weeks, "Inequality Trends in Some Developed OECD countries," in K. S. Jomo and Jacques Baudot (eds.), *Flat World, Big Gaps* (159–174). New York: ZED Books, 2007 (published in association with the United Nations). Department of Treasury, "Income Mobility in the U.S. from 1996 to 2005." November 13, 2007. Web. http://www.treasury.gov/resource-center/tax-policy/Documents/incomemobilitystudy03-08revise.pdf.

5. I will refer to the short title throughout this discussion.

6. Charles A. and Mary R. Beard, *America in Midpassage* (New York: Macmillan, 1939). See the discussion in chapter 6 specifically.

7. Adam Smith, *An Inquiry into the Nature and Causes of the Wealth of Nations* (London: W. Strahan and J. Cadeli, in the Strand, 1776).

8. Karl Marx, *Pre-Capitalist Economic Formations*. Edited by E. J. Hobsbawm, translated by Jack Cohen (New York: International Publishers, 1964).

9. There are other theories as to why the Civil War was fought but underlying each of the theories is the notion that control of the national economy was at the heart of each of the reasons. See Paul Calore, *Causes of the Civil War: The Political, Cultural, Economic and Political Disputes between North and South* (Jefferson, NC: McFarland & Company, Inc., Publishers, 2008). David M. Potter, *The Impending Crisis: America before the Civil War, 1848–1861* (New York: HarperCollins Publishers, 2011).

10. This analogy originated in Jesus' Sermon on the Mount, Mathew 5:14 and used by John Winthrop in his 1630 essay entitled "A Model of Christian Charity." Winthrop's position is that God had chosen the Puritans to populate the New World and they must serve as exemplars of Christianity for the rest of the world referring to their approach to settling in their new homes.

11. One can understand property taxes as rent to the state because if one does not pay these taxes the state does have, under specific circumstances, the option of dispossessing the property holder.

12. To date the only national bank that is currently under federal watch because of their credit card scandal is Wells Fargo.

13. Flores, *The Evolution*.

14. Ibid.

15. Justice Edith Jones of the Fifth Circuit Court of Appeals, for instance, was reprimanded for allegedly making racist comments about African Americans and Hispanics at a speech she gave before the Federalist Society. The judicial behavior panels dismissed the complaint citing lack of evidence in 2015. Justice James Nowlin of the Western District of Texas was reprimanded for *ex parte* communications with a lobbyist during the state house redistricting trial of 1991. Both are and were federal judges who sit in regions where many voting rights cases are heard.

16. Section 2, Article One, *Constitution of the United States*.

17. January 1, 1863.

18. Mark Kanazawa, "Immigration, Exclusion, and Taxation: Anti-Chinese Legislation in Gold Rush California," *The Journal of Economic History* Vol. 65, no. 3 (Sept. 2005): 779–805.

19. The Eugenics Records Office was closed in 1939 due to the controversial nature of their research. See Pat Shipman, *The Evolution of Racism: Human Differences and the Use and Abuse of Science* (New York: Simon & Schuster, 1994).

20. This was discussed in chapter 1.

21. There is no way of accurately counting undocumented individuals because, by definition, they hide from officials. The eleven million figure is based upon the number of apprehensions over a period of many years, but it is not an accurate figure.

22. Fact Sheet.org. A Project of the Annenberg Public Policy Center. "Illegal Immigration Statistics." June 28, 2018.

23. Jeffrey S. Passel and D'Vera Cohn, "Overall Number of U.S. Unauthorized Immigrants holds Steady Since 2009: Decline in Share from Mexico Mostly Offset by Growth from Asia, Central-America and Sub-Saharan Africa," Pew Research Center: Hispanic Trends, September 20, 2016.

24. Jens Manuel Krogstad, Jeffrey S. Passel, and D'Vera Cohn, "5 Facts about Illegal Immigration in the United States." Pew Research Center: Hispanic Trends, November 3, 2016.

25. Bill of Rights, 1688 c. 2 (Regnal. 1_Will_and_Mar_Sess_2).

26. David Hardy, "Book Review: A Well-Regulated Militia: The Founding Fathers and the Origins of Gun Control in America," *Wm. & Mary Bill of Rights Journal 15* (2007). Joyce Lee Malcolm, *To Keep and Bear Arms: The Origins of an Anglo-American Right* (Cambridge, MA: Harvard University Press, 1996). William G. Merkel and H. Richard Uviller, *The Militia and the Right to Arms, Or, How the Second Amendment Fell Silent* (Durham, NC: Duke University Press, 2002). Carl T. Bogus, "The Hidden History of the Second Amendment," *U.C. Davis Law Review* 31, no. 2 (Winter 1998): 309–408. Clayton Cramer, "The Racist Roots of Gun Control," *Kansas Journal of Public Policy* (Winter 1995).

27. Cramer, "The Racist Roots of Gun Control."

28. Second Congress, Chapter XXXIII—*An Act More Effectually to Provide for a National Defence by Establishing an Uniform Militia Throughout the United States*, Section 1, 271.

29. *Dred Scott v. Sandford*, 60 US 393 (1857).

30. "The Constitution of the United States of America: Analysis and Interpretation—1992 Edition—Second Amendment—Bearing Arms." *GPO.gov*. Retrieved June 23, 2017.

31. Michael Waldman, *The Second Amendment: A Biography* (New York: Simon & Schuster, 2014). See particularly Waldman's discussions in the first part of this volume.

32. Ibid.

33. Ibid., *Second Amendment*. See discussion in chapter 4.

34. Ibid., chapters 2–4.

35. Ibid., chapters 2 and 3.

36. Ibid., chapter 7.

37. Dick Anthony Heller, *The Citizens Committee for the Right to Bear Arms: The Common Sense Gun Lobby*. May 1, 2008. www.ccrkba.org/dick-anthony-heller.

38. *Peruta v. County of San Diego*, No. 16-894.

39. Justice Stevens dissent in *McDonald v. Chicago*.

40. *Binderup v. Sessions*, No. 16-847.

41. Samuel C. Patterson and Keith R. Eakins, 1998. "Congress and Gun Control," in John M. Bruce and Clyde Wilcox, *The Changing Politics of Gun Control* (Lanham, MD: Rowman & Littlefield, 1998). Waldman, *The Second Amendment*, chapters 6 and 7.

42. Letter from President George H. W. Bush to Mr. Tom Washington, President of the NRA dated May 3, 1995.

43. All of this information can be found at the National Rifle Association's website together with a list of corporate donors: https://home.nra.org.

44. 554 U.S. 570 (2008).

45. Tom W. Smith and Jaesok Son, *General Social Survey Final Report: Trends in Gun Ownership in the United States, 1972–2014*. NORC at the University of Chicago, March 2015.

46. Ibid., Table 4, p. 6.

47. Ibid.

48. This is the lobbying arm of the NRA.

49. NRA-ILA. "Suicide and Firearms." NRA Factsheet, 1999.

50. When using the term "gun policies" I mean to include both those for and against control, ownership, carry and so forth. In other words, all policies that have to do with the issues that have grown out of the arguments surrounding the Second Amendment.

51. Waldman, *History of Second Amendment*, p. 37.

52. Herbert Aptheker, *American Negro Slave Revolts* (New York: Columbia University Press, 1943). Adam Rothman, *Slave Country: American Expansion and the Origins of the Deep South* (Cambridge, MA: Harvard University Press, 2005). Mary Ann Sternberg, *Along the River Road: Past and Present on Louisiana's Historic Byways* (Baton Rouge: Louisiana State University Press, 2001), 12.

53. Flores, *Latinos and the Voting Rights Act*.

54. Ibid.

55. *South Carolina v. Katzenbach*, 383 U.S. 311 (1966). See also Elizabeth Anderson and Jeffery Jones, "Race, Voting Rights, and Segregation: Direct Disenfranchisement," *The Geography of Race in the United States* (Ann Arbor: University of Michigan Press, 2001).

56. *Thornburg v. Gingles*, 478 U.S. 30 (1986). Section 2 of the VRA of 1965, PL 89-110. NAACP Legal Defense and Educational Fund, Inc. *The Role of Section 2 – Redistricting and Vote Dilution*. Undated.

57. A "covered" population is one specifically protected by a law such as African Americans, Spanish speakers, Asians, and so forth.

58. Some of these activities were uncovered in evidence produced by NAACP experts in *Katherine Harris, et al. v. NAACP, et al.*, which was a lawsuit filed surrounding minority vote dilution during the 2000 presidential election. The case was

settled out of court in April 2001. The author was one of the experts and uncovered some of this evidence during his research for his expert report and testified on the evidence during his deposition that partially led to settlement. The case did not go to trial as all fifteen defendant jurisdictions and agencies settled their portions of the complaints. In Killeen, Texas, an election poll worker informed an African American woman, wife of an army officer, that Congress had rescinded the voting rights of African Americans during general election voting in 2004.

59. Referring to Hispanics or Latinos as a racial or ethnic group is difficult given that the various national origin groups have different racial and ethnic identities.

60. For the use of code words, see Ian Haney López, *Dog Whistle Politics: How Coded Racial Appeals Have Reinvented Racism and Wrecked the Middle Class* (New York: Oxford University Press, 2014). For racial shields, see *Latinos and the Voting Rights Act* by Flores.

61. Geographic Information Services.

62. As many as five state assembly and several state senate districts were also drawn with racial intent using the same methodology as CD 23. This observation was made by the author as he served as a voting rights expert during the trial and uncovered the scheme.

63. See House Journal dated March 22, 2011.

64. Robin Diangelo, *White Fragility: Why It's so Hard for White People to Talk About Racism* (Boston, MA: Beacon Press, 2018).

Chapter 3

The Socioeconomic-Psychological-Ideological Elements of the State Matrix

Here we will explore, as the title implies, the socioeconomic-psychological elements of the state matrix. My operating assumption is that all the state matrix elements work in tandem to form the political, economic, and social place of individuals within the matrix. In other words, these elements determine the social, economic, and political standing of individuals within the state. When I speak of the state, I mean all institutions that perform together to allow the state matrix to function. These institutions include executive officers, legislators, and legal interpreters who make all the decisions necessary for the state matrix to function daily. For instance, executive branch officials would include the president, governors, mayors, school superintendents, and so forth. Legislative officers would include all elected assembly officials at all levels of government including senators, house members, city councils, county commissioners, education boards, and so forth. Finally, the legal interpreters include all judges and justices at every jurisdictional level, attorney generals, city and county attorneys, solicitor generals, and all lawyers working as advisors and councilors to all governmental agencies. All courts at all levels whether dealing with criminal, civil, bankruptcies, immigration, or other topical issues specific to their court.

It should be noted, here that the state matrix does not include simply the institutions of the public sector but also the private sector. The reason the private and public sectors need combining is that in the state matrix both function together in tandem and reflect the interconnected nature of the institutions and all levels of the state matrix. The interaction of both sectors is required to insure the stability, functioning, and growth of the state matrix. One may use a Venn diagram to conceptualize the relationship between both sectors. Although both sectors can act alone and remain relatively autonomous in some of their domains of operations, they cannot function efficiently and successfully without their interconnectedness. Therefore, in many public policy areas both public and private sectors require each other for the functioning of a specific policy area. For instance, all elected officials need to be citizens of the United States. All lawyers must be licensed in and by the state within which they wish to practice. Businesses must follow certain regulatory rules for the production of certain products, meet certain licensing requirements, pay certain taxes or franchise fees established by the government before they can "do business." The policies, laws, regulatory standards created by the state are the conceptual bridges tying together the private and public sectors of the state matrix. Within this matrix and the subjects affected by the interactions of the public-private intra-institutional arrangement are the individuals residing within each of the social strata. Essentially, society's people inhabit and make the matrix function. However, as we discuss each institution and its effects on the quality of life within the state matrix individuals of each stratum are affected differentially than others as the state matrix operates daily.

The institutional elements also determine whether one belongs to a specific social stratum, whether one becomes a member of those who make decisions at specific levels within the matrix, and those who can control the distribution of wealth, or not, also within the state matrix. So, what constituent parts combine to make up each element? How are these parts and elements interconnected? What is the role of psychological effects on the individuals within the state matrix? Where does racial bias fit within this entire structure? These questions will be addressed in this chapter.

THE ELEMENTS OF THE STATE MATRIX

The four elements of the state matrix are the political, economic, social, and psychological. These elements are somewhat tangible as well as not. They are tangible because the elements cannot function without the actions and inputs of human beings. For instance, political offices exist on paper and in the minds of the residents of the state matrix but can only function if an individual is in that office. The same can be said of positions and offices in all elements of the state matrix. A social class cannot exist without individuals belonging to that social class. A bank does not exist without bankers, clerks, janitors working within that institution and so forth.

Each element of the state matrix, then, stands alone and separate yet is linked with the others through culture, history, and ideology. Culture itself is a combination of language, customs, diet, and the general way of life of the persons within the state matrix. History is the compendium of every occurrence that the state matrix and its inhabitants experienced as it matured through time. Ideology, discussed in an earlier chapter, is comprised of the general beliefs shared by all individuals within the matrix. Although the entire population generally shares all culture, history, and ideology, there are sub-elements to each depending on various factors. For instance, many immigrants have entered the state during differing historical periods. The reasons many immigrants came to the United States vary. Some immigrants sought asylum from repressive political regimes, others from rampant street violence, and still others saw no future in their countries and simply wished a better system of opportunities for their children. All immigrants, past and present, came to the United States for security, stability, and the creation of a new and better life for their progeny. I am a living example of this when my grandparents fled Mexico from the Mexican Revolution.

These immigrants transplanted their cultures within the United States that absorbed their culture that eventually melded it into the general overall American culture. For instance, Italians, Germans, Irish, Mexicans, and Indians (there are many more examples) brought their languages, cuisine, music, religions, and histories to America, and all cultures were incorporated into the greater culture changing the general cultural identity of this state matrix. This cultural absorption is what binds these groups to this country. The same cultural absorption can be said of the histories, customs, dress, and ways of life of each group absorbed into the state matrix.

Ideology is extremely important because it is the set of beliefs, opinions, perceptions of life, that one can accomplish throughout their lifetime and so forth. A common ideology is the "glue" that holds the individuals within the state matrix together as a group allowing them to view the world and the state matrix through the same conceptual lenses. This general ideology also includes beliefs in why the state matrix, the social, economic, and political structures are legitimate. There is some variation, for example, some are liberal, others conservative, and some are variations of both. Each sees the state matrix functioning differently when it comes to addressing social or political issues. Yet, the general ideology remains centered in a set of beliefs held in common by all. Without an ideological belief system generally held by all within the state matrix the matrix might be threatened with extinction or, at least, a chaotic moment in time. The belief system must be vague and general enough that it remains open to many interpretations allowing for ideological inclusivity resulting in progressives through conservatives believing in the tenets of the constitution, the country's history, and so forth. This inclusivity builds into the belief or ideological system the spiritual and emotional glue that holds the state matrix together.

The process of socialization for new immigrants includes incorporation of their histories, languages, and religions. Incorporation of all facets of immigrant cultures occurs through the normal machinations of the institutions in the state matrix as it socializes all societal members to the current state ideological belief system. For instance, some holidays, such as Eid-al Fitr, celebrated at the end of Ramadan, have prominent places on commercially sold calendars and the local media often cover the festivities. The same can be said about other holidays of other cultures, such as St. Patrick's Day, Cinco-de-Mayo, Rosh Hashanah, Christmas, and so forth. Assisting to incorporate more and more cultures into the state matrix are the actions of many other members who operate the functionings of the state matrix. Some examples of these cultural assimilationists are attorneys who offer multilingual assistance, doctors who provide services to people of different cultures and language groups, and teachers who provide support services for non-English speaking students so that they can assimilate into the culture of the United States through the educational processes. Even religious institutions in various denominations have incorporated multiple cultures into their religion, community, and services. Some histories of immigrant groups are taught in schools and some significant holidays have even been placed on the national calendars of days of remembrance. Parts of languages have become part of the unique English spoken in the United States and many religions brought by immigrants have found that the belief in religious freedom has protected the ability of immigrant groups to worship in almost any way they wish. This incorporation process is an important characteristic of the matrix state. This process reflects the flexibility a state is required to have to survive. For the state matrix to survive it must remain flexible about incorporating different ideas, belief systems, language groups, and religious beliefs into its structures. Without flexibility built into the state matrix's structures it could not survive. The flexibility allows for the absorption of both internal and external tensions that the matrix state must learn to absorb if it is expected to survive for the future. The passing of great powers and countries has been the result of the inflexibility of their structures and infrastructures.[1]

The Social

The social structure of the state matrix is comprised of classes or strata, within which individuals reside, live, and work. There are, in the United States because all state matrices are different, generally five, some might argue three or four or six, strata to the social structure. There are those considered wealthy, a middle class divided in two or three distinctly different types of classes, the working class, and the poor. One can even state that within the working and poor classes there are sub-classes. The working class can be divided into the skilled working class and the unskilled, while the poor could be the poor working class and the destitute.

The wealthy class is comprised of all those who mostly inherit their wealth and produce individuals who head corporations, major businesses and who either produce the individuals who rule the matrix or can influence the elected and appointed rulers of the matrix in various ways including through their wealth and social standing. The middle class is comprised of the professional middle class, upper middle class, high-level professionals such as lawyers, doctors, full-tenured professors, and so forth or individuals who make secondarily important decisions within the matrix but also play significant roles in how the matrix socially and economically reproduces itself. The lower middle class is comprised of those highly skilled working-class individuals who make a significant amount of money but are not part of the middle class making decisions that allow the matrix to socially reproduce or function. The poor working class is comprised of individuals who work at lower level skilled work that pays a living wage but not much more and whose members are dependent on the work produced by the skilled working class. Finally, the poor or destitute are those who depend on public or private assistance to survive. Some even make their living through unique forms of entrepreneurship such as crude recycling, day labor, and so forth. The underside of this class is that some will survive by committing petty crimes.[2]

Contemporaneously, what creates these social strata are principally social circumstances beyond anyone's control. For instance, a substantial explainer of one's social standing is based on which class one is born into. The era of social mobility, where the United States appeared as the land of opportunity and one, through industriousness and conformation to the cultural norms of society, can achieve wealth and security for themselves and their progeny. This era, described as a myth by some sociologists and economists, helped drive the economy and work force, and either has long since passed or never existed. The general rule of thumb for social mobility is that one is born into a social class from which one most likely will never leave. They may find their social standing and wealth improved over that of their parents but not by much. As a result, if one is born into the wealthy class one can expect to remain there their entire life barring some major economic catastrophe. The wealthy reproduce among themselves because they live separately from other groups, school their children in unique schools, have social connectivity that allows for them to marry within their social group, and obtain positions of power unavailable to others outside their group. The same can be said of the other social groups.

Advancing from one group to another requires having the knowledge and financial wherewithal to afford the advancement. For instance, to live among the wealthy requires the ability to purchase homes costing in the millions, sending their children to schools that cost in the tens of thousands just for the elementary school with costs running into the hundreds of thousands at the university level. Finally, one must be able to purchase memberships in very private and expensive clubs of all types to maintain the social connections required to "fit in" and/or make the social connections required to advance in the economic world. Still an outsider, one who obtained their riches based on hard work, taking advantage of opportunities and luck, might not ever be accepted fully by the others of the wealthy because of their lack of pedigree or coming from the "right" kind of long-established wealth.[3]

The lower down the social structure the more open it is, however, there are rules of admission to these classes unique to each social stratum. One must be born into the class and one must have the wherewithal to survive within that class. Those born into families in each class are raised in schools that serve the neighborhoods where they live although the higher the income the more opportunities for educating their children are available. Therefore, those of the professional classes for instance can sometimes send their children to the same schools as the wealthy or choose private schools where the children of the same class are also educated. Table 3.1 shows the mean incomes for six classes of income levels described above by Domhoff. Besides indicating the differing potential purchasing power of each group, the table reveals some interesting characteristics of the social class system in the United States. The data in the table covers the years 1989 through 2016 and demonstrate that the six income groups have remained separated economically consistently over the reporting period. Although all groups experienced income growth over the twenty-nine-year period depicted in the table, the highest percentile group experienced the most growth, measured in 2016 dollars, at 67 percent between 1989 and 2016. The lowest percentile group increased from a mean of $5,900 to $14,400 during the same period, an increase of 59 percent. As the last column in the table indicates all groups showed increases in mean income levels but the highest group experienced by far the most growth. Additionally, if one peruses the columns showing the dollar differences between each group over the entire reporting period one observes that the gaps between each of the groups has grown substantially over the period depicted in the table. For instance, the gap between the highest and second highest group has grown from $109,000 in 1989 to $376,000 in 2016 or a 71 percent increase difference in 2016 dollars. The data indicate that the percentile groups have remained relatively stagnant over the twenty-nine-year period with the income differences becoming more pronounced. Essentially, the United States is a class society whose social class lines have become broader separating the classes from each other even more in recent years.

Mean incomes, however, only show half the picture. A perusal of the net worth of each group within the six percentile groups is important to understand the social place of each group in relationship to each other. In other words,

Table 3.1 Mean Percentiles of Incomes for Families, 1989–2016 (2016 Dollars)

Income Percentiles	1989	Dif Between Groups	1995	Dif Between Groups	2001	Dif Between Groups	2007	Dif Between Groups	2013	Dif Between Groups	2016	Dif Between Groups	% Inc. 1989-2016
Bottom 20%	$5,900		$6,600		$10,000		$12,300		$13,300		$14,400		59
20–39.9%	$14,700	$8,800	$17,600	$11,000	$24,100	$14,100	$28,300	$16,000	$28,600	$15,300	$31,800	$17,400	54
40–59.9%	$25,900	$11,200	$30,100	$12,500	$40,300	$16,200	$47,300	$19,000	$47,200	$18,600	$53,400	$21,600	51.4
60–79.9%	$40,900	$15,000	$46,300	$16,200	$65,200	$24,900	$75,100	$27,800	$78,500	$31,300	$87,400	$34,000	53.2
80–89.9%	$61,100	$20,200	$69,600	$23,300	$98,100	$32,900	$116,000	$40,900	$124,300	$45,800	$138,700	$51,300	56
90–100%	$170,000	$109,000	$175,300	$105,700	$302,900	$204,800	$397,600	$281,600	$412,000	$287,700	$514,700	$376,000	67
Dif Between Bottom 20% and Top 10%	$164,000		$168,700		$293,900		$385,300		$398,700		$500,300		67

SOURCE: Board of Governors of the Federal Reserve System, "Survey of Consumer Finances, 2016."

the net worth of each group is a major explainer of why the groups remain separated, have differing levels of purchasing power and remain socially segregated. Table 3.2 shows the mean net worths of each of the six groups over the same reporting period as depicted in Table 3.1. The data in Table 3.2 demonstrates the stark differences in net worth among all groups but especially how markedly different the highest tenth percentile group is from the remainder. Similar to the data in Table 3.1 all groups increased their net worth over the twenty-nine-year reporting period but the highest group far surpassed the other groups increasing their net worth 78.4 percent between 1989 and 2016. As the data demonstrate in Table 3.2 the differences in net worth between all groups increased over time indicating a widening of wealth gaps between the groups a phenomenon that increased over time. As the data clearly show the differences in mean net worth are very large and can be difficult to close. The net worth for each group is based upon the total value of assets minus debts of all sorts including mortgages, credit cards, loans, and so forth. This data is presented to demonstrate the financial barrier faced by individuals in each of the lower groups if they wished to move upward in American society. Generally, the data demonstrate that the higher the income levels the higher the net worth. Individuals from the bottom 40 percent cannot afford to live in communities or neighborhoods where the net worth is over $4.5 million dollars. The implications of the gaps themselves are interesting to discuss. In Table 3.1 each income level most likely lives in economically and racially segregated neighborhoods, do not shop in the same stores to purchase consumer goods, and send their children to schools vastly different in the quality of education offered. Domhoff, Wolff, and others who study the social stratification of American society have concluded that these gaps between social strata were established at the beginning of the nation and have remained relatively constant ever since. Indeed, the United States has been a socially stratified society with only minimal movement between classes since the beginning.

The strict social stratification of the state matrix is the most powerful barrier that maintains the social status quo with the large differences between classes unambiguously demonstrated in Table 3.2. It appears that the gaps are pronounced between the lowest three classes with the smallest gap being between the bottom two classes. This suggests that the lowest two classes are closer together than the other groups. The third and fourth classes are the next closest. Therefore, there are significant gaps between the lowest two classes and the third and fourth classes combined. The second highest class, representing the professional class appears to stand alone, while the highest percentile group is by far separated from all groups. Essentially, it would take a lifetime of saving and very steady and secure employment to bring parity to this structure, however several factors mitigate against this possibility. The first factor is that the children born into each group only have opportunities

Table 3.2 Mean Net Worth for Families by Percentiles, 1989–2016 (2016 Dollars)

Percentiles of Net Worth	1989	Dif Between Groups	1995	Dif Between Groups	2001	Dif Between Groups	2007	Dif Between Groups	2013	Dif Between Groups	2016	Dif Between Groups	% Inc 1989–2016
Bottom 20%	$24,700		$44,400		$52,800		$105,300		$86,100		$89,500		72.4
20–39.9%	$65,700	$41,000	$79,100	$34,700	$115,200	$62,400	$134,900	$29,600	$112,700	$26,600	$128,700	$39,200	49
40–59.9%	$101,300	$35,600	$102,300	$23,200	$162,700	$47,500	$210,500	$75,600	$168,600	$55,900	$207,300	$78,600	51
60–79.9%	$136,000	$34,700	$161,300	$59,000	$294,300	$131,600	$375,100	$164,600	$333,600	$165,000	$373,500	$166,200	63.6
80–89.9%	$222,460	$86,460	$257,500	$96,200	$457,300	$163,000	$609,000	$233,900	$635,800	$302,200	$771,000	$397,500	71.1
90–100%	$981,200	$758,740	$1,088,600	$831,100	$2,266,300	$1,809,000	$3,316,500	$2,707,500	$3,307,900	$2,672,100	$4,550,000	$3,779,000	78.4

SOURCE: Board of Governors of the Federal Reserve System, "Survey of Consumer Finances, 2016."

available to them that the income and wealth levels of their parents can afford. For instance, the tuition at some of the most prestigious of American universities are out of reach for the children of all three lower classes and a stretch for the parents of the second class. For instance, according to the National Center for Educational Statistics[4] the average tuition and ancillary fees for the 2013–2014 academic year for public, four-year universities and colleges was $18,632 and the private, four-year colleges and universities was $37,990. Private universities cost twice as much to attend. By academic year 2017–2018, the average tuition alone for the top twenty-five American universities was over $50,000 annually. Adding costs for housing, board, living expenses, and books leaves higher education far out of reach for families in the lowest three net worth classes. This is what I label a "structural barrier" to the advancement of the quality of living of the lower middle, working, and poor classes of the United States.[5]

Failing to obtain a good quality education, regardless of educational level, is a function of the salaries and income of their parents. Individuals of the lower three social classes are, due to lower paying jobs, forcing them to reside in different parts of town than the two upper classes, sending their children to schools that they can afford, and only socializing in the institutions and clubs based upon what they can afford. Without a good quality education that also provides linkages to occupations, work, and social standing, the lower classes will always remain in the stratum to which they were born. Each class will continue residing in social and racially separated neighborhoods, send their children to very different schools with the higher classes having the ability to afford more expensive, better quality education leading to higher paying careers where they can build their net worth. The lower classes are confined to poor and moderate living spaces, educate their children in poorly funded public schools and any higher education that their children obtain will only be funded through scholarships, state or federal funding, work or loans. The loans will only add to the debt burden of these families of the lower classes. The work the children of the poor will achieve, if they manage to obtain some higher education, will be low-level supervisorial or management positions. The state matrix will be organized and controlled by the highest classes in perpetuity where decisions are made controlling the social and economic quality of themselves and the lower classes.

The Economic

Undoubtedly, the social and economic elements of the state matrix are interconnected and go hand in hand. One's social status depends heavily on one's net worth defined earlier as the total assets minus the total liabilities held by a family or individual. Table 3.3 provides the total net worth and financial

Table 3.3 Distribution of Net Worth and Financial Wealth in the United States, 1983–2013

	Total Net Worth		
	Top 1 percent	Next 19 percent	Bottom 80 percent
1983	33.8%	47.5%	18.7%
1989	37.4%	46.2%	16.5%
1992	37.2%	46.6%	16.2%
1995	38.5%	45.4%	16.1%
1998	38.1%	45.3%	16.6%
2001	33.4%	51.0%	15.6%
2004	34.3%	50.3%	15.3%
2007	34.6%	50.5%	15.0%
2010	35.1%	53.5%	11.4%
2013	36.7%	52.2%	11.1%

SOURCE: Board of Governors of the Federal Reserve System, "Survey of Consumer Finances, 2016."

wealth of families in the top 1 percent, next 19 percent, and bottom 80 percent of all individuals and families residing within the state matrix. As the data, clearly indicate the total net worth of the top two groups increased over the thirty-year period while the lowest group has greatly decreased. When one removes the value of their residences from the net worth the Financial (Non-Home) Wealth (Table 3.4) demonstrates how important a residence is to the total net worth of the bottom 80 percent of the population.[6] The higher the net worth the less effect the value of the residence has on the overall net worth of the individuals and families within those groups. Home ownership, then, comprises the core net worth of the bottom 80 percent of the United States population, while that of the top 1 percent's net worth lies in investments, expensive commercial, industrial and residential properties, liquid cash, and so forth. The second 19 percent's core net worth is a combination of personal

Table 3.4 Percent Difference between Wealth Group

	Financial (Non-Home) Wealth		
	Top 1 percent	Next 19 percent	Bottom 80 percent
1983	42.9%	48.4%	8.7%
1989	46.9%	46.5%	6.6%
1992	45.6%	46.7%	7.7%
1995	47.2%	45.9%	7.0%
1998	47.3%	43.6%	9.1%
2001	39.7%	51.5%	8.7%
2004	42.2%	50.3%	7.5%
2007	42.7%	50.3%	7.0%
2010	41.3%	53.5%	5.2%
2013	42.8%	51.9%	5.3%

SOURCE: Board of Governors of the Federal Reserve System, "Survey of Consumer Finances, 2016."

property, middle to small investments, second homes, some commercial properties, and business inventories. Each individual situation varies from person-to-person within each stratum.

What determines the net worth of families within each class and what are the implications? The obvious answer to these questions are that the value of their net worth and salaries are what allow one to exist within each class. A more profound analysis of the data allows one to conclude what effect the net worth of families and individuals in the lower three classes have on their quality of life. For example, besides the costs of higher education being far out of reach for many in these lower classes, the same can be said of their choices of residences. The net worth of the lower classes is not enough to allow them to apply for mortgages of homes that permit them to leave their current neighborhoods and "buy-up." They may be able to leave their neighborhoods in some cases but only move to another that is marginally better. Additionally, the net worth of individuals living in the lower three classes does not provide enough wherewithal to refurbish the new house including the higher property taxes attached to living in a higher priced neighborhood. Finally, the net worth of the lower classes does not leave enough, after the basic purchase of the new residence, to enhance their lifestyle where it will be acceptable to those of the classes above them. The combination of these financial and economic variables acts as a structural barrier to individuals or families attempting to climb out of one class to the one above.

Not being able to move to neighborhoods where property values are higher also leaves lower class families with little or no choice as to the schools they send their children. Consequently, the economic segregation caused by their net worth also leads to the children being segregated into public schools that are poorly funded and do not provide an education of sufficient quality to qualify for admission to higher quality universities and colleges.[7] The cascading or resulting effect also causes these children to develop peer and work group interactions with individuals from their own class. In addition, it happens that these children commonly find occupations that others of their same class aspire to, gaining roughly the same salaries as their peers. These become structural barriers also trapping the three lower classes within their own social groups. Another complexity is that the consumer tastes and purchases, locations of outlets where these classes purchase their consumables (food, clothing, automobiles, and so forth) are the same for the three lower classes.

The upper and second class live separated from the three other classes in suburban subdivisions or isolated communities that cater to those who can afford a home in these neighborhoods. Obviously, the cost of the housing is designed to appeal to the financial well-being of these two classes and their ability to buy with either cash or rolling over other real estate or mortgages. Knowledge of and the ability to manipulate these financial tools allows these two classes to purchase a home or apartment in whichever locale they wish. Essentially, the net worth of these two classes allow for many more options, including residing in other countries, than those of the lower classes. Schooling is also more available to the children of the upper classes beginning with the elementary level through university and post-graduate work. Unlike their lower-class counterparts, the children of the upper two classes make friends and acquaintances, obtain internships in social clubs, have family connections together with professorial support who allow them to enter either public or private institutions at the managerial trainee level and eventually progress to higher levels of management. Eventually, some will become CEOs, high-powered attorneys or doctors, bankers, financial managers, or other types of high salaried occupations that allow them to maintain the quality of life within which they were raised and can provide for their children. Individuals within the second tier find their way into the upper and senior management positions of industry, commerce, finance which, in unison, manage the functioning of the state matrix. Politically, the two upper tiers have a great deal of influence on the state matrix's function through supporting their candidates in the election process or running for office themselves; serving as highly placed advisers or counselors to high elected officials.

Essentially, economic and financial circumstances provide a social and economic "head-start" for those born into the two higher classes. Although some in the second class may be more financially tenuous than others, they still have enough net worth to provide their children with the educations required to advance in society. The children of these two classes, then, have access to better quality education, higher level occupations (with salaries and investments comprising higher levels of compensation), better social connections, and higher valued quality of life circumstances such as residences (sometimes multiple), recreational, and so forth. The three lower classes appear trapped in their classes with little opportunity (there are exceptions to this) to advance. Social class based on net worth appears to be stratified with the stratification almost calcified to the extent that the United States has moved into a situation where classes are well defined and permanent.

Psychological and Ideological

The last two elements of the state matrix are the psychological and ideological. I treat both of these here in the same subsection because they overlap quite a bit in how individuals interpret the world and decide which decisions are the most appropriate in the political, social, and economic institutions of the state matrix. The psychological is complex and is a combination of the metaphysical and ideological mechanisms that tie all, who reside and work within the matrix state, together. Fundamentally, it includes the entire belief system including ontological, metaphysical, ideological, and any other set of beliefs that define one's place within the state matrix and also how they interpret the matrix fitting into the world of nations and societies. Additionally, this includes the interpretation of how one's matrix is interconnected to state matrices external to the state matrix within which the individual resides.

On an individual level this belief structure allows one to understand where one's social, economic, and political place is within the matrix. This causes one to develop a belief as to why they are in the social group or stratum they live in; what their personal capabilities are particularly intellectually; what their relation to the state matrix is; and, what their future and that of their children will be. Those in the top social stratum view the world and their place within the state matrix much differently than those in the lower three or four strata. Those in the top stratum see themselves as being the appropriate class to make decisions that directly affect the well-being of everyone within the state matrix while those in the bottom three strata see themselves working within the matrix to make a place for themselves and the advancement of their children. The upper class, then, develops a feeling of entitlement. This feeling reflects their belief that they should be the ones in control of the state matrix's direction and function because they have managed to acquire a great deal of wealth, defining themselves as successful individuals within the matrix, and therefore know better what is good for the state matrix and its inhabitants. The lower classes feel that they are victims of their own destinies and social existences and need to work hard to maintain their social place within the matrix.

The middle classes, those that exist within the second and upper part of the third stratum become the managers of the various institutions within the state matrix. These individuals, the professionals such as doctors, lawyers, full professors, and so forth, play significant roles in the reproduction of the matrix also insuring that their children will follow in similar roles of their classes. They aspire to wealth, some obtain it most do not, but share social, economic, and political space within the matrix. Sociologists who have studied the behavior of all these classes including Karl Marx, Max Weber, G. William Domhoff, and Eric Olen Wright have already discussed much of this.[8] Although these were the leading thinkers in the development of social class theories there have also been their detractors who feel that class is becoming less and less evident in American society and therefore not a good analytical framework to use in social stratification research.[9] These latter social scientists, however, appear to remain in the minority among their colleagues. As noted earlier in this volume the current state of social stratification research appears that the United States has become a society that is strictly class based with little social mobility between classes. Essentially, the social classes of the United States have calcified into a rigid and highly segregated social structure where individuals within each stratum live separate lives, disassociated from individuals in other classes.

Structured into the socialization of the class dwellers are feelings of privilege and fear, hate, racism, empathy, and other feelings or phobias that keep the structures separated. The feeling of privilege enjoyed by the upper two classes moves them to organize and take action to maintain their privilege and deny access to the lower classes. For instance, lobbying to insure the quality of education for the poor remains underfunded. There is no more clear or classic example of this than the struggles over public school funding that have gripped the State of Texas since the late 1960s and culminated with the now infamous *San Antonio, ISD, v. Rodriguez*, 411 US 1 (1973). In *Rodriguez* the Supreme Court, under Chief Justice Berger with Justice Louis Powell writing the majority opinion, stated unequivocally that education was not a constitutionally protected right and that there was not an identifiable "poor" social class in the United States. The decision relegated public education as not a constitutionally protected right but a state requirement up until a certain age, generally at the completion of one's secondary education, after that all education was the responsibility of the individual. Secondly, the decision made poor people as a class completely disappear under the law. This essentially created a legal situation where indigents could not bring lawsuits based on their status as a class of poor persons; they lacked standing before the law in federal courts. The poor, in effect, were stripped of any constitutional protections as a group. The *Rodriguez* decision was a legal barrier created by the judicial institution of the state matrix defending the educational status quo and constructed a barrier preventing the poor from achieving a quality education. The quality of education in the State of Texas was and still is determined by the value of property lying within the boundaries of each school district. As a result, if a school district is "land rich" possessing large financial districts, commercial, or industrial entities the quality of education would improve. This occurred when Toyota decided to build a large assembly plant on the south side of San Antonio, Texas. The Edgewood School District, where Mr. Rodriguez resided, remains one of the land-poorest school districts in the state and has a great deal of difficulty providing quality education for its children. The *Rodriguez* decision insured that the class structure and the existence of a class of poor persons was nonexistent in American legal culture thereby helping to concretize the relationship between the classes. By denying that a class of poor people existed, the Burger Court helped to maintain the class structure.

An important element of the metaphysical glue that holds American society together, perhaps the most important is that of ideology. Ideology is the shared belief system including political, religious, economic beliefs of all who live in the state matrix of the United States that makes Americans Americans.

The belief system that serves as an essential ingredient in the intellectual, social, and political formation of individuals within the state matrix can be found in the same socialization processes we all undergo as we live our lives. For instance, one receives intense training from their family concerning who they are, what social class they are in, what religious belief system they profess, what their educational goals and career ambitions are, and what their political orientation or ideology is. These beliefs hold throughout one's entire life unless the individual encounters a traumatic event that requires them to restructure their own belief systems, which is extremely difficult and painful for an individual to experience. The difficulty of one's political or ideological transformation is caused because to transform oneself, one must question all her beliefs and the veracity of many she holds as pillars of legitimacy such as her parents, teachers, religious leaders, and so forth.

As these children go through the educational systems their parents can afford, they encounter beliefs of others in their social classes that they share and reinforce what they have been taught by their families. Most importantly, these children are exposed to society's social beliefs as they progress through the educational system. Once in university the children learn more biased information in their lower division classes, switch to professionally biased methodologies at the upper division and graduate school. It is important for these children to learn biased information and methodologies because if they do not, they will not be able to manage and run the corporations their families own or within which they are expected to become high-level managers. This holds true for those going into law, medical, engineering, architectural, or doctoral programs. Any challenge of the belief systems or structures by any of these students or products of the structures is only on the margins. One is never exposed to the possibilities that the entire state matrix requires complete restructuring; or that banks have to be completely overhauled in order to bring fair treatment to their clients; or that the legal system is built only to protect those in power and not the rights of humanity; or that doctors are taught the canon so they are generally not open to nontraditional healing ways thus subject to manipulation by large pharmaceutical companies.

Additionally, as one traverses life, one's beliefs, although sometimes challenged, appear to be more and more reinforced concerning their social place and one's orientation to the state matrix and role within it. The socialization forces or mechanisms also reinforce one's belief as to the nature, orientation, and global place of the state matrix. Many times, these beliefs are reinforced in the cultural and political media, "America First," war movies, reciting the Pledge of Allegiance daily in school, and so forth. This political orientation also allows one to vote a certain way, determines one's ideological orientation and the level of one's nationalism.[10] Ideological orientation also builds into all individuals within the state matrix their perceptions of others within the matrix including those of other races, genders, social classes, and so forth. The next question then becomes why they received their racial beliefs and believed what they do about others.

This is a difficult question because the answer requires that we delve back into history to determine what the origins of and/or why we perceive and define individuals of other races, genders, and social classes the way we do. One can certainly assume that the perception of the lower classes' living arrangements, intelligence levels, and social statuses have evolved through at least the last seven or eight hundred or more years and become an essential element of why an upper-class family, the ones in the upper 1 percent stratum, believe the way they do about the lower classes. Why men, and some women, feel that women are the inferior gender is because of the beliefs that have been passed down by the family, media, and pop culture. The same can be said as to why white persons feel the way they do about non-white individuals. Nevertheless, the question remains, "Where did these perceptions originate and why did they originate the way they did?" These questions are important to the future of the state matrix because they underlie the worth of individuals and the future ability of the state matrix to reproduce itself; this is particularly important for the United States because this state matrix has built these concepts into its state mythology.[11]

Although the origins of why one group, in this case Whites, view others, especially people of color, the way they do, has already been demonstrated earlier in this volume, the psychological or emotional bases of these beliefs are still not clear. As a result, it may be useful to delve into the world of psychology to assist us in developing an understanding of why these perceptions are defined in the manner they are. For instance, although there is substantial evidence to indicate that there is scant scientific support demonstrating that one group is lesser than another, the belief persists that African Americans and Latinos are lesser than whites. Latinos are seen as simple, lazy people lacking in intelligence with little perception of the future or any ambitions to better themselves. These excuses have been used throughout history to demean Latinos through refusing them various services such as education or even a quality education, not allowing them to own higher valued property, and denying them access to higher paying jobs and opportunities. Scientific and legal evidence tells us this is true, but why?

In the introduction, I describe the anger felt by a Texas state senator as he sat in the courtroom galley of the US Circuit Court for the District of Columbia. The longer he heard testimony as to why the Texas state voter ID law that he shepherded through the 2011 Texas legislative session was harmful to Latinos the more angry he got until he reached a point I thought he was going to explode. I posed several possibilities for his extreme anger. Was he angry at being questioned by outsiders he deemed unknowledgeable about Texas politics? Was he angry because his belief system that Latinos were inferior to whites was systematically challenged? Was he angry because two teenage Latinas had sued him? Was he angry because he felt that his privileged position as a white man, in control of the levers of state power, was being challenged and he feared losing them? Or, was it all these reasons? If it was fear that his beliefs were not accurate why was he afraid?

It may well be that the state senator from Texas could not face the possibility that what he learned from his family and reinforced throughout his lifetime including during his tenure in the Texas congress was wrong, that his entire belief system was wrong. If this was the case, then he may have feared several eventualities. The senator may have feared the loss of his white male privilege in society; he may have feared what Latinos would do once in power; or he may have feared what he would do with his life if his belief system failed him. In the final analysis, he may have feared all these things. To change one's ideological framework, although it can be done, is an extremely difficult, arduous, and long process. It is not impossible but extremely problematical and challenging. One would have to question the legitimacy and belief systems of one's parents, the religious institution(s) one was raised in, the educational system that educated one together with all the beliefs of one's peers. At the same time, one would require the courage to not just reject everything they believed but to take a journey to find a belief system that placed one's social reality into a context based on reality and not bad science or irrational unverified and untrue belief systems. Perhaps the state senator lacked the courage to face this journey even when faced with facts in a court of law. Maybe the state senator was confronted with the possibility that his belief system was false but did not where to turn next.

One of the most important, if not the most important assumption underlying this discussion is that the driving force behind racism and racial thinking and intent to control fear is fear itself. What, then, is the linkage, the conceptual bridge if you will, between fear and racism? An ancillary question then arises, What is the linkage between racism and intent to create barriers against the fear of racial minorities? Some psychologists (I am not one, so I am intellectually speculating here) point out that fear of the unknown may be behind racism. The fear that drove the white state senator to the emotional and physical response he was experiencing during that Section 5, VRA hearing in Washington, DC, includes the following:

- The fear of losing his social, political, and economic place as a white, privileged male.
- The fear of minorities seeking reparations or retribution once they gain power in the state government.
- The fear of what he will face socially and economically once out of power.

- The general fear of an unknown future including his loss of social status, work.
- The fear that he will become completely irrelevant.

Let us discuss each of these in turn in order to understand why he creates and assists others in his situation, to build and reinforce barriers to the social, economic, and political advancement of racial minority group members.

White Privilege

The concept of white privilege is defined as the social status including all educational, work, career, and living opportunities that one acquires and possesses because they are considered "white." Individuals who are considered "white" by society usually do not consider themselves abnormal or "white." Some are extremely conscious of their "whiteness" while many simply take it for granted and do not consider all opportunities granted them are given because of their "whiteness." Many "white" persons do not consider it unusual if they are chosen for leadership positions, to be spokespersons for a team or group, to be chosen to run for an elected office just to appease white voters, and are seen racially as clean hygienically, examples of citizenship, better and more qualified than others are, and so forth. These expectations essentially make up what is considered "white privilege."[12]

For many whites, whiteness is seen and defined as the social norm to which other groups in society are measured. White is seen as normal and, in some instances, becomes an essential characteristic of one's society, nation, or state matrix. This was surely the case of the white nationalists at the beginning of the founding of the United States through Charles Davenport, the founder of the Eugenics Record Office at Cold Springs Research Laboratory, and his minions, and many decision makers and white nationalists today. Davenport, using "scientific racism" methodologies that came under fire by international biological communities as unscientific and racist, created the race hierarchy spoken of earlier in this volume. The racial hierarchy placed whites at the top with the bottom being occupied by the Hottentots.[13] Whites were credited with being the most intelligent, creative of all racial groups and responsible for the Great Western culture and all technological, scientific, and artistic creations in history.[14] Over time the belief in white superiority came to be taught in high school and university classrooms, found their way into intellectual conversations in many social science and scientific conferences, and became the norm for how to think and define all racial groups in the world generally and the United States specifically. Whiteness became the norm while all other races were seen as less than normal.

Underlying "white privilege" is the fear lurking in the minds of many "whites," also those who perceivably have "white privilege" but are not white, of losing their privilege to people of color.[15] Some feel, one can hear it currently during debates raging over the treatment of Central Americans seeking political asylum in the United States, that the United States is protecting our culture and heritage by denying entry to immigrants from Central America. This racial fear, created by the right wing, has spread through large segments of American society all the way to the top of the government. Underlying this fear is the theory that once Central Americans gain citizenship they will vote against right-wing interests and ideologies. Even more fearful is that immigrants will seek revenge for their ill-treatment once they are safe from deportation. Both fears were heard during the legislative deliberations surrounding the passage of the Texas State Redistricting Plan in 2011 as well as the voter ID law passed during the same session.

This fear has spread across all geographical areas, where mostly white people reside, like some "mass hysteria" affecting both adults and children. Even though the genetic differences between races, according to "authentic" scientific research indicates very little if any differences, between all races. Among some of the stereotypical beliefs that form part of this "mass illness" include the notion that racial segregation is natural because all races feel comfortable living among their own. Another notion and an important one in defining racial hierarchies is that whites are superior than people of color in all social areas such as educational attainment, employed positions, personal initiative, and the ability to work at long and arduous tasks. An essential facet of racial beliefs is that racial and culturally different people feel comfortable among their own kind because they speak the same language and share the same culture. As a result, racial minorities wish to be segregated so they prefer living in their own neighborhoods and socializing in their own clubs and churches. The totality of these reasons form the basis of a benign racism and are at the heart of how decision makers within the state matrix make daily decisions. Many of these beliefs were first pronounced in much of the white supremacist literature that evolved from the research by scientific racialists such as de Gobineau, Stoddard, Madison Grant, and others. Regardless, like most fears, although based in old, outmoded, and disproven beliefs, these theories are still held by those who fear losing what little imagined privileges they have. Finally, the loss of white privilege is undergirded by the fear of the unknown. The fear that those who lose their privileges will have no privileges after the takeover by people of color or women. Losing their privileges means leaving the control of the economy, political, and legal systems, and all other major institutions in the hands of an uneducated, illiterate, not very smart, and incompetent group of people. This underlying fear is what many white privileged people feel will happen to the economic, political, and social systems if left in the hands of people of color.

As a corollary, once one loses their white privilege what becomes of them? In some cases, these former privileged individuals feel they need to do something to protect themselves against retribution by those who were discriminated against while white privilege was in power. In addition, the loss of privilege may result in the loss of income and social place. As a result, some losers of privilege do not have any idea as to what their future economic and social places will look like. What will their income look like? How will the loss of privilege affect their social standing? On another level, this happens with retirees almost all the time; a feeling of the loss of self-worth may affect their mental health leading to early aging or other physical disorders. In the final analysis, the losers of white privilege may feel that they have become anachronistic and useless to society, essentially fearing the unknown and unseen future.

The psychology of fear then causes those who fear losing white privilege that they must act to prevent the loss of their privileged position in society. What results is the creation of certain structural barriers preventing or inhibiting members of minority groups, in Texas these victims are Latinos and African Americans, to take advantage of political, social, or economic opportunities available to them in the United States. What happens next is that those who fear loss of white privilege and who are in positions of power do what needs to be done to underfund schools for poor children; create a series of barriers inhibiting the right to vote; and, deny citizenship to children born in the United States of immigrants regardless of legal status of their parents or mothers all actions that create barriers to the social advancement of the other racial groups. In this latter category one finds the separation of families, including infants and toddlers and disabled children, declared in an Executive Order by President Trump to intimidate Central American "asylum seekers" from applying for refugee status. The president's rationale was to stop the "infestation" of American society and culture by the Central Americans. Trump used the exact same language as one of his ideological heroes, Adolph Hitler. Hitler used the same language and verbiage as Trump when he spoke of the Jewish question. Many of these barriers have been challenged in the federal courts and generally the courts have sided with the victims. Perhaps the psychology of fear was what made that Texas state senator so angry that sultry afternoon in a DC circuit courtroom. He was angry because the barrier he constructed, the Texas voter ID law, was being attacked and brought down by two teenage Latinas. Or, perhaps his anger was driven by his fear and all it entailed in his own perception.

The Fear of Racial Minorities Seeking Retribution or Reparations Once They Gain Power in the State Government

An essential aspect of the fear of losing a position of white privilege is that once minority groups gain political power due to changing demographics and the increased political efficacy of these groups, they will seek either reparations or retribution for past discrimination. Some of this fear is caused by recent efforts of the African American community seeking reparations from institutions such as universities to repay the local or national Black community for their years in slavery. Brown, Georgetown, and Harvard have recently agreed to repay hundreds of millions of dollars to the descendants of slaves. At one point in history all three universities bought, sold, and used slaves in building their campuses and generally as a form of cheap labor.[16] The fear of retribution, on the other hand, appear unfounded but rests in the minds of some whites.[17] In Texas, at least, the Latino community has never sought reparations, although there has been talk among some community leaders about the possibility of petitioning the government for reparations, but this has never gone beyond the discussion stage. There is no evidence of Latinos planning for any retributive efforts once they gain political power.[18] There were attempts by various parties or individuals, sometimes supported by the Mexican government, to return portions or all of Texas to Mexico in the nineteenth century but all these failed.[19]

The fear of reparations and retribution appears to only arise among some white leaders that fear losing their privileged positions through the loss of a reelection campaign, particularly if they have any discomfort at the way they have treated members of minority groups, in the way they achieved office or how they have acted while in office. Various white leaders speak about these fears openly, they certainly do in the Texas State Legislature. Sometimes you hear it in public discourse, legislative debates, presidential news conferences, television interviews by congressional leaders, and so forth. Sometimes this fear is expressed as a loss of culture, how future governments will be restructured, and some fear undefined retribution.[20] As one member of the Black Panther Party comparing the violence perpetrated by the Ku Klux Klan to that of the Black Panthers. The Panthers have never bombed churches, castrated voter registrars, raped young white women, or lynched anyone. The fear of black or Latino retribution on whites is more a phenomenon driving the actions and beliefs of some whites while the opposite is not true.[21]

The Fear of What He Will Face Socially and Economically Once Out of Power

The "he" in the subtitle above is used to define "all white persons" regardless of gender or ethnicity. This fear is not uncommon but can be experienced by anyone who has lost a spouse, entire family, a job, or career. Anyone who has been attached so intensely to another or group that helps that individual define themselves will tend to feel a great loss, feelings of helplessness, a deep malaise, and a fear of the unknown future. These individuals will sometimes suffer depression or anxiety or deep grief because an important element of their own essentiality has been lost. This leads to a feeling of hopelessness and helplessness because suddenly their lives are, in their perception, worthless. Those with privilege may see themselves without any or little self-worth if minority group members replace them in positions of power, for instance taking their place as heads of boards of directors, governorships, presidents of senates, mayors, and so forth.

If those with white privilege lose their positions of power, they fear what their personal future will look like without the possession of any power. For these persons it is a great fear that begins driving their actions in many areas of their lives, including the professional world or their occupations. They do not realize that most persons, not just African Americans or Latinos, do not have social privilege yet are productive members of today's social, economic, psychological, and ideological structures. Without these latter groups performing their proper functions the state matrix would fall apart. However, the egotism and narcissism of the privileged class do not allow them to define themselves as an "everyman," just the "average, everyday worker," regardless of profession, who works to provide food and shelter for her family, and who provides the services required to make the economy or society move forward. They will not necessarily lose privilege because their "whiteness" will allow them to retain privilege within their professions and social circles. Their new privilege will simply be defined as another type of privilege to one that they held earlier when in control of the state or some of the institutions of the state matrix. This is evident among the working class where whites hold large numbers of supervisory positions and minorities populate street repair, construction, and other similar crews.

Fearing the loss of privilege functions at several, simultaneous, levels. For instance, one may fear the loss of power, an uncertain personal future, loss of income, status, and so forth. These fears acting collectively compound the loss of privilege and intensify the reaction, such as the Texas state senator's, referred to earlier here, extreme anger at two teenage Latinas challenging his voter ID law. He may have felt not just the impending or possible loss of power, he also may simultaneously have felt demeaned that two Latina teenagers may be legally correct and he was not, he also felt that if he lost this trial his position of power within the senate would appear weakened among his peers, he may have feared losing his next election, and he may have feared an unknown future without work that would provide him with a feeling of self-value. An additional layer to this fear is that the senator may have feared what would happen to his state if minorities were to vote all Anglos out of office, an unfounded fear, still very real to the senator. Maybe, most importantly, he feared the perception of his family and friends were he to lose this struggle to two teenage Latinas and a Latino trial team. Essentially, the loss of privilege was perceived by the senator as his loss and everyone else's particularly Mexican Americans' gain. The senator felt his political world coming to an end with the stars of others ascending as he looked on helplessly.

The Feeling of Becoming Completely Irrelevant

It goes without saying that if the loss of privilege is everything mentioned above then the final feeling may be the logical concluding stage of the fear, the loss of relevance to society. This fear of irrelevancy is probably buried deep in our psyches and similar to what many will suffer at the end of our work life or careers. How will each of us feel when we can no longer work regardless of the reasons? Some individuals can make the transition, with good planning, easier than others. Some cannot because they have worked almost an entire lifetime and their entire life has been defined by their work. Some who have achieved great political and economic power then suddenly lose it, due to the loss of an election or retirement, also may feel completely irrelevant and useless to society. This latter group may see society losing its quality because he is not in charge and when he sees signals that he is no longer needed or wanted, and, in his own perception, he slips further into irrelevancy. Additionally, this individual feels that society, his culture and heritage as he defines them, will be replaced by those of the racial groups who replace him.

The loss of privilege, then, can also lead to the fear of irrelevancy and helplessness so individuals in power may wish not to leave and may have to be "pushed" or "pulled" out of their positions because they will refuse to leave voluntarily. If these individuals' self-worth is mostly based in their positions of privilege then, whether they are forced out or leave their positions voluntarily, these persons may feel a sense of irrelevancy, worthlessness, helplessness, less worth and suffer from depression or worse because they have lost a major sense of identity.

Loss of Privilege and Racism

The relationship between the fear of losing one's privileged position and racism appears simple but the relationship between privilege and racism is complex because it involves several emotional variables and their effect on human behavior is still not understood by many in the fields of psychology, psychiatry, and generally the neural sciences. One may argue that my delving into this relationship is beyond my professional scope. However, if political scientists are called on to provide evidence of racial intent by the federal courts in the United States then I must try to understand the relationship between the fear of losing white privilege and racism. In my perception one cannot provide the courts with evidence of racial intent or intent to discriminate unless one provides direct evidence to this effect. In the era of "dog whistle and racial shield politics" direct evidence of racial intent is most often lacking. Technology, language, and refusal on the part of public decision makers to even discuss race makes acting with racial intent easy and legally defensible. Understanding these linkages, placing them in an historical context and providing evidence of the linkages between each to the discriminatory actions of decision makers in a particular situation is the only way in which to provide evidence of racial intent that the court can easily understand and adjudicate decisions. As a result, we must make an effort at understanding human behavior in this context, which means delving into understanding the psychologies of fear and racism and the emotional "triggers" that cause persons to act on the fears of losing privilege and making racist decisions even if they do not think they are acting in a racist manner.

Consequently, one must understand the complexity and pervasiveness of all variables that construct racism and the resulting discriminatory action including white privilege, fear of loss of that privilege, hatred of other races and place them within an historical and situational context. Acting with racial intent is not just the intention of deciding to harm others intentionally, as noted earlier few, in the contemporary era, would openly admit to doing something of this nature. Acting in a racist manner may simply be the result of how one was raised and educated by one's family, educational, work, and peer environments. How we define racism has already been discussed earlier in this volume, how it affects public policy and formation of laws has already been examined when we spoke of the socialization process. What we have yet to discuss is how racism becomes deeply imbedded in those making public policy decisions and how that racism is infused into policies the decision makers, make. Contemporary racial attitudes have become increasingly complex, and multidimensional.[22] "Despite these caveats it can be concluded that social psychology has conceptualized racism to be a normative, often invisible system of social practices, cognitions, emotions and discourses that are perpetuated through all levels (individual, interpersonal, intergroup, institutional) that privilege one social group and disadvantage and marginalize other social groups. These practices can be overt assertions of biological difference, but in today's social and political climate, are more likely to be covert and implicit."[23]

Acting with racial intent, then, is not simply the direct act of taking action that "intentionally" causes harm to a racial group but is a multilayered, complex, and historically based action. This action began at a certain point in history with clear and direct racial intent, became institutionalized, explicit statements of race dissipated but the methodology of the original racial intent constructed policy remained. Consequently, actors may be implementing a decisional process that is infused with racial intent yet it may not appear so on the surface. Some actors may even be acting with racial intent subconsciously and may not even be aware they are. The first indication that a policy was constructed with racial intent is by evaluating the "effects" of the policy. If the effects appear that the policy has an uneven, unequal, or harmful effect on a racial minority group then the next step is to investigate the origins of the policy and the "original intent" intent of the policy. This will result in determining whether the policy itself was designed with racial intent and to see whether the policy has remained substantively the same since its inception. There may have been modifications to the policy but the elements of the decisional process that results in the effects may not have changed. The courts separated "effects" from "intent," however, both are the result of the same process, two sides of the same coin, if you will. In both my undergraduate and graduate classes in public administration, decision theory, or public policy the fundamental rule is that the result (effect) of decisional processes will reflect the goals set forth during the earliest stages of the policy process. For instance, if you assume you will have a goal resulting in objective, equitable results then your policy assumptions, the decisional process and projected effects will reflect the effort to achieve equitable effects and vice-versa.

So, then what would this process, from original racial intent to the resultant present effects, look like? The formation of the policy, one may look at the three policy areas already discussed in this volume to understand this process, is originally placed in the hands of individuals who have been socialized into thinking racially. These individuals, who will become decision makers, have learned how to understand people of racial minority groups by their parents and these observations have been reinforced by their educational, occupational, and work environments and what they view in the media daily. Generally, they have no personal relationships with members of racial minority communities only those fortunate enough to have found their way into the "white" worlds of supervisors, lawyers, corporate managers, and so forth. The members of the racial minority groups who do manage to move into the "supervisorial/management" ranks of society do so because their personal behavior and educational pedigree allow them to be considered almost as equals to whites within those ranks.

The end result is that the decisional processes of the state are reflective of an ideological structure designed to perpetuate the social conditions of the state matrix.

Decisional Processes

So, what do those decisional processes look like? The processes are divided generally on three levels.

1. First Decisional Level

The first level of the decisional process is populating the process with individuals who have been racially socialized. The process of population requires that only a certain pool of individuals is looked at for inclusion in the decisional levels of the matrix state. These individuals are chosen through their attendance and performance at selected schools from secondary through post-graduate education, their performance of standardized examinations at every level, letters of recommendations, social contacts and how they impress their future employers, supervisors, or managers. This process guarantees that all applicants chosen for inclusion at the managerial and eventually the decisional levels of the state matrix think, process information, and reach decisions generally alike. This initial first step in the process, it can be labelled a "selectivity step," occurs through the Human Relations review of résumés, college and university transcripts, letters of recommendation, calls to recommenders and such. This process is generally crowned off with an interview process that also measures the social and ideological compatibility of the candidate. The socialization process guarantees that all individuals who are candidates for the upper echelons of the state matrix have studied the same histories, decisional methodological techniques, economic systems, methods of investment and so forth that are essential to understand and use if one is to become an effective decision maker within the state matrix. There is some variance in thinking, but these individuals view issues and problems together with their solutions based upon similar social, economic, and political assumptions as those reviewing their applications.

This highly generalized process explains, to a great extent, why individuals populating many public and private sector institutions appear to think similarly about issues. This also explains partially why many institutions are populated by conservative-thinking individuals. The opportunities for advancement in the political world are not as great for progressives or liberals because of their general "out-of-the-mainstream" thinking. Conservatives, on the other hand, have learned the vocabulary of the establishment and are more acceptable to those responsible for employment. This eventually results in conservatives generally having control of all political, economic, and social institutions within the state matrix. Without conservativism maintaining control of the state matrix then the state cannot continue along the preferred path. However, one must consider the long-term consequences of this type of linear process that is generally inflexible and not prepared for large changes caused by tensions from outside and inside the state matrix that may affect the matrix's trajectory. This inflexibility causes the state matrix not to respond appropriately to tensions that may threaten the state matrix. The most recent example of this is the 2008 housing bubble that was caused by a few individuals and institutions taking advantage of loose regulatory rules and policies. This was coupled with a complete lack of ethics and moral behavior on the part of the perpetrators together with a lack of empathy for the effects of their trading on the greater society and economy. This behavior is reflective of what these individuals learned in business curriculum or from the behavior of their peers, when making money is considered the fundamental rationale for investing or manipulating investments then only wrong can occur. In the case of the 2008 housing bubble poor investing and lending practices led to global economic problems.[24]

2. The Second Decisional Level

The second policy decisional level include all mechanisms through which a policy must travel in order to become an official policy of the state matrix. These include mechanisms at all decisional levels and nodes that create the policies' substance together with directions for implementation. Generally, these mechanisms operate on two levels: exclusionary and inclusionary. The exclusionary level insures that concepts, ideas, or solutions to problems that do not coincide with the matrix state's general ideological or philosophical belief systems are excluded from the conversation.

An example, one I've used in prior writings because it is so obvious, after the housing bubble of 2008–2009 there was little if any discussion concerning the nationalization of the mortgage lending systems of the United States or at least imposing heavy and strict regulatory measures to insure any future victimization of loan seekers by lending agencies or banks. The nationalization of banks is a topic for academic debate, even there it would only occur in the least traditional of all universities and departments of economics or business schools. Included in the policy debate, however, would be the imposition of strong sanctions or regulatory measures and, maybe, some fines for the most egregious of perpetrators. Still, the basic lending framework would be in place allowing for the predator lenders to "lay low until the dust settles" and then continue their old ways as is currently happening. Although a discussion of nationalization is simple, the actual reorganization under full nationalization would be very complex and not to be carried out without some very dangerous political struggles. Still, after both the exclusionary and inclusionary processes have completed their filtering processes what is left is an idea acceptable to all sides that fits the ideological belief system of the matrix state.

3. The Implementation Process

The third and final stage of the public policy process is the implementation process where the approved policy is fully applied. Those who are responsible for the functioning of the implementation process. At this level of the decisional process, we will stay with the banking example, are the directors of the Federal Reserve banking system, bank managers and directors, and their employees. These banks include all commercial banks and lending agencies that make loans on properties of all sizes including privately owned homes. The granting of loans for single-family households, for instance, requires lenders to use their discretion to decide whether to grant the loan, the amount of the loan, and the percent of interest the borrower will be required to pay over a specified number of years. Most individuals, particularly those at the lower economic levels, the bottom three social strata do not have the knowledge, education, or experience to understand the details of the contracts they are negotiating, nor do they fully understand the consequences if they default on their loan. These individuals are driven by the "great American dream" that the epitome of economic success is to own your own home, they don't understand the actual amount of money they will be paying out over the time frame of the loan, this includes interest, property taxes, maintenance costs, and so forth. What the results are of the banking and lending reforms is that not much will change for several reasons.

The first reason is that lenders have become so socialized into their way of thinking financially that they really know no other way of behaving or making decisions. Although they retain some discretion, their discretionary parameters are set by precedent and stereotypes and perceptions they have of their clientele. Lenders are also driven by the stressors of having to produce more profits for their institutions. This caused a scandal when it was discovered that Wells Fargo Bank, between 2016 and 2018, had been engaged in a series of illegal financial activities including the creation of millions of unauthorized credit card accounts, illegal automobile repossession activities, predator lending to low-income and minority community members, the setting of unrealistic sales goals that created a "pressure-cooker" work environment and retaliation against "whistle-blowing" employees. The bank was assessed approximately more than $1.3 billion in fines and reimbursements to wronged employees and customers. These fines were imposed by the Federal Reserve. More than 5,000 employees lost their jobs, thousands of homeowners lost their homes, and their credit worthiness was weakened.[25] In the final analysis, Wells Fargo continues to function after paying fines, forcing the departure of several top-level executives and reimbursing both employees and consumers for predatory lending practices. As of this writing, Wells Fargo stocks have partially recovered but are valued at $5 more than when they reached a low of $51+ during the scandal. The bank is paying federal taxes on only 25 percent or less of what they made in the last tax year and are on their way to prosperity.[26]

The decisional process, in this example, has worked in favor of the financial institution and against the interests of the communities the bank purported to serve. The bank performed as it did to ensure that it continued making profits thus showing its investors that it was healthy and worth investing more in. The bank also performed in this manner because it was doing everything it could to compete in a very competitive environment, which is one of the tenets of American culture—that we are a country of strong competitive men! In the end, the state matrix's belief system became imbedded within the operational functioning of the bank to the detriment of all except speculative investors. In this latter category are investors seeking opportunities in the market where they will purchase stock of a long-time, large institution that has fallen on some unfortunate days seeking profits in the long run.

Racial Effects of Decisional Process

The racial effects of the policies subject to the decisional process described above can be seen in the three policy areas discussed earlier in this volume. A historical review of voting policies, at least in Texas, indicates that race was at the forefront of every policy regardless of whether it was the "white primary" system, at-large election schemes, racially gerrymandered representational districts, voter purges, or the creation of voter ID laws. The same can be found in the case studies of immigration policies and the lack of gun control laws. All three of these policy areas were dominated by the fear of having members of racial minority groups politically participating in the United States. The fear of allowing racial minority group members to politically participate in any country is due to the fear of what racial minorities will do once in office. As noted earlier this fear is or was based in the imagined possibilities that once in office racial minority group members may very well retaliate against whites for past injustices or at a minimum seek some sort of reparation for the injustices. A second layer of fear was what the racial minority members would do to the government if they were in charge. There are recorded in the newspapers of the times in Texas when consideration of extending the franchise to "Mexicans" the fear that they would create a Mexican form of government and change the basic culture of Texas if they were allowed to govern. As a result, white politicians of the nineteenth, twentieth, and twenty-first centuries in Texas have sought to disenfranchise Latinos and Blacks in order to preserve "the Texan way of life."

The refusal to change gun control laws to outlaw guns generally is based on the fear that African Americans and Latinos will invade the homes of white families, defile the women, and kill everyone in sight. As a result, guns were sold as a way to protect one's home from invasion by minority group members because they are assumed to be wild, uncontrolled, rapists, murderers, and thieves. The "right to carry arms" by private citizens began as a "requirement" to carry arms to repel Indian invaders and rebelling slaves to a constitutionally protected right to protect yourself within your own home particularly in high risk neighborhood. Finally, immigration and naturalization laws have been dominated by algorithms providing individuals from English-speaking and Northern European white countries priorities during the process. This "situational" advantage was built into the laws governing quotas from various countries since the inception of the laws. The US government, influenced heavily by the eugenics community, wrote the laws and quotas to favor white immigrants over others. In some cases, such as the Chinese Exclusion Acts, entire groups of people from specific countries were excluded from applying because the US government did not want its culture and heritage threatened by an influx of people that were just not American enough. Mixing races or in some cases ethnic groups was anathema to American social standards and a threat to the cultural homogeneity of the United States. In the final analysis, it is clear that racism and racial thinking and perception can be imbedded within the decisional processes of the state matrix without even most members of the institutions aware that the system itself is racist. The social assumptions of those functioning within the decisional systems of the state matrix are based in the socialization process and brought to bear, sometimes unconsciously, when constructing public policy in some areas of the law. In the United States this has resulted in racist voting, gun control, and immigration policies.

NOTES

1. Paul Kennedy, *The Rise and Fall of the Great Powers* (New York: Random House, Inc., 1987). Stephen G. Brooks and William C. Wohlforth, "The Rise and Fall of the Great Powers in the Twenty-First Century: China's Rise and the Fate of America's Global Position," *International Security* Vol. 40, no. 3 (Winter 2015/2016): 7–53, the President and Fellows of Harvard College and the Massachusetts Institute of Technology.

2. G. William Domhoff, "Wealth, Income and Power," Who Rules America.net, 2018. Domhoff, borrowing from the work of others and citing U.S. Bureau of the Census data even produces tables indicating wealth figures.

3. G. W. Domhoff, *Who Rules America?* (1st ed.) (Englewood Cliffs, NJ: Prentice-Hall, 1967) (together with all eight editions). G. W. Domhoff, *Fat Cats and Democrats: The Role of the Big Rich in the Party of the Common Man* (Englewood Cliffs, NJ: Prentice-Hall, 1972). G. W. Domhoff, *The Bohemian Grove and Other Retreats: A Study in Ruling-class Cohesiveness* (New York: Harper & Row, 1974). G. W. Domhoff, "Social Clubs, Policy-Planning Groups, and Corporations: A Network Study of Ruling-Class Cohesiveness," *The Insurgent Sociologist*, 5, no. 3 (1975): 173–84.

4. U.S. Department of Education, National Center for Education Statistics, 2016, Digest of Education Statistics, 2015 (NCES 2016-014), Chapter 3.

5. Flores, *Evolution of Liberal Democratic State*.

6. Board of Governors of the Federal Reserve System, "Survey of Consumer Finances, 2016."

7. The unequal funding of public education in Texas has been the subject of litigation for more than forty-five years beginning with *San Antonio Independent School District v. Rodriguez*, 411 U.S. 1(1973).

8. Karl Marx, *Capital: A Critique of Political Economy. Vol. 1* (New York: Vintage, 1977). Max Weber, *Economy and Society*. Translated by G. Roth and C. Wittich (New York: Bedminster Press, 1968). G. William Domhoff, *Who Rules America?* (New York: Yale University Press). Erik Olin Wright, *Class Counts: Comparative Studies in Class Analysis* (Cambridge: Cambridge University Press, 1997).

9. Paul W. Kingston, *The Classless Society* (Palo Alto, CA: Stanford University Press, 2000). Jan Pakulski and Malcolm Waters, 1996. "The Reshaping and Dissolution of Social Class in Advanced Society." *Theory and Society* 25 (1996): 667–91.

10. Göran Therborn, *The Ideology of Power and the Power of Ideology* (London: Verso Press, 1980).

11. State mythologies are important because they also act as part of the metaphysical glue holding society together. Certainly, the expectation that all within the United States were created equal is what keeps a great percentage of the population moving forward, voting and participating within this state matrix. Other social concepts such as the United States having a free press, an open society, rights to voting, choice, assembly, petitioning of the government, and so forth help to insure the general loyalty of Americans to the state matrix.

12. Paula S. Rothenberg, *White Privilege: Essential Readings on the Other Side of Racism*, 5th ed. (New York: Worth Publishers, 2016). Cornel West, *Race Matters* (Boston: Beacon Press, 1993).

13. Different scientific racists produced differing hierarchies, but all agreed that white persons were the exemplars of what society should strive for in the maintenance of culture and intellectuality. Count Joseph Arthur de Gobineau, *Essa.i sur l'inégalité des races humaines* (Essay on the Inequality of the Human Races, 1853–1855) (Paris: Librairie de Fermin Didot Fréres, 1853). Jennifer Michael Hecht, *The End of the Soul: Scientific Modernity, Atheism, and Anthropology in France* (New York: Columbia University Press, 2003). T. Lothrop Stoddard, *The Rising Tide of Color* (New York: Charles Scribner's Sons, 1920), xi.

14. Ibid.

15. *Passim* Rothenberg. *Passim* West. Barry Glassner, *The Culture of Fear: Why Americans are Afraid of the Wrong Things* (New York: Basic Books, 2009). Daniel Gardner, *The Science of Fear: How the Culture of Fear Manipulates Your Brain* (New York: Plume, 2009).

16. Shafaq Hasan, "The Case for Universities Paying Reparations to Descendants of Slavery," NPQ: Nonprofit Quarterly, April 28, 2016.

17. G. Ben Cohen, "McCleskey's Omission: The Racial Geography of Retribution," *Ohio State Journal of Criminal Law* Vol. 10, no. 1 (Dec. 12, 2012). Michael

I. Norton and Samuel R. Sommers, "Whites See Racism as a Zero-Sum Game That They Are Now Losing," *Perspectives on Psychological Science* 6, no. 215 (2011). Brian Resnick, "White Fear of Demographic Change Is a Powerful Psychological Force." *Vox*, Jan. 28, 2017. Rev. Dr. Susan K. Smith, "Whites and the Fear Caused by White Supremacy," *The Blog*, Dec. 29, 2015. Updated Dec. 29, 2016.

18. J. Angelo Corlett, *Race, Racism and Reparations* (New York: Cornell University Press, 2003). David Frum, "The Impossibility of Reparations: Considering the Single Most Important Question about Racial Restitution: How Would It Work?" *The Atlantic*, 2014. David Masci, "Reparations Movement: Should Payments Be Made for Historical Wrongs?" *CQ Researcher*. Washington, DC: CQ Press.

19. Carey McWilliams, *North from Mexico: The Spanish-Speaking People of the United States* (Westport, CT: Praeger Publishers, 1948).

20. Cohen, "McKleskey's Omission." Resnick, "White Fear." Smith, "Whites and the Fear."

21. Steve Chapman, "Column: Black Demands and High Fears," July 13, 2016. www.chicagotribune.com/chapman.

22. S. L. Gaertner and J. F. Dovidio, "The Aversion Form of Racism," in J. F. Dovidio and S. L. Gaetner (Eds.), *Prejudice, Discrimination and Racism: Theory and Practice* (Orlando, FL: Academic Press, 1986). Kathleen Cole, "Thinking Through Race: White Racial Identity, Motivated Cognition and the Unconscious Maintenance of White Supremacy," *Politics, Groups, and Identities* Vol. 6, no. 2 (2018): 181–98.

23. Martha Augoustinos, "Psychological Perspectives on Racism," *InPsych*, Vol. 34, Issue 4 (August 2013). Martha C. Nussbaum, *The Monarchy of Fear: A Philosopher Looks at Our Political Crisis* (New York: Simon & Schuster, 2018).

24. Kuniko Fujita, "Introduction: Cities and Crisis: Challenges for Urban Theory," in her, *Cities and Crisis: New Critical Urban Theory* (London: SAGE Studies in International Sociology, 2013), 62.

25. Jackie Wattles, et al., "Wells Fargo's 20-month Nightmare." *CNNMoney*, April 24, 2018.

26. NY Stock Exchange, "Wells Fargo and Company (WFC)," July 18, 2018.

Chapter 4

How the Public Policy Process Creates a Racial Shield

In a previous chapter we saw how racial thinking and racism can be found in the initial stages of a policy's birth and become essential elements of the policy itself as it evolves throughout its lifetime. Nevertheless, one must ask what is it about the public policy process that allows for racial thinking to become implanted in the decisional processes and structures of the state? To unravel this enigma, one must first develop an understanding of how the process becomes ideologically biased because the ideological bias of the process is the principle reason for the creation of policies that act as racial shields. In turn, racial shields conceal decisions based on racial or racist assumptions. This chapter begins with an overview of the policy process, including the decisional and institutional structures and how these structures become ideologically biased. This is followed by how the racial shield is constructed in the policy areas already discussed, immigration, gun control, and voting. The chapter culminates with proscriptions as to how to cleave through the racial shield to uncover the racist machinations of the policy makers in each area. The definition and extended discussion of "racial shields" will also be presented here.

THE PUBLIC POLICY PROCESS

In earlier works I detailed my understanding of the public policy process from the abstract to the concrete[1] so I will not regurgitate my thoughts here. I will, however, provide a "refresher" of the most important aspects of my deliberations on the public policy process in order to assist in presenting my thoughts on how racial thinking and/or racism become embedded in the policy process.

The public policy process serves, as I pointed out earlier, as an institutional selection mechanism; it is a decisional filtering system that performs three functions: (1) it structures social attitudes and value systems in such a way as to prevent certain policy choices from arising during the decisional process; (2) it gives certain policy choices priority over others; and (3) systematically excludes policy choices not perceived to be the fault of systemic failure or oversight but rather are reflective of human weaknesses such as poverty, racism, sexism, hunger, and unemployment to name a few conditions attributed as the fault of the individual rather than the system or structures of the matrix. The first two functions are derivatives of the socialization processes. The first builds the value structures all individuals are imbued with as they proceed through life and interact with each of the socialization agents such as the family, schools, media, peer groups, and so forth. The second function results as decision makers sift through and prioritize policy choices, ranking certain choices above others using professionally acceptable decisional tools. For instance, a common consensus builder is to consider first "best practices" in a discipline and industry and then build one's policy choices around those best practices. During both functions policy alternatives that are not acceptable to a society's norms, customs, traditions, philosophical, or ideological standards are either discarded or not even considered. In this latter instance some choices are not considered because they are simply not part of a society's value structure. The most obvious example of this is that when the United States has faced a banking crisis one policy alternative that is never discussed or considered is the nationalization of banks. This option is not a capitalist norm but one that would belong to a socialist or communist planning process. As a result, it's excluded from consideration during the policy process seeking alternatives to a banking crisis in any liberal democracy.

These policy choices from the filtering process or selective institutional mechanisms become institutionalized as essential elements of any decisional process and deemed to serve society yet give certain institutions and individuals decisional "head starts" when a policy is implemented. For instance, economic development decisions by city governments in the United States are designed to give developers, certain types of financiers, and certain land owners advantages based upon tax breaks or incentives, loans at preferred rates, discounts on building materials, and so forth that are not available to small business persons. Some small businesses may even go bankrupt or must quit and relocate under certain circumstances because of overly intrusive construction efforts or eminent domain actions required during large scale developments. So, the advantages to large scale economic development efforts go to large businesses because the policy is written in their favor. This policy alternative was favored over any other because the local government wanted to encourage a type of development that would bring greater revenues to the city and more jobs over the short and long runs than other types of developmental activities. Thus, large businesses have a public policy head start under these types of circumstances.

The public policy process itself of any state is composed of all decisional processes and decisional structures and ideological mechanisms confined within the state. These include all legislative bodies and the rules, procedures and traditions that govern their operations. Also included are all executive institutions and their decisional structures including rules, policies, traditions, and customs that allow the institutions to function. Substantiating institutions, within a liberal democracy are the court and legal systems as well as accompanying laws, customs, traditions, policies, and procedures. Legal institutions substantiate the process because their interpretations of the process and subsequent decisions mystify the entire process by creating the appearance that all is a democratic and fair functioning process. And, finally, the ideological mechanisms provide the glue that holds a nation together. Ideological mechanisms, sometimes referred to as socialization agents, include parents, families and familial structures, educational systems including teachers, curricula, and so forth, religious institutions and their teachings, the media and other cultural propagators, the work place together with professional rules and regulations, and finally one's peers at every stage of one's development. Essentially, the public policy process of any state is not simply composed of the institutions where policy is formulated but includes every single variable that can possibly affect the outcome of any policy including the personal biases of individuals working on the development of any given policy. These biases are formed through the exposure of individuals to the various socialization agents throughout their lifetimes.

The public policy process does not, however, operate within a vacuum nor is it static. The process is affected by the actions of other states and their processes daily if not hourly. Compounding this is that the public policy process is subject to historical forces as well as internal and external economic and social tensions. The economic and social tensions are created by the normal functioning of people and institutions inside the state matrix and interconnected matrices placing demands on the internal decisional processes. For instance, the passage of the Civil Rights Acts of 1965 were brought about through decades of agitation by individuals to force the national government to act. These internal pressures, tensions if you will, were compounded by criticism the United States received internationally for the poor way African Americans were being treated by a society deemed to be a shining beacon of democracy. Policy is not simply created out of thin air spontaneously but is generally the result of long-standing interactions between many groups, individuals, and societal forces that have been ongoing for years or even centuries. As the discussion in the last chapter pointed out, immigration, gun, and voting policies that exist today have historical antecedents and policies in all three areas were composed in a biased fashion giving some groups a policy advantage over others.

As noted, the policy process is also not simply the actions of institutions performing robotically but rather the actions of the individuals who have populated the various institutions within the process. The substance of public policy is the result of humans thinking about, defining, and creating solutions to some perceived societal need. The perceived societal need, as defined by the policy makers at various stages of the debate over immigration policy, was and is to insure Western civilization prospered and survived the onslaught of non-European, non-English speaking people. From a demographic perspective this would be a giant step toward insuring that "white" persons remained the majority population in the United States. Even in contemporary times the president of the United States has called for immigration reform that can perpetuate the European, white basis of American society.[2] One lingering fear of whites in the United States is that their privileged position as the demographic majority is waning and they will be a minority by 2044 this results in more and more racial bias.[3]

The policy process begins when some individual, interest group, or institution sets forth a perceived need for a policy. In the realm of politics, it has become apparent that sometimes the need for policy is not necessarily based on fact but rather fabrications such as when supporters base the need for voter identification laws on the notion that there is a great deal of voter fraud being perpetrated in the United States when all empirical information reveals just the opposite. Still, many states have passed some form of voter identification law regardless of the reality surrounding the issue. The need for a voting rights act was documented through a long history of the exclusion of African Americans from the voting booths of America. Ironically, during the 2018 general elections questionable voter purges were conducted in several states raising the efficacy of several elections coupled with the consequences suffered in the aftermath of the *Shelby County* decision has resulted in a call for a new federal voting rights act, which the 2019 National Congress may consider. Although, there are deaths by firearms daily in the United States there has yet been an outcry by policy makers of a perceived need to regulate guns even though a majority of Americans want some sort of gun control legislation, mostly to curtail the sale of automatic and military grade weapons. In a recent Pew Research Center poll it was found that 57 percent of all Americans, including gun owners, wanted gun control laws.[4] More than 80 percent of respondents also indicated they preferred background checks banning gun sales to individuals with histories of mental health problems, criminal records, and so forth. Some states have some types of gun regulations but generally the United States is a country with minimal gun control laws.

Generally, at both the national and state levels the proposal for a law begins winding its way through the legislative processes and is modified at almost every stage. Eventually, if the law passes both chambers at the national level it goes to the executive branch for approval and implementation. This was generally the case with all immigration and voting laws at the national level and all gun control proposals. The finished products of each law, however, reflected the ideological orientations of the various and most powerful of the political actors at every stage, modified as representatives of special interests intervened in the process. For instance, the initial immigration and naturalization laws were heavily influenced by leaders of the eugenics movement. Eugenicists encouraged the national congress to establish the immigration ratio systems giving White Northern Europeans an advantage over immigrants from other countries. This racially tinged system remained in place until the 1960s where immigration policies are still being lobbied by anti-immigration organizations such as the Federation for American Immigration Reform. National gun laws were established to ensure that white males owned guns to protect against Indian attacks and slave revolts and this law became imbedded in the national constitution and has evolved into a constitutionally protected right. Contemporary gun ownership and culture is still overwhelmingly dominated by white males who argue that gun ownership is essential to the protection of life and home. Voting rights were initially the purview of white males and the nation has slowly and painfully extended the franchise to more and more groups beginning with African Americans and women. As noted earlier, Latinos have been considered citizens with the right to vote granted as part of various treaty provisions. Still, legislative bodies throughout history have tried to minimize the political influence of Latinos through the development of various legal instruments including the poll tax, voter registration laws, gerrymandering, forced or coerced voting, and the creation of prohibitive voter identification laws.

Once laws have been passed, they are implemented or fail to be implemented completely. Sometimes the laws, given changing social mores, are modified or even eliminated. On occasion the laws are rendered stronger or weaker due to interpretive findings by the Supreme Court such as in the *Shelby County* decision that weakened the enforcement provisions of Section 4 of the Voting Rights Act. Sometimes the Court will expand the scope of the law as it did in the *McDonald* decision where it indicated that the right to bear arms was a constitutionally protected right that extended to all states not just the District of Columbia. Finally, the laws can be redesigned completely as illustrated by the history of the immigration laws of the United States.

RACE AND PUBLIC POLICY

By now it should be clear that I feel that the only way in which to understand the infusion of racism or racial thinking into an area of public policy is to understand the relationship between the two historically. Fundamentally, one cannot understand how racial thinking or racism becomes an essential element of a policy without understanding the historical context within which the policy was initiated. So, one must begin by asking if there were racial considerations when the policy was being initially discussed and were these concerns included as reasons for the creation of the policy or law. The brief reviews of the three policy areas presented here, immigration, gun control, and voting rights have shown that indeed racial considerations were at the heart of the arguments surrounding the need for policies in these areas.

As pointed out earlier, fear of Indian attacks and slave revolts led to the first gun ownership laws, the suppression of the votes of African Americans led to the passage of the Voting Rights Act, and the need to insure a white, European culture in the United States led to the various iterations of immigration laws. In each case race was at the forefront of the policies. Each of the policies and subsequent laws were composed with racial intent. The law requiring white men to carry guns was necessitated because of the perceived threat of Indians attempting to reclaim the lands that had been taken from them. The fear of the savage "red man" pillaging, burning, raping white women and taking back their land drove the law makers to enact the requirement for all white men to be armed. The fear of slave revolts, the fear of wild black natives running amok pillaging, burning, raping white women and killing white folks was a companion fear that drove the national government to pass the gun requirement law.

The Voting Rights Act was just the opposite and is the only policy area of the three that was passed with the intention of expanding the franchise and making Black persons full participants in American democracy. The Voting Rights Act of 1965 was essentially the implementing law for the Fifteenth Amendment to the Constitution of the United States. It was passed after evidence was presented to Congress of the many decades where diverse jurisdictions, principally states, had used various "devices" to prevent African Americans from voting. Some of the devices were literacy tests, refusing to allow people to vote if they could not recite the Constitution, not allowing Blacks to register to vote for a myriad of reasons, and so forth. Latinos were included under the protection of the Voting Rights Act in 1975 when it was extended by Congress to cover language minority groups. Latinos were included for many of the same reasons Blacks had been included in the original act because many jurisdictions, particularly in Texas, had placed barriers against political participation such as poll taxes, at-large election schemes, prohibition of language assistance, among others. The barriers that had been placed to inhibit both Black and Latino voting were placed there so non-white people could not express their opinions at the polls and elect candidates that represented their communities. The fear that drove the creation of these barriers was a combination that people of color would seek revenge or reparations once in office or would compose and pass laws that would change the very fabric of the American political process into something that was not American. So, the Voting Rights Act was passed for racially inclusive reasons rather than the opposite.

The immigration laws, as noted earlier in this volume, were almost all composed with racial intent to exclude those groups from entering the United States that did not appear white and European. It was clear from all the testimony in the hearings that the fear of tainting America's white, European cultural foundation was the reason for many of the exclusionary laws. In some iterations of the passage of various immigration laws throughout the history of the United States the laws were composed to halt the importation of certain national origin groups to perform specific labor such as the Chinese and Japanese and to prevent migrations of people from countries that had been devastated by wars, famine, or economic travails. Most recently there have been calls for prohibiting the immigration of persons from Muslim-dominated countries as a way of preventing the entry of Middle Eastern terrorists from entering the United States. Regardless of the reason, each law was tailored to control the entry of those populations that did not meet the ideal of what was perceived as American—white and European. The fear driving Congress and those who supported, still do, more restrictive immigration laws is that whites will become the numerical minority in the United States and then they will be subject to the dictates of those groups who have been discriminated against for hundreds of years. Additionally, there is the unwarranted fear that once in office minority group legislators or political leaders will pass laws that are not "white" and American. This latter fear is generally shouted out by white supremacists and nationalists. Still, the fear is reflective of the deep-seated racism that still infects American society.

In these policy areas race was a conscious and explicit reason to compose these laws. However, once race was infused into the decisional processes that governed the creation of these laws it became a central element of the decisional process; racism became institutionalized. Race and racial thinking became part of the structure allowing decision makers not to ever have to use the terms explicitly again. Instead, substitutions replaced any reference to race such as the need to create voting barriers to prevent "voter fraud" particular on the part of undocumented immigrants, creating barriers to immigrants who most likely would harbor "terrorists" or "criminals," and finally, allowing gun ownership to protect one's hearth and home from "gangs," "drug dealers," and "home invaders." Who can argue against fraud or crime? In the debates over the need for the voter identification cards in Texas, the need for "proper" identification was based initially on inhibiting undocumented immigrants from south of the border crossing over and voting in Texas elections. This reflected a historical fear of Texans going back to the inception of the nation in the 1850s. The term "undocumented immigrants" was a polite substitution for "wetbacks," which was a derogatory term used by Anglo Texans to describe not just Mexicans from across the border but also Mexican Americans. So, when the Texas legislature was speaking of preventing "undocumented immigrants" from voting they were also referring, subconsciously, to Mexican Americans. In urban areas African American communities have long been associated, by society generally, with high crime rates so social perception associates "gangs," "drug dealers," and home invaders" with African Americans. As a result, guns for the protection of hearth and home are subconsciously being purchased for protection against African Americans. As gun ownership data presented in an earlier chapter demonstrate, Anglos or Whites own guns at much higher rates than either Blacks or Latinos. Essentially, nonracial terms were substituted for references to race as the laws or non-laws found their way through the legislature and were finalized.

Race itself becomes part of the public policy process because it morphs into one of the variables understood as belonging to the normal algorithms of the decisional process as new decisions are made. For instance, law makers will argue that voting should just be limited to citizens and, without saying, has sent a signal that considering including noncitizens as eligible voters is not an option when it is understood that most noncitizens are Latinos. Or, owning guns for self-defense must be a constitutionally protected right sending a signal that one needs to possess guns in order to protect against African Americans and Latinos. Or, building a wall on the southern border of the United States to protect against undocumented immigrants from swarming the United States is clearly a racially tinged reference against Latinos. If the anti-immigrant forces wished to appear even in their pursuit of building walls to prevent undocumented immigrants from entering the United States then they should also be willing to champion a wall on the northern border preventing Canadians from illegally entering the United States.

Stereotypical images and misunderstandings of racial groups become bits of the information that are essential elements of the decisional processes. These bits are elements of what sociologist Joe Feagin has labelled a "white racial frame."[5] This frame is made up of "images, stories, interpretations, omissions, silences—that are passed along from one person and group to the next, and from one generation to the next."[6] These images are passed on through all the socialization mechanisms of society, television, online, movies, and so forth and become reinforced parts of decision makers' perceptual screens. These screens act to allow decision makers to interpret and interpolate information that is either included or excluded from a decision. The "white racial frame" permeates the decisional processes of every level of the state and explains how biases become part of the decisional structures of the states' institutions. In short, the institutionalization of race and racism is a necessary part of society's "white racial frame."

STRUCTURES WITHIN STRUCTURES

The public policy process, then, is not just a structure wherein and through which decisions are made but is itself composed of the belief structures that individuals working within the structure bring with them supplemented by the different decisional tools used in one's profession. As a result, the policy process is composed of traditional methodologies, decisional designs, data gathering processes, research methods, and implementation designs and methods. Conventional decisional tools such as troubleshooting techniques, queuing models, linear programming models, best practices, and so forth are used daily to identify problems as issues to be addressed, determining ways in which to treat the issues or problems and, finally, deciding implementation methods. Subsequently, implementation methods have their own process structures as well that include professional methods and standards brought from their professions by engineers, builders, codes, police enforcement practices, laws, and so forth. Each of these processes and techniques are biased in their own unique ways.

Nevertheless, the policy process is a structure where public decisions are made, laws, policies, programs are written. So, decision makers define issues that need to be addressed, they determine how to address the issues and then establish what policies or laws need to be written to address those issues. During this process, decision makers bring their personal perceptions to bear in defining and identifying the issue. Personal biases coupled with professional standards and processes bias the decisional process giving certain variables or choices a decisional head start, placing some preferences over others. As I pointed out earlier this is the stage where choices not acceptable to the norms of society are excluded from consideration either subconsciously or consciously. For instance, to solve the housing and mortgage crisis of 2008 the only solution to the problem was to allow two large institutions to fail because they had violated the rules of the market in becoming so far over-leveraged that they could not recover, even with governmental intervention, so normal market forces led to their demise. Others were saved by infusions of large amounts of capital from the federal government. Only one low-level financial executive went to jail, high-level executives and CEOs managed to escape any jail time for any of their transgressions.[7] The solution to the problem was to modify and change some of the rules for designing investment instruments, fining certain companies, dissolving others such as Arthur Anderson, the accounting firm, which was supposed to audit and manage the accounting of the investment process or Bear Stearns a global investment bank that secured a large number of the investment instruments, but no jailings of high executives responsible for the decisions that caused the "housing bubble to burst." Why no high-level executives were prosecuted for their part in the 2008 financial fiasco is part of the "white racial frame." It is a belief that prosecuting and jailing high-level executives of banks or corporations will endanger the national and global economies. Where low-level street crime offenses can get one terms of as much as thirty years of hard prison time, high-level corporate crimes that can ruin the lives of thousands get only "slaps on the wrist" and fines that one corporate executive likened to the "price of doing business."[8]

What was eliminated, excluded, or missing from the dialogue that proffered solutions to the financial downturn of 2008 was any consideration of the federal government gaining control of the investment houses or banks that were the culprits or the imprisonment of the executives responsible for the crisis. One of the chief tenets of the American economic belief system is that government does not do business, at best it can only regulate business. Business ownership is the sole purview of the private sector in capitalism, to think otherwise is tantamount to heresy or, at least, sacrilegious thinking. Government ownership of business is so foreign to American thought that it is not even discussed in economics or business classes. Any politician who would even offer this as a policy alternative would run the risk of losing their next reelection attempt or become a political pariah.

The policy choices that were included or excluded in the three policy areas discussed in this volume vary but generally run the gamut of either total inclusion of groups or total exclusion. For instance, in gun control legislation there are few laws, although some exist in some states and local jurisdictions that exclude thorough background checks. In Texas for example, a five-minute phone call or very quick "computer check," conducted out of the view of the gun purchaser, clears the purchase. In some states mental health or felony records are either not checked or overlooked during the background check process. To obtain an open carry permit one can simply apply online to one state, Virginia, who has reciprocal agreements with other states who then will issue the permit without further checks. The author went through both processes so has firsthand knowledge of this process. Gun ownership is encouraged as both a means of enjoying a sporting lifestyle but also as added insurance against crime and a way of protecting one's family and home. Laws governing such loose regulations were excluded or are not considered because gun ownership is seen as an almost completely protected constitutional right without limitations, a fundamental right. Arguments concerning violence, increasing numbers of murders, suicides, or mass shootings are disregarded whenever anyone wishes to bring debate restricting gun ownership.

Excluded from the policy debates, generally, is any information that would create hindrances to gun ownership, while included are only those arguments supporting gun ownership.

What has been excluded from the debates over voting rights is any consideration of universal suffrage. Although this position flies in the face of conventional wisdom there is some logic to this consideration. It is based upon a legal principle expounded by the Supreme Court in *Plyler v. Doe*[9] that all persons subject to the equal protection provisions of the Fourteenth Amendment, which includes all individuals, regardless of citizenship status, also have the responsibility of obeying all laws while in the jurisdictional boundaries and control of the US government and any sub jurisdiction. If this is the case, then it makes perfect sense that all persons within the jurisdictional control of the United States and subject to its laws should have the right to vote for anyone passing those laws; they should have representation under those laws. This can even be expanded to consider that because undocumented individuals pay taxes of all sorts then they are being taxed without representation. As a result, an argument can be made logically to extend the franchise to all under the jurisdiction of the United States regardless of status. Nevertheless, this notion is never included in the discussion for protecting the franchise and, if and when the Voting Rights Act is rewritten by future Congresses, noncitizen voting will be excluded from all debates. Another topic that will be excluded from debate and has never been included to date is appropriate punishment for those who violate the law by preventing voters of color from voting. There are penalties for committing voter fraud such as voting in place of another voter, carrying bundled ballots, or over assistance of voters to the extent there is undue influence over ballot choices.[10] Some of these and other offenses listed in Texas's anti-voter fraud bill have penalties of as long as ten years in prison plus fines. There were four persons indicted in 2018 on thirty counts of voter fraud in Texas for offenses in the 2016 general election and are awaiting trial. These are felony offenses, so each can expect to spend some time in prison.[11] The case is yet to be heard so it's not clear if these individuals are guilty of the violations. These types of penalties for these types of voter fraud have been included in voting laws. What has been excluded are similar types of punishments for those law makers who intentionally violate the voting rights of Latinos or Black voters through racial gerrymandering or other devices. These should also be considered felonies and punishable with prison time and fines because they have the potential of violating the rights of thousands of individuals, but this like the government ownership of banks runs counter to society's cultural norms, it is an essential part of the "white racial frame," so will not be included in the conversations when the new Voting Rights Act or other voting laws are being considered.

Finally, as the United States debates the need for immigration reform one option will never be included in policy discussions or debates and that is the notion of open borders and universal asylum. The arguments against are that the United States must maintain its national sovereignty by controlling its borders, must protect against terrorism, and must insure that only desirable aliens are allowed into the country in a controlled manner. The last argument is based on the notion that the United States does not wish to be overpopulated by individuals who cannot be productive members of society. Therefore, any reform of the country's immigration laws will be based upon exclusionary considerations, for example immigrants from certain countries will be excluded from consideration, immigrants only having certain levels of education and specific skills will be included, and so forth.

In the three policy areas that form the core of this book's discussion racial beliefs were at the center of each policy decision. Each policy was filtered through the decisional structures of the national government in their historical era. Each set of policies were designed with the explicit notion that certain races, for whatever reason, would be targeted by the policies. Why certain races were included was based upon racial beliefs and stereotypes of those groups that included beliefs about intelligence levels, behavioral characteristics, and hygienic assumptions of each group. Included were only negative connotations, excluded were any redeeming values for each of the excluded or discriminated against groups. The values that were included justified the creation of policies for the ownership of guns, excluding persons from voting and denial of entry into the United States.

The public policy process, then, involving seeking solutions to crises such as the financial crisis mentioned above as well as of the three policy areas of the book include not just the actual structural process through which decisions are reached but the values and beliefs of the decision makers as they reach their decisions. The beliefs are born from values, learned through the socialization process, allowing decision makers to include or exclude policy choices that will be included in the final decision becoming fundamental parts of the overall decisional structure.

RACIAL INTENT

The discussion of the policy process notwithstanding, another focus of this chapter is to uncover the nexus between "racial purpose or intent" and "disparate effect." The relationship between the legal concepts of "racial purpose or intent" and "racial shields" is important to understand in the context of this discussion because it lies at the heart of the difficulty in attempting to prove that a racially discriminatory act has occurred. Racial shields, which will be defined shortly, are designed and constructed to hide intentional racially discriminatory actions resulting in the disparate effects of public policy on a social group covered by the Voting Rights Act or the Civil Rights Acts. However, it is important to understand the nexus between the two concepts because they are the central focus of every law suit claiming racial discrimination not just in the area of voting rights. In the public policy process, legislating for example, overt racial intentions of decision makers are concealed by the legislative and parliamentary processes of the state assembly. The consequent policy, presented in language that is racially neutral, is structured in such a manner as to result in disparate effects or treatment of a covered group. When the Texas state assembly designed the congressional and state house redistricting maps in 2011, they diluted the voting strength of Latinos in several congressional and house districts. The intention to racially gerrymander led directly to unequal effects. Thus, the linkage between "intent" and "effect," then, is important to understand because the two concepts are "two sides of the same coin," they are both facets of the same concept. One cannot have unequal effects without the intention to create them. The courts in recent rulings only wish to look at effects and refuse to look at racial intent. Why this is the case is unclear? Nevertheless, intent and effect have been divided into two concepts by the legal establishment. Although some will argue that the unequal effects are unintended consequences of an unbiased decision, a phenomenon such as this can still be controlled through conscious effort by the decision makers. All that is necessary is a complete and thorough consideration of all variables and all possible scenarios of outcomes that might result from a decision. The unintended consequence(s) can be easily identified if caught early enough when building the redistricting methodology or when evaluating outcomes prior to implementation. Normally, before implementation of any policy, decision makers perform tests or experiments to determine what the outcomes will look like and can adjustment the policy prior to implementation. Unwilling to understand that unequal effects are byproducts of the decisional process, that can be controlled, infects the evidentiary rules in lawsuits where racial discrimination is alleged and during legislative bargaining in the national legislature when negotiating the reauthorization of Section 5 of the Voting Rights Act. The refusal to understand the linkage between "intent" and "effects" serves to maintain an evidentiary and legal separation between the two concepts. Isolating the two concepts presents evidentiary difficulties for plaintiffs because the courts have been vague as to whether one must produce evidence on both concepts or on only one.

The separation of "effect" and "intent" was established initially in *Bolden v. City of Mobile*, 446 U.S. 55 (1980), where the US Supreme Court held that disproportionate effects alone were insufficient to establish a claim of racial discrimination affecting voting. The evidence on disproportionate impact or effect needed to be substantiated with evidence of "intent" to discriminate. So, in a voting rights lawsuit a plaintiff had to show that the guilty jurisdiction had intended to discriminate against a "covered" group through changing parts or all its election structures besides providing evidence of racial effect. The thinking behind the court's decision, essentially, was that other variables might explain why there may be disparate effects in some of the socioeconomic-status variables presented in support of the petition to the courts. In the end, Chief Justice Warren Burger rejected the Fifteenth Amendment claims concluding that "action by a State that is racially neutral on its face violates the Fifteenth Amendment only if motivated by a discriminatory purpose."[12]

The national legislature has written the Voting Rights Act so that evidence only needs to be proffered for one of the concepts to prove a law unconstitutional. More recently, however, some courts are beginning to edge their way toward a time when evidence on both concepts was required for plaintiffs to prevail.[13] This is accomplished because the courts are willing to rule on the effects standard but then make a statement to the effect that they will not rule on the intent standard. Thus, the courts in their unwillingness to address the intent standard are creating a situation where they are unknowingly creating a separate standard. Providing evidence for both standards is both time-consuming and expensive. The standards for disparate effect are not difficult to prove in that one only needs to provide empirical evidence that the policy has a dilutive effect on minority communities by demonstrating unequal effects. This evidence is provided using standard statistical analyses of racially contested elections or other implemented policies within jurisdictions having large concentrations of covered populations.[14] The proof lies in demonstrating that covered groups, such as Latinos or African Americans, vote differently and prefer different candidates than do white or Anglo voters, neighborhoods, or racially segregated or there are large racial disparities among incarcerated populations and so forth. Additionally, evidence must be brought forth indicating that white voters "usually" vote as a block preventing Latinos from electing their candidate of choice and they do not "crossover" and vote for Latino candidates allowing Latinos to prevail in elections normally. In other policy areas all one needs to demonstrate is that minority populations live very differently than White populations by demonstrating differences in educational, income, occupational, residential, and public health areas, for instance. Generally, plaintiffs must present evidence of these disparate patterns existing throughout a substantial number of elections or over a long period of time.[15]

The "racial intent" standard is another issue altogether and the evidence, both qualitative and quantitative, is difficult to identify and gather.

Determining the evidence, together with its sufficiency, is a decision rendered vague by the courts. Nevertheless, almost all decisions where evidence of racial intent is submitted and discussed are guided by the variables identified in *Arlington Heights*[16] as well as the "Senate Factors" set forth in *Gingles*.[17] In *Arlington Heights* the Supreme Court identified eleven variables, including one *et alia* that might be used to prove racial intent. The variables overlap in some cases, are not clear in others, and the court gives no guidance as to what evidentiary threshold is preferred. The court appeared to say that you didn't have to prove all of them but not exactly how many. As a result, petitioners are left guessing as to the exact types and amounts of evidence required under the Court's standard while the expert hired to gather the data is left to construct the data parameters herself. In *Gingles*, the Supreme Court identified seven factors that include some of the variables identified in *Arlington Heights*.

Diverging for a moment, the *Arlington Heights* variables were included in the decision as important evidentiary standards that had to be met if the petitioners charged racial discrimination. The Court ruled that the plaintiffs first had to prove that the injured party incurred a legal injury because of the decision (effect standard) but the plaintiffs also had to provide evidence that the defendants had acted with racial intent. The Court identified several variables, not all but most of which had to be met by the petitioners, to prove racial intent. The Court concluded that because the petitioners had not provided evidence for any of the variables then they could not rule in the plaintiffs' favor. As a result, they concluded that no racial intent had occurred.

The Supreme Court, in *Arlington Heights*, ruled that the effect standard was only the starting point of the inquiry besides providing evidence of racial effect or disparate treatment the plaintiffs needed to provide "direct" or "indirect" evidence that the governing body had acted with racial intent. "Direct" evidence is difficult to uncover because sometimes it includes verbal communications of racial intent which no one is willing to provide or written documents showing that certain decision makers intended to discriminate against a covered group this is, in most cases, difficult to uncover. On occasion, direct evidence is behind closed doors conversations with no written record thus impossible to obtain unless the individuals involved are subpoenaed and then they may even deny any such conversation occurred. So, a petitioner is left relying on "indirect" evidence such as a clear pattern of discrimination that is unexplainable on grounds other than race, from the effect of the state action even when the governing legislation appears neutral on its face.[18] However, as noted earlier, the Court made it clear that impact alone is not determinative, and the Court must look to other evidence.

The Supreme Court continued with its observations noting that the historical background of the decision is one evidentiary source, particularly if it reveals a series of official actions taken for invidious purposes.[19] The next variable is specific to the sequence of events leading up to the challenged decision. Essentially, did the jurisdiction in question deviate from its normal decision-making process in reaching its decision?[20] Departures from the normal procedural sequence also might afford evidence that improper purposes are playing a role. Substantive departures, too, may be relevant, particularly if the factors usually considered important by the decision maker strongly favor a decision contrary to the one reached. The legislative or administrative history may be highly relevant, especially where there are contemporary statements by members of the decision-making body, minutes of its meetings, or reports indicating that a departure from legislative or bureaucratic norms and procedures resulted in discrimination. In some extraordinary instances, the legislative or elected members might be called to the stand at trial to testify concerning the purpose of the official action, although even then such testimony frequently will be barred by privilege.[21] Generally, courts are reluctant to cross the divide between branches so are hesitant to require elected officials to testify. Some legislators may offer to testify but they are normally not called. This "courtesy" also acts as a shield protecting elected officials who may have acted inappropriately or illegally. If an ethics violation is found to have occurred by an elected official, they will either be subject to censure by their body or the case may be referred to the local district attorney for investigation.

Attorneys and jurists may see keeping intent and effect separate as appropriate from a legal perspective because it makes for a clear and easily understandable explanation. However, keeping the two concepts separate becomes a methodological nightmare for plaintiffs. Maintaining the separation of the two concepts is the result of attorneys compromising and judges adjudicating in the course of trials where a test of discriminatory intent is applied; this was the case in the *Arlington Heights* decision. However, the Court in *Arlington Heights* created a methodological quagmire for litigation experts and plaintiffs and their attorneys when they did so.[22] Separating the two concepts is designed to make it still more difficult for plaintiffs to argue their claim and easier for the defendant, the institution, or person accused of discrimination, to defend themselves, another example of how a racial shield functions. Insinuating that the unequal effects were caused by some variable(s) other than a racial intention masks the reality of racial intent thus the insinuation shields the truth under the cover of legal reasoning. Finally, social convention dictates that those being accused of discrimination, particularly if they hold an official governmental position, should not openly or publicly be accused of being racists. Generally, a plaintiff bringing a lawsuit claiming racial discrimination must charge someone or some institution with being racist in the way in which they wrote or implemented a specific policy. Nevertheless, polite convention requires that plaintiffs, usually representing a racial minority group, indistinguishable to the decision makers from the lower classes of society, dare not be rude by calling someone of higher social status, such as the governor, president, or some ruling institution such as the state government or legislature, racist. Challenges by individuals from a lower social strata are perceived as attacks and threats to the social institutions governing liberal democracy and the cultural status quo. Or, sometimes poor people are accused of perceiving discrimination where there really is not any and being overly defensive. In order to protect the social status quo and make it more difficult for the voices of discriminated individuals to be heard the concepts of racial intent and disparate effect must be held as separate concepts. The courts, then, create a situation where simply proving that one has been treated unequally by the state or some individual is insufficient, one must also prove that the defendant acted with intent to discriminate. In other words, plaintiffs must show that they are not just being treated unequally but must demonstrate that the discriminators acted with explicit intention to discriminate against the offended group, that the defendants are intentionally treating plaintiffs unequally. The courts have concluded that disparate effect can be the result of a decisional system functioning normally and the inequality is not intentional but simply as an unintended consequence of a normally functioning deliberative process. As a result, the political actors involved in propagating the policy that holds "racial purpose or intent" and "disparate effect" as separate concepts do so because they are following established precedent and social convention.

The Conceptual Problem

From a conceptual perspective the justice who composed the *Arlington Heights* standard did so unknowingly in order to "shield" the notion that some public policy decisions can be structurally discriminatory.[23] What Justice Thurgood Marshall, in an earlier opinion *Washington v. Davis*,[24] recognized that the actual structure of a law could produce disparate effects and so it was not necessarily required to seek whether decision makers had acted with racial intent. Rather than accuse the justice of consciously creating a barrier to the proof of discrimination, the justice, given the benefit of the doubt, may simply have been trying to be judicious and fair in setting forth the eleven variable standard that has come to be known as *The Arlington Heights Factors*. Essentially, the justice, in this case Lewis Powell who was a former corporate attorney, split one concept and created two. Racial intent or purposeful discrimination and disparate effect, I argue, are substantively two sides of the same concept. One cannot have one without the other.

When anyone, group of persons or an institution or group of institutions, wish to create a policy they do so because they are trying to accomplish a specific goal or objective. The goal or objective, in a discriminatory situation, may not appear to be biased but is structured in such a way to produce disparate effects. Discrimination, whether racial or not, is an essential element of any decision made by humans. When making decisions one is choosing among various options or one that will allow one to achieve a desired end, goal, or objective. Sorting through the various choices on the way to designing the policy one discards some options at various stages of the decisional process. Some choices are discarded due to various constraints placed on the process that are political, social, or fiscal in nature. Other choices are discarded because they are not acceptable choices within the realm of the decision makers' ideological orientation. Choices excluded by one's ideological orientation may not necessarily be excluded consciously but may have been excluded in the consciousness of the decision makers through the regular socialization process they were exposed to throughout their lifetime as mentioned earlier and are unconsciously or subconsciously excluded. Another possible explanation is that excluded choices during the normal functioning of a decisional process may have been constructed with the idea that they would necessarily have disparate effects on certain populations without an explicit statement. These may be excluded because they appear explicitly biased, they would not be acceptable to all the decision makers. Consequently, these would be discarded in order to give the impression, mystify, the process as democratic and not prejudicial. Nevertheless, decisional structures are designed to create policy a certain way, to give birth to policies with very specific goals or objectives and any disparate effect is a known byproduct of the process and can be avoided if the decision makers wish to. The argument in this chapter, however, is that the two concepts are not separate concepts but two facets of the same concept. The law has deemed to conceptually split one concept into two. Why they chose to do this without speaking to the authors of *Arlington Heights* is not clear. Regardless, the splitting makes it difficult for individuals or groups claiming discrimination to prove a claim and, therefore, act as a racial shield constructed to protect discriminatory policies. In other words, the Court intentionally made it more difficult to bring a racial discrimination claim because of the evidentiary standards they created. The Court, either intentionally or unknowingly, constructed a racial shield to protect racially discriminatory actions from being uncovered.

Although the two concepts in question appear completely different from each other, it is my contention that both concepts are actually "two sides of the same coin." Without intent one cannot have an effect and without an effect one cannot have intent. If one evaluates both from a conceptual perspective, then one can reach a position that lends clarity to the entire discussion. If one considers that both are different facets of the same concept then, if the courts accept this argument, the evidentiary standards required to be met in a racial discrimination petition are clearer and not too difficult to meet. It appears that conceptually we can see three options of how to view the "intent" versus "effect" conundrum. One argument is that for an effective legal petition to be presented by the aggrieved party, usually the plaintiffs, one must present evidence of both an individual or institutional intent to discriminate as well as evidence of a disparate effect of that discrimination. Another argument is that evidence of only one concept is required; still, another argument is that one must have evidence of intent as opposed to effect. However, if the Court were to accept the notion that "intent" and "effect" are two facets of the same concept then, as Justice Marshall noted, only disparate effect evidence would be enough to prove discrimination had occurred. Or, perhaps the Court is like the prisoner in Plato's Cave who can only see images rather than reality because they are chained down by their legal and social perceptions and thinking at the bottom of their judicial cave. To understand Justice Marshall's observation the Court needs to break those chains allowing them to comprehend the totality of racial discrimination.

A WORD CONCERNING RACIAL SHIELDS

A racial shield can be conceived as an opaque veil, seemingly diaphanous, covering the machinations of a policy process. Although this may appear contradictory, the veil appears to be somewhat translucent, but this is deceptive because the veil really hides a dark truth. The veil is set in place, mystifying the actual, real, planning, maneuvering, intrigue surrounding the policy process. This mystification I have labelled a "racial shield" because it hides the racial intent and thinking behind some process or substance of a given policy. The shield itself is race neutral. In other words, the process is hidden by the language and vocabulary describing the process and structures. The policy or decisional language is race neutral with adjectives or descriptors suggesting that a democratically acceptable process has occurred. The process appears transparent, but the diaphanous veil hides an invidious process resulting in discriminatory outcomes. Thus, the connotation that the process is both opaque, while being diaphanous simultaneously, and functioning in an objective manner producing policy that will serve the entire community equitably. The overt language describing the process is objective-appearing, however, the activity, the reality of the legislators' or decision makers' intentions and subsequent actions, are quite the opposite. Sometimes words such as "equality," "equity," "efficiency," "best practices," and so forth are used to cover or shield the true intent and the language leaves the impression that they are acting on behalf of the entire community. In fact, the legislators or decision makers are acting in their own or the self-interests of others that remain hidden from public view and scrutiny. Covering this process with the diaphanous veil of democratic principles together with processes functioning within democratic institutions acts as the racial shield referred to earlier in this discussion.

Two examples of this can be found during the 2011 congressional redistricting process in Texas where the state legislature was involved in the normal and usual redrawing of lines delineating all thirty-six districts. The other was the passage of Senate Bill 14, the voter ID bill which occurred during the same legislative session. On the surface all appeared to be going as normal as any redistricting process could be going. Countless groups lobbied various members of the legislature and redistricting committees offered their versions of statewide redistricting plans. Other groups wanted to ensure that the legislature created districts that would not divide "communities of interest" whether they be at the neighborhood, city, or county levels. The deliberative process, replete with public and legislative hearings and debate gave the appearance and impression that an open and fair decisional process was functioning. What the various petitioners did not see, not even the media, was that a small group of individuals who oversaw the actual drawing were colluding to ensure that precincts where Latino voters played prominent electoral roles or were a substantial part of the population were manipulated. This insured that the redesigned congressional districts would elect Republican candidates while making certain representative districts had majority Hispanic populations.[25] These individuals ignored all public pleadings and petitions and pursued a redistricting strategy that would elect only Republican candidates while making the process appear democratic and objective. These decision makers wished to make the voters feel like they had elected the Republican candidate when, in effect, the district was drawn giving the Republican candidate an advantage that was not easily overcome. Essentially, the districts were designed to have a majority Latino voting age population but the turnout levels of Latinos in the precincts chosen for inclusion in the new districts were so low that the Anglo, heavily Republican minority of voters, would and did outvote Latinos. This would result in the Republican preferred candidate being elected over that of the Latino voters. This is a classic example of what the federal courts have labelled as "vote dilution" or diluting the potential voting strength of Latino voters. Exacerbating the voting patterns in these "racially gerrymandered" districts was the fact that there were not enough Anglo voters who sided with Latino voters and assist in electing a Latino preferred candidate. In voting rights jargon this latter situation is an indication of an intense level of "racial polarization" existing among the electorate in this newly drawn district. In other words, Anglo voters cast their ballots overwhelmingly for Anglo voters while, in the same election, Latino voters vote overwhelmingly for the candidate of their choice, this choice may be of any racial or ethnic group. This dichotomous voting is particularly deleterious to Latino voters when the population is such that the Anglo voting bloc submerges or overcomes the Latino vote and creates a condition where Latinos rarely have a chance to elect a candidate of their choice.[26] This submergence is legally labelled as "diluting" the Latino vote. The dilution occurs because the Anglo majority voting population votes almost exclusively for white or Anglo candidates. At the same time enough white voters do not "crossover" and vote for Latino candidates. This not only reflects racial polarization but also demonstrates that Latinos cannot garner enough support within the Anglo community to have an electoral chance to elect a candidate of their choice. Racial polarization is the manifestation of years, decades or centuries of racial tensions that have existed, and still do in many communities, between Anglos and Latinos. This tension cannot be relieved until racism and the accompanying perceptions of racial stereotypes are eliminated from society generally. This can only be achieved through a resocialization of the younger generations or the reeducation of older generations who may be open to understanding the unique and positive differences between people of different cultures.

The intention to manipulate the Latino population by Republican operatives was clear as was their rationale. This was revealed in internal legislative memos that were used as evidence of "racial intent" during the redistricting trials to insure the election or reelection of Republicans to the US Congress or state senate or house seats. The operatives pointed out in some of the memos that Latinos would not vote for Republican candidates anyway so why not manipulate them to the advantage of GOP candidates. The State of Texas argued that this was simply partisan gerrymandering, however, making partisan gerrymandering viable was the manipulation of Latino voters. Essentially, Republicans could not partisan gerrymander without diluting the Latino vote. Without eliminating high participating Latino voting precincts from the congressional district and substituting them with low-participation Latino precincts, the racial gerrymander would not have worked in favor of the Republican Party candidate. Thus, the partisan nature of the gerrymander could not have been accomplished without the racial gerrymander.

The passage of Senate Bill 14 was debated and passed without a single reference to race, Hispanics or Latinos. Even when questioned by Latino members of the legislature during floor debate if the voter ID bill would prove deleterious to Latino voters the sponsors simply responded by stating that they "had not been so informed" and then tabled the discussion. In another instance responding to a Latino legislator's query as to whether their actions that day violated any federal law or the provisions of the Voting Rights Act the sponsor responded by stating that it was not their role as legislators to determine the legality of any bill, that role belonged solely to the Supreme

Court.[27] Several months after passage of the Voter ID Bill a three-judge panel of the Federal District Court sitting in Washington, DC, did indeed rule on Senate Bill 14's legality finding it in violation of Section 5 of the Voting Rights Act. The court ruled that the types of identification cards required by the law weighed against young, low-income, and the aged populations thus the law was discriminatory by design. The court did not rule on the racial intent issue even though extensive evidence on this was brought forward by the plaintiffs.

This decision, however, was negated by the *Shelby County*[28] decision that rendered the enforcement provisions in Sec. 4(b) of the Voting Rights Act outdated and therefore unconstitutional. Although the district courts hearing the redistricting and voter ID lawsuit failed to rule on the racial intent behind both laws, they did find them injurious to the political interests of Latinos and ordered the State of Texas to redraw and rewrite both laws. Essentially, the court ignored racial intent and reached their decision solely on the effect standard. Still, the two concepts remained as two singularly separate concepts and were treated as such by the courts. As of this writing both laws are still being debated between the state, various federal judicial panels, and the plaintiffs with no resolution in sight because the plaintiffs have asked the courts to rule that Texas acted with racial intent in both cases. If the court rules in favor of the plaintiffs, opining that racial intent was the reason behind the legislation, then Texas will be placed under Section 5 scrutiny until it can prove that it has mended its ways of discriminating against Latinos, as well as African Americans, in the areas of election law covered by the Voting Rights Act.

The racial shields in both cases proved to be the decisional processes that hid the racial intent behind both laws. The processes were not manipulated or structured to give one group an advantage over the other. The processes were the normal legislative machinations through which a bill must travel in order to become law. The process entails every step detailed in a Texas high school government textbook. What the textbook does not include are the behind the scenes deal making, collusion, and racism that occur surrounding the passage of some bills. The average citizen is completely unaware of how intensely the contestation for political power is among politicians and the extents they will go to win and keep political power. The racial gerrymandering that occurs in Texas is basically political operatives manipulating the system to ensure that the jurisdictions, districts they draw or redraw will give their political party an advantage over the other. It is racial gerrymandering because Latinos are victimized in the process because their populations are divided or stuffed into districts in order to give one political party a political advantage or head start over the other. However, in the racial gerrymandering case the veil was ripped away from racial intent by the appearance of the memo. In the case of the voter ID case, the racial shield proved to be the way in which the law was argued in the state legislature without a hint of racial language or intent. Although a case could be made that the conscious intent to avoid discussing race was evidence of racial intent, the legislature avoided all attempts to make them face the possibility that they were acting with racial intent. The Voter ID Law remains racially neutral except for the specification of which identification cards were acceptable and then one could only demonstrate that some groups had easier access to various cards thus the law itself was discriminatory.

CLEAVING THE RACIAL SHIELD

Cleaving the racial shield and revealing the racially infused decisional processes of the matrix state requires solutions at varying levels and most likely years, if not decades, of toil. Immediately, it behooves legislatures at all levels of government to admit that racial thinking lies beneath how decisions in certain policy areas are formed. With this in mind, the legislatures must then consciously compose laws that are non-racial and truly objective. This process would also require not allowing interest groups that are racially motivated and a desire to discriminate against protected groups to participate in the process. So, for instance not allowing FAIR to have input into the writing of immigration laws or not allowing the participation of partisan politicos from participating in the redistricting process and not allowing the National Rifle Association or gun manufacturing interests from being present at the decisional table when gun control legislation is being considered.

On a more complex level cleaving the racial shield requires a society to restructure its socialization process insuring that any racial thinking is removed from vocabulary, school curricula, from the media, social communications software, and so forth. Laws prohibiting the use of hurtful racist language must be passed and enforced forcefully. Finally, laws punishing not just those using racist language but the political and private decision makers who perpetuate the use of racism to promote their interests.

Although these proscriptions appear to violate some of America's fundamental laws such as the First and Fourteenth Amendments to the US Constitution for example, justification on grounds that racist behavior and language are doing more harm to the victims than any punishment would do to individual perpetrators. One is weighing, much like Lady Justice does, the harm done to millions of persons versus the punishment of a few. The punishment of the few fundamentally protects the overall welfare and healthy future of American society and the continued existence of the state matrix.

NOTES

1. Flores, *Evolution of the Liberal Democratic State* (2007) and *Latinos and the Voting Rights Act* (2017).
2. President Trump speech, August 3, 2017, Huntington Beach, VA.
3. Maureen A. Craig and Jennifer A. Richeson, "More Diverse Yet Less Tolerant? How the Increasingly Diverse Racial Landscape Affects White Americans' Racial Attitudes," *Personality and Social Psychology Bulletin* Vol. 40, Issue 6 (March 13, 2014).
4. John Gramlich, "7 Facts About Guns in the U.S.," *Pew Research Center*, December 7, 2018.
5. Faegin, *The White Racial Frame: Centuries of Racial Framing and Counter-Framing* (New York: Routledge, 2013).
6. Diangelo, *White Fragility*, p. 34.
7. Jesse Eisinger, "Why Only One Top Banker Went to Jail for the Financial Crisis," *New Times Magazine*, April 30, 2014.
8. Ibid.
9. 457 U.S. 202, 216 (1982).
10. Senate Bill 5, 2017. State of Texas.
11. Anna M. Tinsley and Dianna Boyd, "Four Women in 'Voter Fraud Ring' Arrested. They Targeted Seniors on City's North Side," *Fort Worth Star-Telegram*, October 12, 2018, updated October 24, 2018.
12. 446 US 62.
13. Ibid @ 66-68.
14. A covered population according the Voting Rights Act of 1965 and its amendments such as African Americans, Latinos, Asian, Pacific Islanders, and so forth.
15. *Thornburg v. Gingles*, 478 U.S. 30 (1986).
16. *Village of Arlington Heights v. Metropolitan Housing Development Corp.*, 429 US 252 (1977).
17. Ibid.
18. *Yick Wo v. Hopkins*, 118 U. S. 356 (1886); *Guinn v. United States*, 238 U. S. 347 (1915); *Lane v. Wilson*, 307 U. S. 268 (1939); *Gomillion v. Lightfoot*, 364 U. S. 339 (1960).
19. *Lane v. Wilson*, supra; *Griffin v. School Board*, 377 U. S. 218 (1964); *Davis v. Schnell*, 81 F.Supp. 872 (SD Ala.), aff'd per curiam, 336 U.S. 933 (1949); cf. *Keyes v. School Dist. No. 1, Denver Colo. supra* at 413 U. S. 207.
20. *Reitman v. Mulkey*, 387 U. S. 369, 387 U. S. 373-376 (1967); *Grosjean v. American Press Co.*, 297 U. S. 233, 297 U. S. 250 (1936).
21. *Tenney v. Brandhove*, 341 U. S. 367 (1951); *United States v. Nixon*, 418 U. S. 683, 418 U. S. 705 (1974); 8 J. Wigmore, Evidence § 2371 (McNaughton rev. ed.1961).
22. I identified each of the variables and suggested the types of data required to meet the evidentiary standards in *Arlington Heights* in *Latinos and the Voting Rights Act: The Search for Racial Purpose* (New York: Lexington Press, 2015).

23. This argument was made by Justice Thurgood Marshall in his famous *Mobile v. Bolden* decent. He pointed out that the court failed to consider that a decision could be structurally discriminatory. 446 U.S. 55, 83-85.
24. 426 U.S. 248.
25. Memo from Opiela to Interiano.
26. An "opportunity to elect a candidate of choice" originally appears in *Gingles v. Thornburg*, 478 US 30 (1986).
27. House Journal, March 23, 2011.
28. *Shelby County v. Holder*, 570 U.S. 2 (2013).

Chapter 5

Racial Intent Revisited and Some Concluding Thoughts

The previous chapters of this volume have presented the definition of racism, how racist ideas or racial thinking have become imbedded in the way we think about the world and how the public policy process is influenced by racial thinking. Another theme of this volume is to allow us to rethink the way in which the courts interpret "racial intent" in cases involving racial discrimination. My concern is that the Court does not understand what racism is and how it is manifested today or, at least it appears they do not, in some of their most noted decisions. For instance, the Court's rulings, particularly in *Shelby County*, make it abundantly clear that the Court is either unwilling or unable to recognize what contemporary racism looks like and that it even exists.

In the *Shelby* ruling the Court ruled Section 4(b) of the 1965 Voting Rights Act unconstitutional because it stated 4(b) was based on outdated information. Essentially, 4(b) was the section of the Voting Rights Act that set forth the requirements that "triggered" coverage under the preclearance provisions of Section 5. Before the *Shelby County* ruling, if a jurisdiction met any of the specifications set forth in Section 4(b), such as whether a jurisdiction had used any devices to inhibit the right to vote, then that jurisdiction would have to preclear any changes to their election system in the future, or until they could prove to the Department of Justice or of a US District Court in Washington, DC, that they were no longer utilizing the offending device.

The first four chapters of this book have attempted to present racism for what it is and has become. Although, substantively, racism is a constant and its definition will remain unchanged, the discriminatory methods and racist language have changed with the times. Where two hundred years ago the language was clear, distasteful, hurtful, and intentional today it is opaque, distasteful, hurtful, and intentional; where racist laws once were clearly stated they are not today. The effects of the racist laws remain the same resulting in uneven effects for various racial and ethnic groups. The Court, however, ruled that only those laws and languages that were overt and used in recent historical periods count toward the proof of discriminatory behavior. The courts ruled that no discrimination exists, lacking explicitly racist laws or language saying that the laws were composed with the explicit intent to create uneven outcomes. Even if the outcomes or effects of the laws fall unevenly upon different racial groups the Court says that there is no discrimination because there was or is no explicit intent.

This position by the Court belies the depth of racism and racist intent. This is particularly relevant in this day because of the varied and inconsistent history the courts have created in the treatment of this concept. A review of the Court's treatment of racial intent[1] has demonstrated how the Court has continuously changed their position on this notion. Essentially, the courts have yet to develop a final legal definition of racial intent or the effects of that intent. At several times throughout the courts' struggles at understanding racial intent it has become clear that they were not sure as to whether one should simply look at "intent" separate from "effect"; whether the two concepts were inextricably bound together; or, whether the two were so different from each other that one had no other choice but to treat them differently. This is important at the present time because the courts are on the verge of addressing some decisions in this area of the law that will have far ranging implications for public access in the United States. Additionally, the 116th Congress has indicated that they intend rewriting the Voting Rights Act during the 2019–2020 session. It is also equally important, however, that a definitive treatment of "racial intent" be presented that can assist the courts in reaching more accurate and meaningful decisions. A more in-depth discussion of this quandary forms an important part of this final chapter.

Most concluding chapters present conclusions, observations, questions for additional research, and so forth. This one, however, will have all of that as well as speak to some additional thoughts that arose as I was composing the other parts of this volume. Some of these thoughts are just that, thoughts, while others, hopefully, present some other thinker with ideas for future work in this area. I do believe there will be additional work in that race and racism have come to define a great deal of our social interactions in America today and will do so into the future. Without a doubt America is changing demographically. At one point it was pictured as "small-town, white and average" as depicted in many Norman Rockwell paintings. However, immigration from all over the world over the last fifty years has created an America that speaks many different languages besides English and is composed of people from countries far and wide. The new America is one where the old America must learn to accommodate and incorporate the new or else America will cease to exist. At the heart of this change must be deeper understandings of race and of the different people who make up the new America.

One of these new ideas I wish to put forth requiring additional research beyond the parameters of this book is that I feel that issues such as the racism permeating the public policy processes of the United States locally or across states are really manifestations of the same problems internationally. The racism I speak of in this volume is a symptom of even greater and larger problems globally. Although racism in voting rights, immigration and gun control policies are seen by Americans as local and national issues they are really much larger than that. For instance, corrupt voting systems abound throughout the world manipulated by politicians allowing them to maintain control of the state levers of power. These are not unique to third-world countries or little "banana republics" but are common in the United States where state legislatures and the national government contrive to prevent people from becoming eligible to vote or preventing them from voting altogether. One can argue that the American electoral system is designed to discourage people from participating rather than encouraging greater turnout. This is certainly the case in the State of Georgia where during the recent 2018 mid-term elections the secretary of state purged more than 340,000 voters from the roles stating they had moved when, in fact, research by the American Civil Liberties Union proved that not one of the purged individuals had changed their address. The struggles over immigration policies we see in the news every day in the United States are not unique to us but are a global phenomenon and present problems for all countries of Europe, Asia, and the Americas. Finally, the lack of gun control laws is a foil that allows gun manufacturers to sell their products based on the fear of whites and others that people of color will invade their properties and take their land and status.

Although this may, at first glance, appear as a bit of a conceptual leap requiring a great deal of faith (my apologies to Heidegger) it does have a theoretical foundation in the manner in which I see the interconnected layers of the global state matrix. What? This is another thought that came to mind as I was working my way through this volume. The arguments I presented earlier concerning the state matrix only spoke of the matrix as including the local, state (provincial), and national levels of government and of three policy areas. However, the increasing global nature of the economy and the subsequent effects of local activities on global weather and subsequent population phenomenon have made it clear that what happens locally politically, may have long lasting global implications. In turn these implications may go beyond the ability of any one matrix state to solve and may place so many external tensions on a state matrix that they will engender major changes within those state matrices. In other words, local problems can cascade upward through all levels of a matrix and cause tensions beyond the nation-state. At the same time those tensions may cascade back down to the local levels, compounding already complex problems for the local state. A situation such as this is most evident in the realm of natural disasters, which know no boundaries, or wide-spread famine or environmental disasters. However, this interconnectedness can also be found in the realm of civil rights. Local discrimination problems in the Southeastern regions of the United States caused a reaction globally that it helped generate support for the passage of the Civil Rights Acts of 1965. This, in turn, resulted in much needed election, housing, and public accommodations reforms throughout the South. At the same time the ethos of the American civil rights movement spread to other countries such as South Africa, the People's Republic of China, and Eastern Europe driving the democracy movements in those countries. As these brief examples demonstrate, each of these issues or problems could begin at the local level and eventually spread to the national and global levels. At the same time global and national responses to the problems at the local level might add other difficulties on the local state as outside assistance and governance play more important roles at the local levels as well as oversight of the implementation of needed reforms.

Without further digression, the chapter will conclude with some thoughts concerning the theory of the state in relationship to how the state matrix achieves sophisticated levels of interconnectivity. Without interconnectivity the state cannot hold together whether on a global or national level. This is currently being threatened by the global struggles over race that dominate global politics today and will continue to dominate them well into the future.

RACE AND RACISM AS ARTIFICIAL CONSTRUCTS

We also began this discussion, in the first chapter, with the definition of racism as a theoretical construct designed on false premises and propagated through the normal and natural socialization processes that we all undergo. This construct was created by human beings, was grounded in non-scientifically based opinions about people of different colors. These perceptions and opinions eventually were found throughout the world as Western civilization expanded and exploited the world's resources through the use of slave labor. Racism was and is an infection of the mind allowing individuals to justify, to themselves and the greater world, their unequal treatment of individuals unlike themselves. This was true as justifications for slavery were sought during the sixteenth and seventeenth centuries. The justifications for the mistreatment of those deemed lesser were based on the notion that lesser individuals were born to serve those of higher social orders. As a result, it was normal to exploit the lesser people to the advantage of those on the higher rungs of the racial ladder. Simply, it was necessary to the maintenance of the existing social order. Consequently, other racial barriers were established throughout history insuring that those of the lower social orders remained in their places and continued to serve those of the higher social orders. Some of these barriers were the withholding of education, health care, proper nourishment, adequate housing, and oppressive working conditions.

Returning to our original discussion, that of the artificiality of race, we discovered that the concept of race and the hierarchical belief in the superiority of some races over others was a social construct designed and propagated by European aristocrats to justify the existence of African slavery that was the backbone of both European and early American wealth. The excuses that were used to propagate the racial superiority of European Whites was that the Africans were not much more than primitive savages that, through the imposition of slavery, could be eventually Christianized. The Christianization process would occur as the Africans labored under their slaver taskmasters. The racial constructs were given birth by aristocrats such as de Gobineau who perceived slavery as good for all, the slaves would benefit through their Christian conversion and the aristocrats would economically prosper from the labor of the slaves. It was simply a "win-win" situation in his perception. Of course, no one asked the opinions of the slaves or the poor and working classes who worked alongside the slaves, many of whom were indentured and worked to pay off their debts to the aristocrats.

Nevertheless, the concept of racism was developed to understand the differences between what were perceived as racial groups. Although the discipline of anthropology was not even in its nascent form and would not be born until the late nineteenth and early twentieth centuries, the perceptions of aristocratic opinions and those having access to the media of the day propagated their opinions of the differences between racial groups that laid the foundation for future racial discriminatory attitudes and actions. White racial thinkers attributed all inventions and creations in the sciences and mathematics to Europeans because that is all they knew. Yet to be discovered were the advances in medicine, the general sciences, astronomy, and mathematics of the ancient Greeks, Americans (Mayans for instance), Egyptians, Chinese, Africans, Arabians, and so forth. These discoveries would not be known until the late nineteenth and the entirety of the twentieth centuries and are still being uncovered through modern anthropological research. I'm not sure what the European aristocrats would have thought or done or how it would have affected their perceptions of race if they had discovered that some of the scientific and mathematical work being conducted in these "savage and romantic" societies surpassed some of the work that the Europeans were conducting in the same disciplines.

Still, the Europeans, based on their own primitive beliefs, constructed the hierarchy of races placing themselves at the apex and relegating all others to rungs lower on the hierarchical ladder. The only basis for placing any "racial" group on a particular level was their color. The closer to "white" one was the higher up the racial ladder one found themselves. In more contemporary times one finds persons of color accepted by whites who believe in this type of construct. This allows the person of color to believe like a white racist and is accepted by the whites as one of their own but not quite as good because of their different color. This manner of contemporaneous thinking is subsumed under the ideological construct of "conservatism." Those persons of color who deny the superiority of whites are perceived today as "trouble makers, revolutionaries" and threats to the social, political, and economic status quo. Essentially, differing views abound among various groups of people. Some believe in the social hierarchical theory, others do not, some believe that all are equal, and that skin color is a biological difference and nothing else. Still, there is a belief among enough "whites" that people of color are biologically inferior and not capable of performing intellectually at the same level or higher levels than whites. A sufficiently large enough number of white people believe in their superiority over people of color that racial discrimination is very much a difficult problem to overcome in contemporary society.

These thoughts and premises of racism were and still are passed down through the generations where they are reinforced with contemporary phobias about the loss of sociopolitical place by white people. The loss of political place forebodes the loss of social and economic place for racist thinkers. In other words, they fear not just losing control of political power but also the possibilities that they will also lose economic and social standing within their respective communities. This fear also extends to the possibility that the persons that have been subordinated for generations will seek either reparations, may retaliate in some manner, or attempt to place white people in a subordinate social position. Obviously, there are exceptions, not all white persons are racists and not all people of color believe they are subordinate to whites. Nevertheless, there is a sufficient number of white persons in American society that fear people of color and have a sense of their own self-superiority that they manage to support racist politicians and who, in turn, can be appealed to for their support. This sense of white superiority and attempting to deal with the loss of political place led to the creation of public policies that were designed with racial intent originally. As these policies became institutionalized and social mores changed, racist verbiage and language were removed from the laws. The laws themselves remained unchanged and passed through the years and decades as policies that, superficially, have no or little mention of race. The lack of overt racial appeals in the law or around passage of these laws results in the observation by many responsible for administering or adjudicating law that there has been no racial discrimination when the laws are implemented. Some jurists even go so far as stating that times have changed, and racism is no longer a problem in the United States. Even though victims can easily provide evidence that disparate effects have occurred when the laws are implemented, they run up against a wall because explicit racist or racial language is missing from the law rendering the law as non-racist or written without racial intent. Justice Thurgood Marshall in his dissent in the *Bolden* decision made this latter argument in his disagreement with the majority opinion.[2] He argued that racism can become institutionalized to the extent that a policy process by itself, having been created with the intention of racially disadvantaging a group of people, may provide discriminatory legislation. Essentially, that a decisional structure can be racist and result in discriminatory decisions without decision makers necessarily intending to do so.

One of the most significant controversies in the racial intent discussion is whether there is a relationship between racial intent and effect. In a now infamous Supreme Court decision, *Mobile v. Bolden*,[3] the Court ruled that without evidence of "invidious discrimination" unequal effects could be artifacts of other decisional variables. Although the Court in *Bolden* was attempting to be judicious and logical it rendered an ahistorical, superficial, and trivial opinion. In other words, the Court failed to take into account Justice Marshall's concerns in his *Washington v. Davis* dissent. Essentially, Marshall argued that a policy can be created making it appear racially neutral but that the policy's structure, once implemented, can lead to unequal outcomes. So, one must inquire into how and why the policy was structured in the manner in which it was, in order to determine whether or not there was discriminatory intent. Lacking this inquiry, we are left empty handed and left only to conclude that no discrimination occurred when, in fact it may have. Still, Marshall raised an important issue, one that lies at the heart of public policy theory. One does not construct, design, or compose a policy without determining what outcomes one wishes. If you wish a policy to produce equal outcomes, then you structure the policy so that the implementation will yield equal outcomes. If you wish outcomes that are unequal or to feature a specific outcome a certain way, then you structure the policy accordingly. As a result, any policy resulting in unequal outcomes was created to do just that, create unequal outcomes therefore is discriminatory by definition.

The belief of a racial hierarchy and the threat of the status quo from those people or groups residing on the lower racial levels of the hierarchy then, were, and are still controlled in various ways. In the early eras of the American republic control was exerted through various means, only allowing people of color certain levels of education or none, slavery, bondage labor, cheap contract labor, denial of the vote, holding political office, residential restrictions, the passage of anti-miscegenation laws, and the passage of immigration laws that minimized the entry of people not deemed white. Although many of these devices or laws have been stricken down over the last several hundred years by the Supreme Court or passage of laws by Congress, they still remain in the hearts and minds of many legislators because of the socialization processes they experienced in their lifetimes. As a result, many legislators in the state or national legislatures still believe they must pass laws to preserve, protect, and defend their culture, language, way of life, heritage, however they define their ontology.

The belief in racial inequality was the foundation for not just the maintenance of the system of slavery but also for the failure to provide educational, health, economic (jobs, benefits, housing, etc.), and nutritional support to people of color. The belief in racial superiority became the excuse for the creation of separate educational and public accommodation systems, segregated neighborhoods, occupations that were deemed appropriate for certain racial groups, and so forth. The racial hierarchical structure became the foundation for many of the racial stereotypical beliefs held by society today. Some beliefs crept their way into the political world and were the basis for creating barriers against voting, working in the public sector, holding elective office, and so forth. This resulted in the current situation in the United States where people of color lag behind whites in almost every socioeconomic category. In short, racial beliefs and the belief in racial hierarchies, artificial constructs, are at the heart of social, economic, and political inequality in the United States.

THE DECISIONAL PROCESS OF THE STATE AND INFUSION OF RACIST BELIEFS

The underlying theme of this work is that racial beliefs have become infused in the public policy process. The subsidiary questions include, Why is this the case? And, How did this happen? The answer to the first question is one that is at the heart of the role race plays in the political culture of the United States. Race is the central identifying variable of everyday social interactions at all levels and areas of American society. Most germane to this discussion is that race has found a prominent place within the public policy processes of the American political milieu. It formed the foundation of the creation of the three policies discussed in this volume as well as many other policies throughout the history of the American political state.

Public policies and their subsequent specific programs and laws are created to solve or address an issue important to the state. The decisional processes of the state are structured in such a manner to ensure that the policies or laws progress through a process insuring that the appropriate institutions bring forth their expertise assisting in the creation or construction of the laws. In this volume I only spoke to three areas of public policy that I hoped would serve as examples of my proposal. The three areas were chosen because they appear from the less obviously racial, the lack of gun control laws, to the most obvious, immigration laws with voting rights falling somewhere in between. The lack of gun control laws for instance were designed to allow free access to weapons for protection. In the beginning gun ownership was sanctioned by the government and was required but only of white males between the ages of 18 and 45, for protection against Indians and African slaves. One could seek an exception on religious grounds to this requirement. The Indians were fighting to reclaim the lands that had been taken from them and the Africans were trying to unleash the bonds of slavery, both logical concerns. The only defense as perceived by the national and local authorities was allowing white men to own guns if they could afford them. So, gun ownership was perceived as a barrier against a threat to their existence, culture, and attempts to grow a nation. This protection was against people of lower races who were seen as having no education, no Christian intentions, and brutal and savage ways of adjudicating disputes. These savages of color needed controlling and the only way was through reliance on fire arms.

In the Second Amendment to the Constitution there is a statement concerning a "well ordered militia" but this referred to local groups that were to be mustered to bolster a small standing army estimated to be no larger than 3,000 at the beginning of the republic. Americans of the late eighteenth century were wary of large-standing armies, such as the British Army that they had just defeated, so wrote the militia provision into the Second Amendment as a counter to the American regular army. The need for militias was superseded later with the creation of state national guards first in 1903 with the passage of the Dick Act and further formalized in1933 in the National Guard Mobilization Act.

The vague status of gun ownership was begun to be clarified by the "right-wing" members of the National Rifle Association when they took control of that organization in 1974. This leadership group began a campaign, culminating with the *Chicago* and *Heller* decisions in 2010 and 2008, respectively, where the Court held that gun ownership was a constitutionally protected right and that right extended to the entire nation. The initial decision, *Heller*, was based on a right to bear arms for protection against lurking dangers in Mr. Heller's neighborhood, a neighborhood in the inner city of Washington, DC. In other words, the Supreme Court saw the Second Amendment protections as a matter of self-defense and the protection of "hearth and home" or one's private property. Later *McDonald v. Chicago*[4] extended this right to all states. The plaintiff in the *McDonald* lawsuit also argued that his neighborhood had changed and "gangs and drug dealers" had moved into his neighborhood so he needed a handgun for protection.

The debates over the imposition of gun control laws, then, morphed into a struggle over the "second amendment right to bear arms" to protect one's body from harm and one's home from invasion and damage from one of controlling raiding Native Americans and African slaves seeking their freedom. The interesting historical footnote, albeit an important one, is that there were no legislative attempts to change the racial interpretations. Imbedded within the Second Amendment right, then, is the need to bear arms against the minions of crime who are emotionally defined as people of color. The stereotypical images of Black men seeking to ravage white womanhood and steal the property of whites and knife-wielding Latinos bent on perpetrating the same damage as Blacks underlies the need to bear arms. Protecting one's property is the contemporary way of saying that one is protecting one's property and women from people of color, particularly minority men of color. On another level, the right to bear arms is the most recent attempt at protecting one's privileged social status. This is a particularly interesting point if one considers white privilege as property requiring protection.

In the matter of voting rights, Latinos and African Americans or Blacks have been denied the franchise through several mechanisms throughout the history of the United States. The rationale, in every historical era, has been and continues to be the fear of what would happen to the government and the prevailing cultural environment if Latinos or Blacks were to take over the reins of government. Going as far back as 1854 when Texans were concerned with who would have the right to vote as they were contemplating their new constitution, it was clear that Mexicans would not be allowed to vote because then as many as 50,000 would cross the border to vote and pass Mexican laws. This was an era when rumors were ripe with various conspiracies to take Texas back for Mexico. Through the use of political parties as private clubs, poll taxes, at-large elections schemes, racial gerrymandering, and the imposition of voter identification laws, the state has made attempts at minimizing or diluting the voting strength of mostly Latinos because of our growing numbers in the population. False claims of voter fraud, illegal registrations, illegal ownership of citizenship documents and passports, denial of birth certificates to infants born in the United States, and passports to Latino citizens living along the border have also become parts of the voting barriers created to deny Latinos the right to vote in Texas.

Finally, the immigration laws of the United States have always been racially based since their inception. The initial immigration laws were even composed with the consultation of Madison Grant the American "father" of scientific racism. His racial hierarchy was clearly evident in the early two or three iterations of the nation's main immigration laws. Since then, various amendments or rewrites of the original laws have explicitly excluded residents of certain countries not deemed white enough, that is, Eastern

European, African, Chinese, and Middle Easterners. Again, the fear is that the influx of these lesser than white individuals, speaking strange languages, worshipping different religions could disrupt if not completely change the culture of the United States. Furthermore, once these disparate groups gained citizenship they would outvote, together with the other people of color, Latinos and Blacks, Whites, and then the government of the United States would become something "foreign."

In all three policy areas, there could be more, it is clear that to understand the place of race within each one must begin the investigation at the origins of each policy area. If one were to simply look at the last ten, fifteen, or twenty years of each policy one would see, except for immigration laws, no discussions of race. This results in individuals at various levels of the decisional process or the average, everyday individual of not understanding and even denying that each policy area was racially inspired. Many will admit that the immigration laws need to be racially based, or at least nationally or religiously based, insuring that "terrorists, rapists, and criminals" are not allowed to infect America. At least, this is what President Trump declared when he espoused the need to build a wall on the southern border.

IMPORTANCE OF ORIGINAL INTENT IN RACIAL DISCRIMINATION CASES

It has already become obvious that to understand racial intent in any law requires returning to the original intent of the composers of the policy area or laws emanating from the policy area. Those who feel that racial discrimination is determined by only observing whether or not a discriminator acted with explicit racial intent over the last few years are only seeking a superficial answer to their query. In this day and age of "dog whistle politics" or the use of "racial shields" to filter or inhibit one from uncovering the racial intent of the perpetrators one must utilize the most stringent observational techniques available. When looking at a policy area one does not look halfway through the lifespan of the policy to seek its intent; one must go to the beginning of the policy's formation in order to understand all the intents and goals of the policy in question. One must understand why and how a policy was constructed in the way it was in order to achieve the outcomes it did. Unequal or equal outcomes are not accidental artifacts of a policy but the result of how a policy is structured.

An important adage of public administration is that if one wishes to compose a policy, program, or law designed to address a specific problem or issue area the first step is to state your goals and/or objectives of what that policy is supposed to achieve. State your intent for creating the policy in the first place. If there is no intent, there are no goals, subsequently no need for a policy or law. If there are perceived needs, fear of Indian or slave attacks, protection of home, hearth, and self, controlling voting participation to insure continued control and the prevention of alien cultures from invading your home land, then you compose policies to meet those goals. Each of the above goals requires the control or attempted control of groups of people deemed threats to society. Therefore, the laws were and are written to enforce sanctions against those people. Required outcomes requires specific goals; specific goals require specific strictures. Racial intent is normally inserted at the birth of a policy, not at the end. The explicit implementation of the policies loses the explicitness of race as social norms change the manner in which races are understood and treated. Racial thinking and racism still remain in the hearts, minds, and eyes of the beholders and can only be reversed through intense exposure to the people of other races, learning about them, living among them, and knowing them as fellow human beings. However, the fear of miscegenation prevents this from happening. It is a taboo that has begun to fall by the wayside, that people of different races and cultures should not intermarry or produce children. This has been perceived as the denigration of the predominant culture in the United States and prevented by other state and national laws.

In the final analysis, racial intent in any law or policy area is best determined by investigating the original intent of the statute or policy area. So, to those lawyers and judges who declare that "history is *passé*" I simply say you are heavily mistaken and not interested in taking a thorough and complete look into the origin of racial discrimination within specific areas of law. I'm not sure if these types of statements that I have heard in federal courtrooms are just flippant statements meant to hide the truth or they are just statements of laziness on the part of the declarant, or the individuals are afraid to discover the truth.

RACIAL INTENT AS AN ARTIFACT OF THE SOCIALIZATION PROCESS

A deeper and more difficult question to answer is, Why racial intent? Why do individuals act with racial intent or animus? I feel that this can only be understood as an artifact of the socialization process. Racial thinking about other races is learned in the socialization process, principally from the family unit. Understanding of other races is learned as the child either hears close relatives, principally their parents, speaking about the perceived traits, habits, and work ethos of the other groups. Pete Simi and Robert Futrell relate in their research how the children of white nationalists, skinheads, and neo-Nazis are indoctrinated with the hatred of the parents even to the extent of redesigning toys and teaching them derogatory names for people of other racial groups.[5] These attitudes receive reinforcement throughout their education by belonging to groups who share their own perceptions and then refined through their professional associations also chosen because they have found the exact "fit" for their career advancement. During this rather average lifespan there is little opportunity for these individuals to challenge their racial thinking, so their biases and perceptions remain unchanged throughout their lifespan.[6]

After one matures professionally and obtains a position within the state or private matrices and is required to make decisions concerning a different racial group, opinions about that group on old and biased perceptions of the group are made. Racism becomes an essential element in the way the problem is perceived, solutions determined, and the policy designed and written. The language used in the composition of the design is sometimes infused with racist and racial assumptions, which become part of the decisional process. Racism, then, becomes spliced into the decisional structure itself. So, Blacks become gangs and drug dealers, Latinos become rapists, and so forth. Belief in the stereotypical behavioral traits of these groups lurk in the minds of the decision makers as excuses for excluding the groups from benefiting from the decision. This results in often deleterious decisions about the state of the racial minority groups' educational, financial, or employment statuses resulting in the expansion of educational and learning gaps between racial groups, the maintenance of economic and income gaps among members of all racial groups, and so forth. Neighborhoods remain segregated because fewer members of racial minority groups possess the financial wherewithal to purchase a home in upscale neighborhoods, send their children to the "best" of schools, and obtain those high-level jobs that allow them to advance their family's fortunes. In the world of voting rights, laws are made that do not value the votes of racial minority groups the same as those of white voters. So, minorities find themselves undercounted in censuses, racially gerrymandered, or denied the vote out of fear that they will bring their culture in competition with that of "white person's cultural values." And, gun control laws are phrased and implemented to protect one's family and hearth from invasion by people of color who tend to have higher criminal elements than white persons. And, immigration laws are made more stringent in order to preserve the dominant culture from being tainted by the "brown" invasions from the south and Middle East. Underlying racial intent, then, is fear of loss of privilege, property, and one's way of life. Finally, the fear that racial minority group members will take control of the state and private matrices and turn them into something other than what the traditional matrices were intent to provide and control.

Chapter 5

FEAR AND RACIAL THINKING

As noted throughout this volume fear plays an important role in racial thinking and racist actions. The OED definition quoted at the beginning of this volume clearly indicates that fear drives racism, prejudice, and discrimination. The fear of loss of status or privilege is underlain by a subconscious fear of the unknown or "the other." This latter aspect of fear is embedded in a person's psyche through early interactions with family members who transfer their fear to their children who, previously, received their fear from their parents.

All values, perceptions, attitudes, opinions, and fears are embedded in human beings through the normal socialization process. All of these, when aggregated, become the ideological and philosophical framework through which one views, interprets, and interacts with the world and the state. When one ascends to an office of importance within the state or the private sector matrices, one brings the ideological and philosophical perceptions to bear. So, they write and compose laws, journal articles, make judicial decisions, or corporate decisions that bias the laws, academic thinking, legal precedents, and production, investment and financial decisions affecting all lives within their respective matrices. These, in turn, directly or indirectly, affect the general populations of the matrix state and sometimes in adjacent matrices as well. This latter situation depends upon which level within the matrix one sits. For instance, if you are the president of the United States and deciding international trade policies and your decision will affect import/export levels of trade and the amount of taxes rendered on the goods and subsequent price of the goods, then your decision will, in turn, cascade down to the production levels. If this policy is a tariff on steel or grain production, then it affects not just investors and consumers it will also affect the jobs and income opportunities of the workers producing the goods and perishables. A lack of production will cascade backward to consumers in the markets in other matrices who purchase the goods with higher prices because of the lack of supply. This will, in turn, cause consumers to vote against those who imposed the tariff in the first place. So, a policy that begins in one matrix can spill over and affect the population in other matrices. This, in turn, can "boomerang" and affect the populations in the initial matrix. All matrices are interconnected because the world has evolved into a global community of interconnected national matrices.

What one fears also becomes part of the decisions made within and outside of the matrices affecting all populations. For instance, during the Kavanaugh confirmation hearings one saw the fear of loss of privilege and status being spoken about openly. Simultaneously, the leader of the Senate, Mitch McConnell, set forth his fear of the loss of conservatism if Kavanaugh were not to be appointed. The loss of privilege and status, on the part of Brett Kavanaugh, was perceived as a loss of white, male control over the laws of the land. As a result, one can perceive, it may not happen but we can perceive, that *Roe v. Wade*[7] will be overturned, voting rights laws will be ignored even more, no gun control laws will survive, and immigration laws will become more restrictive. As I said, these may not come to pass but if Mr. Kavanaugh brings his conservatism to bear, they may.

Messer. Kavanaugh's and McConnell's ideological and philosophical foundations were learned within the family structure and reinforced and refined as they progressed through their educational and professional careers. Their belief structures are such an essential part of their identity and how they view the world that they cannot accept other beliefs as authentic. For these two individuals or anyone to change they must encounter a life-altering situation that forces them to question their entire belief system. A situation so powerful would include experiencing a divorce as a participant in the divorce or experiencing the fracturing of the family unit as a child or as the parent of a child's divorce. Experiencing the traumas of war, whether a participant or a non-combatant emotionally tied to someone who had experienced the trauma. Being a victim of a life or near-death situation where one survives but is allowed in time to face their own mortality during the recovery stage. Or, the political world within which one lives becomes so hypocritical or contrary to one's beliefs that they begin challenging their own beliefs. This has happened recently as individuals such as the former mayor of New York City changing his party affiliation from Republican to Democrat because of President Trump's behavior to cite one example of many. Nevertheless, these are just several examples of how an individual may question their own philosophical or ideological perceptions based on what they experienced in each of these traumatic events. They may not change, but these types of situations allow an individual to arrive at the moment where they have the opportunity to question much of what they believe as well as the opportunity to change ideologically and philosophically.

To change one's perceptions of individuals of other races necessitates establishing close relations with individuals of other cultures and learning a great deal about those cultures. This requires studying about those cultures, perhaps evening learning their languages and understanding that group's fears and perceptions of the world and white persons. In order to understand people of other races it requires not only reading about the group but speaking with journalists, intellectuals, and the average person about their perceptions of society, white people, and trying to understand their fears, ambitions, expectations, their views of the nation, and the world. Of course, this is difficult given the highly segregated nature of our societies. This process may not change the minds of the investigator, but it certainly will reveal that there are perceptions other than their own in society and that people think very differently about the world than just the way they do.

THOUGHTS ABOUT SOCIAL STRUCTURES AND THE STATE

Throughout this extended volume I've used the word "structure" to describe the state, the decisional process, and belief systems. My thinking about structures has evolved some since I began this exercise. As a result, I feel I need to make some clarifying, if not defining, comments before I conclude this work.

Structures as we understand them can be material but here what we are speaking of also goes beyond the material. Structures in this discussion include belief systems, subjective by nature, that describe the political, social, and economic place of groups of people and their relationship between each other. These belief structures bias the decisional processes of the public policy process resulting in the creation of policies biased in favor of one group over another. The favoritism appears as not necessarily placing a group in a subordinate position but of creating conditions that gives some groups a decisional "head start" over others. So, for instance, the lack of gun control policies favors those who can afford guns over those who cannot; racial gerrymandering favors those who are not gerrymandered; and, immigration policies favor those who are not the subject of the laws. Nothing is said of these excluded groups, but the law favors them nonetheless because they are written by individuals who are and think just like them. This is the case because those composing the laws have the privilege of being in a position to compose the laws and they can define them whichever way they wish. They usually define, design and/or compose the laws based upon their own experiences, perceptions, and beliefs. This describes the biased nature of the decisional process. They cannot understand the perceptions and beliefs of individuals from other groups because either they do not wish to or they cannot fully comprehend that those other groups do have perceptions and beliefs different from their own. Essentially, decision makers tend to be solipsistic in nature and just cannot understand why anyone else could be any other way than the "norms" demanded by society. A white decision maker cannot see or understand, for instance, the desperation of a mother wanting to bring her child to the United States to escape poverty and danger in her homeland. The decision maker does not understand her desperation only his perception that he is trying to protect the sovereignty of his country. Supporters of unlimited gun ownership cannot understand why Latinos and African Americans generally do not wish to see guns in the hands of individuals. White legislators have no empathy for the needs of Latino voters and see their gerrymandering as only a way of maintaining the levers of political power.

The decisional process defined above is a process where white males are in a privileged position to design, write, and pass the laws. White males are structured into the top of the decisional process. As a result, the ideas, beliefs, opinions, and perceptions of white males define what the laws will look like. This allows for the laws or policies, imbued with racial ideas and perceptions, to be composed in nonracial terms. This, subsequently, results in laws and policies that appear nonracial superficially but result in unequal effects that disfavor minority communities. Consequently, the structures that we speak of here include the way in which the process is dominated by white males, their thoughts, beliefs, and ideas and how the decisions are reached. Decisional structures in the public policy process can and are, at least in the cases of the three policy areas discussed here, biased in the way they are constructed and the beliefs that permeate the process.

WHY RACISM CANNOT BE DEFEATED

The racism that guides decision makers when composing and later defending public policies cannot be eradicated because of the powerful forces that made them believe racial thinking in the first place. Their actions are the prisoners of their own consciousness, a Gordian knot that defies undoing. I've often pointed out that the single, most important and powerful institution in the United States is its socialization process. The process that makes us all Americans. I'm not a cultural anthropologist but I've studied enough throughout my lifetime about the socialization process and have written several pieces on it to understand how powerful a grip it has on individuals in any society. As I pointed out earlier it is what makes Americans Americans, Mexicans Mexicans, Russians Russians, and so forth. Without this powerful "glue" a society cannot maintain itself as a society or nation.

If one looks back through one's lifetime one can discover that the most powerful values one holds were breed into them by the family unit. Values of what one defines as "good/bad," "right/wrong," and "social standing" are taught to children through the family structure. The relations to other racial and social/class groups, status of women, and so forth are also learned inside the family. Some sociologists have surmised that by the time a child reaches the age of six their basic orientation to the world and the children or groups of people around them have already been formed. These basic beliefs are reinforced through the educational system the child goes through on the way to their career. How they choose a university, social groupings in university or college, career patterns have already been influenced by their parents and reinforced by the peer groups they socialize with throughout their young lives. When choosing a job opportunity an important part of their job interview is to make themselves appear suitable for acceptance by the employer and his or her employees. The big question is "Does she belong?" The universities and professional schools, such as law or medical schools, are as much about further refining socialization so these young folks can "fit in" than they are about teaching the basics of their chosen fields. After I passed my PhD orals this was made abundantly clear by one of my mentors when I asked on what basis I was being evaluated and her response was simple. She said, "We were making sure we wanted you as a colleague." Throughout one's professional career one adheres to the canons or standards of one's profession whether it's in the fields of law, medicine, financial management, banking, engineering, or the academy. If one strays there are ways in which the individual is brought to bear, disciplined if you will, or they will be excluded socially from the better law firms, hospitals, universities, journals, and so forth.

To allow one to "think outside the envelope," be intellectually curious or thorough in their investigation of the basis for a social problem is not looked upon favorably. Creative, revolutionary, out of the box thinkers are perceived as possibly dangerous, trouble makers, or someone just wanting to open old wounds. As a result, all who go through or went through the rigors of graduate or professional schools are taught the canons by older generations of academics and professors still trapped in ways that tend to perpetuate conservative thinking. The fear of what would happen to the traditional way of thinking if new innovative ways of thinking is unbearable to traditional or conservative thinkers. Here conservatism means the preservation of a canon, methodologies, or assumptions in public policy. To dramatically change the canons or traditional ways of thinking about "things or issues" is perceived as marginal thinking at best. If traditions or traditional thinking or scholarship is changed it is changed by experienced professionals who have achieved some standing within their professions.

As a result, by the time an individual attains sufficient status to be placed in a position to dominate the public policy decisional process they are long imbued with the beliefs, ideologies, methodologies, and perceptions of generations before them. This system has been designed by conservative, old, white males who proceeded the generations of current decision makers. This has been demonstrated in the discussion of how racist thinking was born in the imagination of de Gobineau and nurtured through the ages by other thinkers until it has become imbedded in the consciousness of the world. To change this structure requires the resocialization of the globe let alone an entire society. Changes in the educational, pop-cultural, social, religious, and political systems are essential. Changes to change a system where decisional processes will result in equal effects requires changing the structures both socially and ideologically. Because of this I strongly feel that racial thinking and decision-making will remain the norm for a while until younger generations of people can enter into the system and restructure both the processes and the way we think about social issues and problems. Of course, these younger generations must also have the courage to question and challenge the old, traditional beliefs and ways of thinking and making public policy decisions.

NOTES

1. I presented this in *Latinos and the VRA* (2015).
2. 446 U.S. 55, 104. (1980).
3. Ibid.
4. 561 U.S. 742 (2010).
5. Simi and Futrell, *American Swastika: Inside the White Power Movement's Hidden Spaces of Hate* (New York: Rowman & Littlefield, 2010).
6. Diangelo, *White Fragility* (2018).
7. 410 U.S. 113 (1973).

Bibliography

Acuña, Rodolfo. 2015. *Occupied America: A History of Chicanos* (8th edition). New York: Longman Publishing Group.
Agoustinous, Martha. August 2013. "Psychological Perspectives on Racism." *InPsych* Vol. 34, Issue 4.
Anderson, Elizabeth, and Jeffrey Jones. September 2002. "Race, Voting Rights and Segregation: Direct Disenfranchisement." In *The Geography of Race in the United States*. Ann Arbor: University of Michigan Press.
Aptheker, Herbert. 1943. *American Negro Slave Revolts*. New York: Columbia University Press.
Banfield, Edward. 1970. Revised, 1990. *The Unheavenly City Revisited*. Prospect Heights, IL: Waveland Press
Barken, Elizar. 1993. *The Retreat of Scientific Racism: Changing Concepts of Race in Britain and the United States Between the First World Wars*. Cambridge: Cambridge University Press.
Barber, William J., and Jonathan Wilson Hartgrove. 2016. *The Third Reconstruction: Moral Mondays, Fusion Politics, and the Rise of a New Justice Movement*. Boston: Beacon Press.
Beard, Charles, and Mary R. 1939. *America in Midpassage*. New York: Macmillan.
Berman, Ari. 2015. *Give Us the Ballot: The Modern Struggle for Voting Rights in America*. New York: Farrar, Straus and Giroux.
Bilbo, Theodore G. 1947. *Take Your Choice: Separation or Mongrelization*. Poplarville, MS: Dream House Publishing Company. Burlington, VT: Ostara Publications, 2012.
Binderup v. Sessions, No. 16-983 (2016).
Bogus, Carl T. Winter 1998. "The Hidden History of the Second Amendment." *University of California Law Review* 31, no. 2: 309–408.
Bolden v. City of Mobile, 446 U.S. 55 (1980).

Brooks, Stephen G., and William C. Wohlforth. Winter 2015. "The Rise and Fall of the Great Powers in the Twenty-First Century: China's Rise and Fate of America's Colonial Position." *International Security* Vol. 40, no. 3.
Calore, Paul. 2008. *Causes of the Civil War: The Political, Cultural, Economic and Political Disputes between North and South.* Jefferson, NC: McFarland and Company.
Chapman, Steve. July 31, 2016. "Black Demands and High Fears." www.chicagotribune.com/chapman.
Chomsky, Aviva, Barry Carr, and Pamela Maria Smorkaloff, eds. 2004. *The Cuba Reader: History, Culture, Politics.* Durham, NC: Duke University Press.
Cohen, G. Ben. December 12, 2012. "McKleskey's Omission: The Racial Geography of Retribution." *Ohio State Journal of Criminal Law* Vol. 1.
Cole, Kathleen. 2018. "Thinking Through Race: White Racial Identity, Motivated Cognition and the Unconscious Maintenance of White Supremacy." *Politics, Groups and Identities* Vol. 6, no. 2.
Corlett, J. Angelo. 2003. *Race, Racism and Reparations.* Ithaca, NY: Cornell University Press.
Cox, Earnest Sevier. 1923. Revised, 1937. *White America: The American Racial Problem as Seen in a Worldwide Perspective.* Burlington, VT: Ostara Publications, 2012.
Coyne, Jerry A. 2012. "Are There Human Races?" *Why Evolution Is True.* New York: Viking Penguin Press.
Craig, Maureen A., and Jennifer A. Richeson. March 13, 2014. "More Diverse yet Less Tolerant? How the Increasingly Diverse Racial Landscape Affects White America's Racial Attitudes." *Personality and Social Psychology Bulletin* Vol. 40, Issue 6.
Cramer, Clayton. Winter 1995. "The Racist Roots of Gun Control." *Kansas Journal of Public Policy.*
Davidson, Chandler, Tanya Dunlap, Gale Kenny, and Benjamin Wise. 2014. "Republican Ballot Security Programs: Vote Protection or Minority Vote Suppression—or Both?" *A Report to the Center for Voting Rights and Protection.* Washington, DC.
Darwin, Charles. 1859. *On the Origin of Species by Means of Natural Selection.* London: John Murray.
Davis v. Bandemer, 478 U.S. 109 (1986).
DeLéon, Arnoldo. 1979. *In Re Ricardo Rodriguez: An Attempt of Chicano Disfranchisement, 1896–1897.* San Antonio, TX: Caravel Press.
Diangelo, Robin. 2018. *White Fragility: Why It's So Hard for White People to Talk About Racism.* Boston: Beacon Press.
Domhoff, G. W. 1967. *Who Rules America?* (1st edition). Englewood Cliffs, NJ: Prentice-Hall.
———. 1972. *Fat Cats and Democrats: The Role of the Big Rich in the Party of the Common Man.* Englewood Cliffs, NJ: Prentice-Hall.
———. 1974. *The Bohemian Grove and Other Retreats: A Study in Ruling-Class Cohesiveness.* New York: Harper and Row.

———. 1975. "Social Clubs, Policy-Planning Groups, and Corporations: A Network Study of Ruling-Class Cohesiveness." *The Insurgent Sociologist* 5, no. 3.

———. 1983. *Who Rules America Now?* (4th edition). New York: Simon & Schuster.

———. 2018. "Wealth, Income and Power." Who Rules America.net.

Dred Scott v. Sandford, 60 U.S. 393 (1857).

Eisinger, Jesse. April 30, 2014. "Why Only One Top Banker Went to Jail for the Financial Crisis." *New York Times*.

Faegin, Joe. 2013. *The White Racial Frame: Centuries of Racial Framing and Counter- Framing*. New York: Routledge.

Fairchild, Harry P. 1925. *Immigration*. Charleston, SC: Nabu Press, 2009, reprinted from original.

Fernandez, Randall. 1996. *The Disenchanted Island: Puerto Rico and the United States in The Twentieth Century* (2nd edition). New York: Praeger Paperback.

Fitzgerald, David Scott, and David Cook-Martin. 2014. *Culling the Masses: The Democratic Origins of Racist Immigration Policy in America*. Cambridge, MA: Harvard University Press.

Flores, Henry. 2003. *The Evolution of the Liberal Democratic State with a Case Study of Latinos in San Antonio, TX*. Lewiston, NY: The Edwin Mellen Press.

———. 2015. *Latinos and the Voting Rights Act: The Search for Racial Purpose*. Lanham, MD: Lexington Books.

Fredrickson, George M. 2002. *Racism: A Short History*. Princeton, NJ: Princeton University Press.

Fromm, Erich. 1965. *The Heart of Man: Its Genius for Good and Evil*. New York: Harper and Row Publishers.

Frum, David. 2014. "The Impossibility of Reparations: Considering the Single Most Important Question about Racial Reparations: How Would It Work?" *The Atlantic*.

Fuerst, Joh. June 18, 2015. "The Nature of Race: The Genealogy of the Concept and the Biological Construct's Contemporaneous Utility." *Open Behavioral Genetics*.

Fujita, Kumiko. 2013. *Cities and Crisis: New Critical Urban Theory*. London: SAGE Studies in International Sociology.

Garcia, Carolina. May 25, 2012. "*39.000 euros para cada víctima de esterilizacíon forzada*." *El Pais*.

———. July 12, 2013. "*Los mexicanos, principales víctimas de las esterilizacíon forzada*." *El Pais*.

Gaertner, Samuel L., and John A. Dovidio, eds. 1986. *Prejudice, Discrimination and Racism: Theory and Research*. Orlando, FL: Academic Press.

Gamble, Richard M. 2012. *In Search of the City on a Hill: The Making and Unmaking of an American Myth*. New York: Bloomsbury Academic.

Gardner, Daniel. 2009. *The Science of Fear How the Culture of Fear Manipulates Your Brain*. New York: PLUME.

Garis, Roy L. 1927. *Immigration Restriction: A Study of the Opposition to and Regulation of Immigration into the United States*. New York: Macmillan.

Gilbert, Dennis. 2002. *The American Class Structure: In an Age of Growing Inequality*. Belmont, CA: Wadsworth.

Glassner, Barry. 2009. *The Culture of Fear: Why Americans Are Afraid of the Wrong Things*. New York: Basic Books.

Glazer, Nathan, with Daniel Moynahan. 1963. Second expanded edition, 1970. *Beyond the Melting Pot: The Negroes, Puerto Ricans, Jews, Italians and Irish of New York City*. Cambridge, MA: MIT Press.

Gobineau, Joseph Arthur, Comte de Gobineau. 1856. *Essai sur l'inégalitédes races humaines (Essay on the Inequality of the Human Races, 1853–1855)*. Published in English as *The Moral and Intellectual Diversity of Races*. J. B. Lippincott. New York: Garland Publishing, 1984.

Goldenberg, David M. 2009. *The Curse of Ham: Race and Slavery in Early Judaism, Christianity and Islam*. Princeton, NJ: Princeton University Press.

Gomillion v. Lightfoot, 364 U.S. 339 (1960).

Gossett, Thomas F. 1997. *Race: The History of an Idea in America*. New Edition. Oxford: Oxford University Press.

Gould, Stephan Jay. 1981. *The Measurement of Man*. New York: W. W. Norton.

Grant, Madison. 1916. *The Passing of the Great Race*. New York: Charles Scribner's Sons.

Griffin v. School Board, 377 U.S. 218 (1964).

Grosjean v. American Press Co., 297 U.S. 233 (1936).

Guinier, Lani, and Gerald Torres. 2002. *The Miner's Canary: Enlisting Race, Resisting Power, Transforming Democracy*. Cambridge, MA: Harvard University Press.

Guinn v. United States, 238 U.S. 347 (1915).

Hardy, David. 2007. "Book Review: A Well-Regulated Militia: The Founding Fathers and the Origins of Gun Control in America." *William and Mary Bill of Rights Journal*, 15.

Hasan, Shafaq. April 28, 2016. "The Case of Universities Paying Reparations to Descendants of Slavery." *NPQ: Nonprofit Quarterly*.

Hecht, Jennifer Michael. 2003. *The End of the Soul: Scientific Modernity, Atheism and Anthropology in France*. New York: Columbia University Press.

Hernandez v. Texas, 347 U.S. 475 (1954).

Herrnstein, Richard J., and Charles Murray. 1994. *The Bell Curve: Intelligence and Class Structure in American Life*. New York: Basic Books.

Hitler, Adolph. 1939. *Mein Kampf*. English translation by Deitrick Eckart. London: Hurst and Blackett, Ltd.

Hobsbawm, E. J., ed. 1964. *Pre-Capitalist Economic Formations*. Translated by Jack Cohen. New York: International Publishers.

Holder v. Texas, 1:2012cv00128 (2012).

In Re Ricardo Rodriguez, 81 F. 337 (W.D. Tex. 1897).

Jefferson, Thomas. 1781. *Notes on the State of Virginia*. Philadelphia, PA: Printed and sold by Richard and Hall. William Peden, ed. Chapel Hill, NC: University of North Carolina Press.

Jensen, Arthur R. 1969. "How Much Can We Boost IQ and Achievement?" *Harvard Educational Review* 39, 1–123.

Jiménez, de Wagenheim, Olga, and Karl Wagenheim. 2002. *The Puerto Ricans: A Documentary History*. Princeton, NJ: Markes Weiner Publishers.

Jomo, K. S., and Jacques Baudot, eds. 2007. *Flat World, Big Groups: Economic Liberalization, Gobalization, Poverty and Inequality.* London: Zen Books Published in association with the United Nations.
Kahneman, Daniel. 2011. *Thinking, Fast and Slow.* New York: Farrar, Straus and Giroux.
Kanazawa, Mark. September 2005. "Immigration and Taxation: Anti-Chinese Legislation in Gold Rush California." *The Journal of Economic History* Vol. 65, Issue no. 3.
Katherine Harris, et al. v. NAACP, et al., 01-CIV-120-GOLD (2000).
Kennedy, Paul. 1987. *The Rise and Fall of the Great Powers.* New York: Random House.
Keyes v. School District No. 1, Denver, CO, 413 U.S. 207 (1973).
Kingston, Paul. 2000. *The Classless Society.* Palo Alto, CA: Stanford University Press.
Kirkpatrick, Clifford. 1927. "Intelligence and Immigration." *The Psychological Review* 14: 363–64.
Kousser, J. Morgan. 1999. *Colorblind Justice: Minority Voting Rights and the Undoing of the Second Reconstruction.* Chapel Hill: The University of North Carolina Press.
Krogstad, Jens Michael, Jeffrey Passel, and D'Vera Cohn. November 3, 2016. "5 Facts about Illegal Immigration in the United States." Pew Research Center: Hispanic Tends.
Kühl, Stefan. 1994. *The Nazi Connection: Eugenics, American Racism and German National Socialism.* Oxford: Oxford University Press.
Lasch, Christopher. 1979. *The Culture of Narcissism: American Life in an Age of Diminishing Expectations.* New York: W. W. Norton.
Lewis, Oscar, Ruth M. Lewis, and Margaret Mead. 1959. *Five Families: Mexican Case Studies in the Culture of Poverty.* New York: Basic Books.
López, Ian Haney. 2014. *Dog Whistle Politics: How Coded Racial Appeals Have Reinvented Racism and Wrecked the Middle Class.* London: Oxford University Press.
Loving v. Virginia, 388 U.S. 1 (1967).
LULAC v. Perry, 548 U.S. 399 (2006).
Malcolm, Joyce Lee. 1996. *To Keep and Bear Arms: The Origins of an Anglo-American Right.* Cambridge, MA: Harvard University Press.
Marx, Karl. 1857. Translated by Jack Cohen 1964. *Pre-Capitalist Economic Formations.* New York: International Publishers. 1867. Translated by Samuel Moore and Edward Aveling. 1995. *Capital: A Critique of Political Economy.* Moscow: Progress Publishers.
Masci, David. 2018. "Reparations Movement: Should Payments be made for Historical Wrongs?" *CQ Researcher.* Washington, DC: CQ Press.
Mayer, Jane. 2016. *Dark Money: The Hidden History of the Billionaires Behind the Rise of the Radical Right.* New York: The Knopf Publishing Group.
McDonald v. Chicago, 561 U.S. 3025 (2010).
McWilliams, Carey. 1948. *North from Mexico: The Spanish-Speaking People of the United States.* Westport, CT: Praeger Publishers.

Merkel, William G., and H. Richard Uviller. 2002. *The Militia and the Right to Arms, Or, How the Second Amendment Fell Silent*. Durham, NC: Duke University Press.

Miller, Stuart Creighton. 1969. *The Unwelcome Immigrant: The American Image of the Chinese*. Berkeley: University of California Press.

Montejano, David. 1987. *Anglos and Mexicans in the Making of Texas, 1836–1986*. Austin: The University of Texas Press.

Morales Carrión, Arturo. 1984. *Puerto Rico: A Political and Cultural History*. New York: W. W. Norton.

Murray, Charles, and Richard J. Herrnstein. 1994. *The Bell Curve: Intelligence and Class Structure in American Life*. New York: The Free Press.

National Association for the Advancement of Colored People (NAACP). n.d. *The Role of Section 2—Redistricting and Vote Dilution*.

National Rifle Association-Institute for Legislative Action (NRA-ILA). 1999. "Suicide and Firearms." *NRA Factsheet*.

Norton, Michael I., and Samuel R. Summers. 2011. "Whites See Racism as a Zero-Sum Game That they are Now Losing." *Perspectives on Psychological Science*.

Nussbaum, Martha C. 2018. *The Monarchy of Fear: A Philosopher Looks at our Political Crisis*. New York: Simon & Schuster.

Oxford English Dictionary, 3rd edition. Oxford: Oxford University Press.

Pakulski, Jan, and Malcolm Waters. 1996. "The Reshaping and Dissolution of Social Class in Advanced Society." *Theory and Society*.

Passel, Jeffrey S., and D'Vera Cohn. September 20, 2016. "Overall Number of U.S. Unauthorized Immigrants Holds Steady since 2009: Decline in Share From Mexico Mostly Offset by Growth from Asia, Central-America and Sub-Saharan Africa." Pew Research Center Hispanic Trends.

Patterson, Samuel, and Keith R. Eakins. 1998. "Congress and Gun Control." In John M. Bruce and Clyde Wilcox (eds.), *The Changing Politics of Gun Control*. Lanham, MD: Rowman & Littlefield.

Peruta v. County of San Diego, 824 F. 3rd 919 (2016).

Phillips, Patrick. 2016. *Blood at the Root: A Racial Cleansing in America*. New York: W. W. Norton.

Plato. 1951. Translated by Francis M. Cornford. *The Republic*. London: Oxford University Press.

Potter, David M. 2011. *The Impending Crisis: America before the Civil War, 1848–1861*. New York: HarperCollins.

Reitman v. Mulkey, 387 U.S. 369 (1967).

Resnick, Brian. January 28, 2017. "White Fear of Demographic Change is a Powerful Psychological Force." *Vox*.

Rodriguez v. San Antonio Independent School District, 411 U.S. 1 (1973).

Rothenberg, Paula S. 2016. *White Privilege: Essential Readings on the Other Side of Racism*, 5th edition. New York: Worth Publishers.

Rothman, Adam. 2005. *Slave Country: American Expansion and the Origins of the Deep South*. Cambridge, MA: Harvard University Press.

Rosenberg, Alfred. 1930. *Der mythus des zwanzigsten Jahrhunderts* or *The Myth of the Twentieth Century: An Evaluation of the Spiritual-Intellectual Confrontation of our Age*. Publisher unknown.

Rushton, J. Philippe, and Arthur R. Jensen. 2005. "Thirty Years of Research on Race Differences in Cognitive Ability." *Psychology, Public Policy, and Law* Vol. 11, no. 2: 235–94.
Schnell v. Davis, 336 U.S. 933 (1949).
Scott, John. 1972. *Internalization of Norms: A Sociological Theory of Moral Commitment.* London: Prentice-Hall.
Seller, Maxine S. 1984. "Historical Perspectives on American Immigration Policy: Case Studies and Current Implications." *U.S. Immigration Policy.* Edited by Richard Hofstetter. Chapel Hill: The University of North Carolina Press.
Shelby County v. Holder, 570 U.S. _____ (2013).
Shipman, Pat. 1994. *The Evolution of Racism: Human Differences and the Use and Abuse of Science.* New York: Charles Scribner's Sons.
Simi, Pete, and Robert Futrell. 2010. *American Swastika: Inside the White Racist Movement's Hidden Spaces of Hate.* New York: Rowman & Littlefield.
Smith, Adam. 1776. *An Inquiry into the Nature and Causes of the Wealth of Nations.* W. Strahan and J. Cadeli in the Strand.
Smith, Rev. Susan K. December 29, 2015. "Whites and Fear Caused by White Supremacy." *The Blog.*
Smith, Tom W., and Son Jaesok. 2015. *General Social Survey Final Report: Trends in Gun Ownership in the United States, 1972–2014.* NORC at the University of Chicago.
South Carolina v. Katzenbach, 383 U.S. 311 (1966).
Spiro, Jonathan P. 2009. *Defending the Master Race: Conservatism, Eugenics, and the Legacy Of Madison Grant.* Burlington, VT: University of Vermont Press published by University Press of New England, Lebanon, NH.
State of Texas. 2017. Senate Bill 5. "Relating to Requiring a Voter to Present Proof of Identification; Providing a Criminal Penalty and Increasing a Criminal Penalty."
———. 2011. House of Representatives. Daily Journal, March 22.
Sternberg, Mary Ann. 2001. *Along the River Road: Past and Present Louisiana's Historic Byways.* Baton Rouge: Louisiana State University Press.
Stoddard, T. Lothrop. 1922. *The Revolt against Civilization or the Menace of the Underman.* Burlington, VT: Ostara Publications.
Sussman, Robert Wald. 2014. *The Myth of Race: The Troubling Perspective of an Unscientific Idea.* Cambridge, MA: Harvard University Press.
Tenney v. Brandhove, 341 U.S. 367 (1951).
The Holy Bible. 2017. New International Version. Grand Rapids, MI: Zondervan.
Therborn, Göran. 1980. *The Ideology of Power and the Power of Ideology.* London: Verso Press.
Thompson, William E., and Joseph V. Hickey. 2005. *Society in Focus.* Boston: Pearson, Allyn and Bacon.
Thornburg v. Gingles, 478 U.S. 30 (1986).
Tinsley, Anna M., and Dianna Boyd. October 24, 2018. "Four Women in 'Voter Fraud Ring' Arrested. They Targeted Seniors on City's North Side." *Fort-Worth Star-Telegram.*
Traditionalistsamericanknights.com.

Upchurch, Thomas Adams. 2004. *Legislating Racism: The Billion Dollar Congress and the Birth of Jim Crow*. Lexington: University Press of Kentucky.

United States. Second Congress, Chapter XXXIII – "An Act to More Effectively Provide For a National Defence by Establishing a Uniform Militia throughout the United States."

———. 1778. Constitution of the United States.

———. 1992. Edition. The Constitution of the United States of America Analysis and Interpretation—Second Amendment—Bearing Arms. Gpo.gov. Retrieved June 23, 2017.

———. 1965. Voting Rights Act, PL 89-110.

———. Department of Education. National Center for Education Statistics. *Digest of Education Statistics*, 2015 (NCES 2016-014).

———. Department of the Treasury. "Income Mobility in the U.S. From 1996 to 2005." November 13, 2007. Downloaded from http://www.treasury.gov/resource-center/tax- Policy/Documents/incompatibilitystudy03-08revise.pdf.

———. House of Representatives. Congressional Record, S2817-S2818 (February 9, 1928).

United States v. Nixon, 418 U.S. 683 (1974).

Veasey v. Abbott, 796 F. 3rd 487 (5th Cir. 2015).

Village of Arlington Heights v. Metropolitan Housing Development Corporation, 429 U.S. 252 (1977).

Waldman, Michael. 2014. *The Second Amendment: A Biography*. New York: Simon & Schuster.

Washington v. Davis, 426 U.S. 248 (1976).

Washington, DC, v. Heller, 554 U.S. 570 (2008).

Wattles, Jackie, et al. April 24, 2018. "Wells Fargo 20-Month Nightmare." *CNN Money*.

Weber, Max. 1968. Translated by G. Roth and C. Wittich. *Economy and Society*. Cambridge, MA: Harvard University Press.

Weeks, John. 2007. "Inequality Trends in Some Developed OECD Countries." DESA Working Paper #6. *Economic and Social Affairs*.

West, Cornel. 1993. *Race Matters*. Boston: Beacon Press.

Winthrop, John. 1630. *A Model of Christian Charity*. Published in 1838 by Boston. 1968 by Evergreen Publishers.

Wolff, Edward N. 2017. *A Century of Wealth in America*. Cambridge, MA: Harvard University Press.

Woolston, Howard. 1923. "Wanted—An Immigration Policy." *Journal of Social Forces* Vol. 2, (1923–1924): 666–70.

Wright, Eric Olin. 1997. *Class Counts: Comparative Studies in Class Analysis*. Cambridge: Cambridge University Press.

Yick Wo v. Hopkins, 118 U.S. 356 (1886).

Index

Abbott, Gregg, 40
African Americans, 11, 17–19, 36–37, 46, 58–59, 78, 80, 88–89, 124, 140, 146, 168
Age of Enlightenment, 16
Alexander the Great, 53, 63
American Anthropological Association, 18
American Civil Liberties Union, 161
American Civil Rights Movement, 162
American Historical Society, 21
American Political Science Association, 21
American Renaissance, 32
anti-miscegenation, 20
Aptheker, Herbert, 87
Arlington Heights Factors, 43, 52n95, 147–48, 149–50
Arthur Anderson, 141
Aryan/white/anglo, 18, 22, 45, 153
Asian, 69, 77

Banfield, Edward, 24
banking system, 61–62
Bear Stearns, 142
belief structures, 31, 173
The Bell Curve, 25
Bilbo, Theodore G., 22, 32, 48n29

Bill of Rights, 79–80
Black Panthers, 120
Boas, Franz, 24
Bolden v. City of Mobile, 145, 157n23, 165
Box, John, 33
Bretton Woods Agreement, 57
Burger Court, 113
Bush, George H. W., 47n1, 84

Cato Institute, 82, 162
Chamberlain, Houston S., 19
Chinese Exclusion Laws, 75, 182
Christianization, 163
"city on a hill," 67
Civil Rights Act of 1965, 42, 59, 68, 135, 145, 162
Civil Rights Amendments, 69, 79
culture of poverty, 24

Darwin, Charles, 3, 21
Davenport, Charles B., 19, 24, 117
Davis v. Bandemer, 4
decisional processes, 40, 65, 88, 124–29, 135, 166–69, 175
decisional structures, 46, 135, 175
de Gobineau, Joseph Arthur, Comte, 17, 32, 44
discrimination, 68, 145, 172

disparate effect, 144, 146, 149
Domhoff, G. William, 54, 93n3, 106, 112, 129n2

Eastern Europeans, 23, 34, 77
Edgewood School District, 113
effect standard, 43, 147, 154
Ellis Island, 69
English Bill of Rights of 1689, 78
equal protection clause, 5, 83
Essay on the Inequality of the Human Races, 17
eugenics, 17, 21, 129, 137
Eugenics Record Office, 19, 23, 76, 117
The Evolution of the Liberal Democratic State, 56
exclusion mechanism, 68–69

FAIR. *See* Federation for American Immigration Reform
Feagin, Joe, 140
fear, 25–30, 81, 116–17, 172–74
Federal Reserve, 127
Federation for American Immigration Reform (FAIR), 137, 155
Fifteenth Amendment, 42, 68, 89, 90, 138, 146
First Amendment, 6, 42, 155
Five Families: Mexican Case Studies in the Culture of Poverty, 24
Fourteenth Amendment, 39, 42, 68, 83, 143, 155
Fredrickson, George M., 3
French Revolution, 58
Fromm, Eric, 32
Futrell, Robert, 170

Gadsden Purchase of 1854, 39
Galton, Francis, 3, 21
Galton Institute, 18
Gates, Louis, 29
Geary Act of 1891, 69
Gerry, Elbridge, 79

Goebbels, Joseph, 19
Goldwater, Barry, 41
Gordian knot, 46, 53–54, 93, 175
Gore v. Bush, 41
Gossett, T. F., 3, 24
Gould, Stephen Jay, 40
Grant, Madison, 18, 20–22, 32, 44, 118, 168
Great Depression, 55
gun control, 69, 77–89, 168

Heller, Dick Anthony, 82, 167
Henry, Patrick, 79, 87
Herrnstein, Richard J., 20, 25
Hispanics, 36–37, 45, 58, 85, 87, 91, 124, 153, 168, 175
HUD. *See* United States Department of Housing and Urban Development

ideology, 31, 59–63, 101
ideological culture, 62
ideological matrix, 66–68
ideological mechanism, 64, 135
ideological structure, 15
immigration, 69, 75–77
Immigration Act of 1891, 69
Immigration Act of 1924, 18, 32–36
In Re Ricardo Rodriguez, 37
intent, 88, 170. *See also* racial intent
Iyer, Ragahavan, 5

Jews, 19
Jewish Question, 119
Jensen, Arthur R., 25
Jim Crow laws, 7n4, 11, 26, 90
Jones-Shaforth Act, 89

Kavanaugh, Brett, 173
Ku Klux Klan (KKK), 16, 22, 120

Latin Americans, 77
Latin American immigration, 76
Laughlin, Harry H., 19, 33, 76

Laws of Nature, 20
Lewis, Oscar, 24
Lincoln, Abraham, 68
Loving v. Virginia, 18, 20
LULAC v. Perry, 4

Madison, James, 79
Marshall, Thurgood, 149, 151, 157n23, 165
Marx, Karl, 57, 112
Mason, George, 79
matrix, 53, 66, 125. *See also* state matrix
McConnell, Mitch, 172
McDonald v. Chicago, 82–84, 137
The Measurement of Man, 39
Melting Pot, 22
Mexican, 22
Mexican Americans, 39, 89, 91, 140, 146
Mexican American War of 1848, 38
Mexican women, 19
Mexico, 101
militias, 79–80
mongrelized, 18
Monroe Doctrine, 34
Moynihan, Daniel P., 24
Murray, Charles, 4, 20

National Center for Educational Statistics, 108
National Guard, 80, 82
National Rifle Association (NRA), 82, 83, 155, 167
National Socialist Movement, 32
nationalization, 60, 61
Native Americans, 80, 88
Naturalization Act of 1790, 69
Naturalization Act of 1870, 69
Naturalization Act of 1906, 76
Nazis, 11, 19, 22–23
Nixon, Richard, 41
Nordic theory, 19

NRA. *See* National Rifle Association

Obama, Barack, 40, 59
On the Origin of Species, 3
Oxford English Dictionary (OED), 3–4, 20, 32, 44

Passing of the Great Race, The, 18–20, 22
Perry, Rick, 42
Peruta, Edward, 83
Pew Research Center, 76, 136
Plato's Cave, 151
Plyler v. Doe, 143
Powell, Louis, 15, 149
Powell Memorandum, 15
public policy process, 133–34, 137, 141–45, 165
Puerto Ricans, 91
purposeful intent, 88

race, 162
race betterment, 21
Race Matters, 28
racial discrimination, 148
racial integrity, 9
Racial Integrity Act of 1924, 18
racial intent, 124, 144–48, 155, 159–60
racial polarization, 153
racial shields, 5, 122, 133, 151, 154–55, 169
racial thinking, 84, 139, 176
racism, 162, 171–72, 175
racist, 26
Ramos, Nelva Gonzalez, 42–43
Ramadan, 102
Rehnquist, William, 41
Republic of Texas, 38
Republican Party (GOP), 2, 26, 41–42, 86, 153
Roberts, John, 43
Rodriguez v. SAISD, 15, 113, 130n7

Roe v. Wade, 173
Romani, 19
Rosenberg, Alfred, 19
Russian Revolution, 58, 75

Scalia, Antonin, 43, 83
Second Amendment, 5, 79, 81, 83, 87, 168
Section 2, Voting Rights Act of 1965, 42
Section 4(b), Voting Rights Act of 1965, 154, 159
Section 5, Voting Rights Act of 1965, 1, 40, 145, 159
segregation, 46
selective mechanisms, 65
Senate Bill 14, 92, 152, 155. *See also* Voter ID Law
Senate Factors, 147
Shelby County v. Holder, 1, 42, 136, 137, 154, 159
Shockley, William, 25
Simi, Peter, 170
slave trade, 16
Smith, Adam, 57
socialization agents, 135
Southern Strategy, 41
state matrix, 99, 125, 135
sterilization, 20
Stoddard, T. Lothrop, 21–22
structured intent, 88
Supreme White Alliance, 32
Sussman, Robert N., 3

Teutonic, 20
Texas, 3, 39
Therborn, Goran, 30
Third Reconstruction, 26
Thirteenth Amendment, 68
Thornburg v. Gingles, 147
Treaty of Guadalupe Hidalgo, 89

Trump, Donald, 27, 119, 169
Turner, Nat, 87

United States Fifth Circuit Court of Appeals, 43, 94n15
United States Ninth Circuit Court of Appeals, 83–84
United States Congress, House Committee on Immigration and Naturalization, 33
United States Department of Commerce, 56
United States Department of Defense, 56
United States Department of Housing and Urban Development (HUD), 56
United States Department of Labor, 56
United States Department of War, 56
United States District Court for the District of Columbia, 41–42
United States Supreme Court, 43

voter fraud, 139
voter ID law, 1, 5, 40, 42–44, 118, 128
voting rights, 36, 37, 90
Voting Rights Act of 1965, 1, 40, 90

Waldman, Michael, 79
War of Secession, 39
Washington, George, 37
Washington v. Davis, 149, 165
Washington, DC v. Heller, 82
Weber, Max, 112
White America: The American Racial Problem as Seen in a Worldwide Perspective, 21
white racial frame, 140
World War II, 7
Wright, Eric Olen, 112

xenophobia, 81

About the Author

Henry Flores, PhD, is Distinguished University Research Professor Emeritus of Political Science at St. Mary's University in San Antonio, Texas. He is currently composing a biography of the late congressman Henry B. Gonzalez (D-TX). Dr. Flores taught at St. Mary's for thirty-five years, has been a litigation voting rights expert for more than thirty years, and has published several books including *Latinos and the Voting Rights Act* (2015). He is a combat veteran of the Vietnam War and holder of the Bronze Star.

www.ingramcontent.com/pod-product-compliance
Lightning Source LLC
Chambersburg PA
CBHW050907300426
44111CB00010B/1412